ALL THE WORLD'S ANIMALS
SONGBIRDS

ALL THE WORLD'S ANIMALS
SONGBIRDS

TORSTAR BOOKS
New York · Toronto

CONTRIBUTORS

MA   Mark Avery PhD
Edward Grey Institute of Field
Ornithology
University of Oxford
England

JCB   Jon C. Barlow PhD
Royal Ontario Museum
Toronto, Ontario
Canada

MEB   Michael E. Birkhead DPhil
Edward Grey Institute of Field
Ornithology
University of Oxford
England

MDB   Murray D. Bruce
National Parks and Wildlife
Service
New South Wales
Australia

PRC   P.R. Colston
British Museum (Natural
History)
Sub-department of
Ornithology
Tring, Hertfordshire
England

WRJD   W.R.J. Dean
Knysna
South Africa

SME   Stewart M. Evans PhD
University of Newcastle-
upon-Tyne
England

CJF   Chris J. Feare PhD
Ministry of Agriculture,
Fisheries and Food
Worplesdon, Surrey
England

JWF   John W. Fitzpatrick PhD
Field Museum of Natural
History
Chicago, Illinois
USA

HAF   Hugh A. Ford PhD
University of New England
Armidale, New South Wales
Australia

CBF   Clifford B. Frith PhD
Paluma via Townsville
Queensland
Australia

EFJG   Ernest F.J. Garcia DPhil
Guildford, Surrey
England

PJG   Peter J. Garson DPhil
University of Newcastle-
upon-Tyne
England

AJG   Anthony J. Gaston DPhil
Canadian Wildlife Service
Ottawa, Ontario
Canada

FBG   Frank B. Gill PhD
Academy of Natural Sciences
Philadelphia, Pennsylvania
USA

LGG   Llewellyn G. Grimes BSc MSc
PhD
Warwick
England

DTH   David T. Holyoak PhD
University of Nottingham
England

AMH   A.M. Hutson
Fauna and Flora
Preservation Society
London
England

CBK   Cameron B. Kepler PhD
US Fish and Wildlife Service
Kula, Hawaii
USA

JKi   Jiro Kikkawa DSc
University of Queensland
Brisbane, Queensland
Australia

RWK   Richard W. Knapton PhD
Brock University
St Catherine's, Ontario
Canada

DRL   Derek R. Langslow MA PhD
Nature Conservancy Council
Huntingdon
England

AL   Alan Lill PhD
Monash University
Clayton, Victoria
Australia

HL   Hans Löhrl PhD
Egenhausen
West Germany

ALu   Arne Lundberg PhD
Uppsala University
Sweden

CJM   Christopher J. Mead PhD
British Trust for Ornithology
Tring, Hertfordshire
England

DHM   Douglass H. Morse PhD
Brown University
Providence, Rhode Island
USA

IN   Ian Newton PhD
Institute for Terrestrial
Ecology
Abbot's Ripton
Cambridgeshire
England

RAN   Richard A. Noske PhD
Canberra College of
Advanced Education
Australia

GHO   Gordon H. Orians PhD
University of Washington
Seattle, Washington
USA

CMP   Christopher M. Perrins DPhil
Edward Grey Institute of Field
Ornithology
University of Oxford
England

IR   Ian Rowley B Agr Sc
CSIRO, Wildlife and
Rangelands Research
Australia

GHS   Greg H. Sherley
University of Canterbury
Christchurch
New Zealand

AFS   Alexander F. Skutch PhD
San Isidro
Costa Rica

GTS   G.T. Smith PhD
CSIRO, Wildlife and
Rangelands Research
Australia

DWS   David W. Snow DSc
British Museum (Natural
History)
Sub-department of
Ortithology
Tring, Hertfordshire
England

AKT   Angela K. Turner PhD
University of Glasgow
Scotland

CW   Cliff Waller
Blythburgh, Suffolk
England

DRW   D.R. Wells PhD
University of Malaya
Kuala Lumpur
Malaysia

BW   Brian Wood PhD
University College
London
England

RDW   Ron D. Wooller PhD
Murdoch University
Murdoch, Western Australia
Australia

**ALL THE WORLD'S ANIMALS
SONGBIRDS**

TORSTAR BOOKS INC.
300 E. 42nd Street,
New York, NY 10017

Project Editor: Graham Bateman
Editors: Peter Forbes, Bill Mackeith, Robert Peberdy
Art Editor: Jerry Burman
Art Assistant: Carol Wells
Picture Research: Alison Renney
Production: Barry Baker
Design: Chris Munday

Originally planned and produced by:
Equinox (Oxford) Ltd
Mayfield House, 256 Banbury Road
Oxford, OX2 7DH, England

Copyright © Equinox (Oxford) Ltd, 1985

On the cover: Green-headed tanager
page 1: Blue jay
pages 2–3: Golden palm weaver
pages 4–5: Brassy-breasted tanager
pages 6–7: Schlegal's twinspot
pages 8–9: American goldfinch

Editors
Dr Christopher M. Perrins
Edward Grey Institute of Field Ornithology
University of Oxford
England

Dr L. A. Middleton
Associate Professor of Zoology
University of Guelph
Ontario, Canada

Artwork Panels
Norman Arlott
Trevor Boyer
Ad Cameron
Sean Milne
Denys Ovenden
Laurel Tucker
Ian Willis

Library of Congress Cataloging in Publication Data

ISBN 0–920269–72–9 (Series: All the World's
Animals)
ISBN 0–920269–77–X (Songbirds)

CONTENTS

FOREWORD

Of all Nature's creatures, birds have the greatest appeal for mankind. Their soaring flight symbolizes freedom, their song delights our ears, their bright feathers, our eyes. Distributed all over the globe, they are the most readily visible of wild animals. This book, with its lucid text and vivid illustrations, brings the songbirds' world to life.

Almost 60 percent of all living species of bird are included in the group of the Songbirds, or Passerines. Ranging from the dainty wrens and abundant, common sparrows to the raucous crows and the exotic birds of paradise, this group includes at once some of the most familiar and the most extraordinary members of the bird world.

As their name suggests, it is their voices that mark out the songbirds from their relatives in the bird world; their song, like the human voice, is vital to communication. As it sings, a bird tells its friends, its enemies and its mate (or potential mate) where it is. Songbirds also possess remarkable powers of hearing. They can distinguish sounds which are much closer in time than humans can. So what to us sounds like a single note may be heard by a bird as, say, ten separate notes. A snatch of "simple" bird song may thus convey to a bird much more than seems possible to our ears.

How this book is organized

Bird classification, even for the professional zoologist, can be a thorny problem, and one on which there is scant agreement between experts. Here we have used a widely accepted classification, based, with only a few exceptions, on the so-called Wetmore order employed in *Checklist of Birds of the World* by J. L. Peters. Other taxonomic works referred to are listed in the Bibliography.

The layout of the book follows a fairly simple structure. Each article deals with a single family or with several related families or subfamilies. The text gives details, where relevant, of physical features, distribution, evolutionary history, classification, breeding, diet and feeding behavior typical of that family. Social dynamics and spatial organization, conservation and relationships with man are also covered. Color artwork in the text illustrates representative species engaged in characteristic activities.

Preceding the discussion of each family or group of families is a panel of text that provides basic data about size, habitat, plumage, voice, nests, eggs and diet. Where a number of families are considered, a supplementary table gives this detailed information for each family (or in some cases subfamilies). For each family, there is a map of natural distribution (not introductions to other areas by man.) Unless otherwise stated, this is the global distribution of the family and includes breeding and wintering grounds for migratory birds. For each family, there is a scale drawing comparing the size of a representative species with that of a six-foot man or a 12-inch human foot. Where there are silhouettes of two birds, they are the largest and smallest representatives of the family. Generally, dimensions given are for both males and females. Where sexes differ in size, the scale drawings show the larger sex.

Every so often a really remarkable study of a species or behavior pattern emerges. Some of these studies are so distinctive that they have been allocated two whole pages, enabling the authors to develop their stories. The topics of these special features give insight into evolutionary processes at work in the world of songbirds and span social organization, foraging behavior, breeding biology and conservation. Similar themes are devoloped in smaller "box features" alongside the main text.

As you read these pages, you will marvel as each story unfolds. But as well as relishing the beauty of these birds you should also be fearful for them. Again and again authors return to the need to conserve species threatened with extinction. In *Songbirds*, the following symbols are used to show the status accorded to species at risk as listed by the International Council for Bird Preservation (ICBP) at the time of going to press. ⒺⓍ = Endangered—in danger of extinction unless causal factors (such as habitat destruction) are modified. Ⓥ = Vulnerable—likely to become endangered in the near future. Ⓡ = Rare, but neither endangered nor vulnerable at present. Ⓘ = Indeterminate —insufficient information available, but known to be in one of the above categories. (Some species that have become extinct within the past 100 years are indicated by the symbol ⒺⓍ.)

However, not all songbird species listed as threatened by the ICPB are discussed in this book, and information about the total number of threatened species in each family is included as follows: where all such species are included in the summary panel or table of species devoted to a particular family, no further comment is added. Otherwise, a figure for the "total threatened species" is given, either at the end of the list of representative species or, where the list is divided into subfamilies or other groups, at the head of the tabulated information on the family.

BROADBILLS

Family: Eurylaimidae
Order: Passeriformes (suborder Eurylaimi).
Fourteen species in 8 genera.
Distribution: Sino-Himalaya to SE Asia; Africa
S of the Sahara.

Habitat: tropical forests and thickets.

Size: length 5–11in
(12.5–28cm), weight 0.7–5.6oz
(20.5–160g). Little difference
between sexes.

Plumage: browns with gray to black; or green,
red, black or silvery gray with areas of bright
color contrast, often including the bill. Little or
no difference between sexes. Juveniles resemble
adults except that colors are duller.

Voice: screaming whistles, explosive trills,
cooing rattles, croaks.

Nest: large, domed, suspended.

Eggs: 2–3, more in Sino-Himalayan
populations; white to pinkish, unmarked or
speckled purple or reddish.

Diet: chiefly arthropods or fruit.

Species: **African green broadbill**
(*Pseudocalyptomena graueri*), **Banded broadbill**
(*Eurylaimus javanicus*), **Black-and-red broadbill**
(*Cymbirhynchus macrorhynchus*), **Black-and-
yellow broadbill** (*Eurylaimus ochromalus*),
Black-capped broadbill (*Smithornis capensis*),
Dusky broadbill (*Corydon sumatranus*), **Gray-
headed broadbill** (*Smithornis sharpei*), **Green
broadbill** (*Calyptomena viridis*), **Hose's broadbill**
(*C. hosei*), **Long-tailed broadbill** (*Psarisomus
dalhousiae*), **Philippine broadbill** (*Eurylaimus
steerii*), **Rufous-sided broadbill** (*Smithornis
rufolateralis*), **Silver-breasted broadbill**
(*Serilophus lunatus*), **Whitehead's broadbill**
(*Calyptomena whiteheadi*).

BROADBILLS are sturdy birds whose squat
appearance is accentuated by a rather
short, square tail, except in the Long-tailed
broadbill which has a fine-pointed tail. The
family is named for the great width of the
mouth, which reaches a grotesque extreme
among passerines in the outsize pink bill of
the Dusky broadbill. Broadbills inhabit
chiefly the interior of evergreen or semiever-
green broad-leaved lowland forest. Only two
species are exclusive mountain dwellers
although Long-tailed and Silver-breasted
broadbills are restricted to mountainsides in
inner tropical Southeast Asia.

No genus is common to both areas of the
broadbills' distribution and the diminutive,
mainly brown, ventrally streaked Black-
capped, Rufous-sided and Gray-headed
broadbills look so different from their gaudy
Asian relatives that they were long classified
as flycatchers—shape of bill not withstand-
ing. Anatomical studies exposed this
apparent error, adding broadbills to the African bird stock in 1914, though 19 more
years elapsed before the discovery of the
African green broadbill. Three genera are
green with black, blue or yellow on the
head, wings, belly or tail. Long-tailed, Hose's
and occasional male Green broadbills have
all of these colors. The Banded broadbill is
wine-red with a blue bill, and other species
are black with areas of red, lilac, yellow and/
or white. Black is replaced by rich chestnut
in the Philippine broadbill.

For all their color, however, bright
plumages are not especially conspicuous in
forest and the most prominent feature of, for
example, the Black-and-red broadbill, sitting in the shade of a waterside thicket, is
its almost luminous pale blue and yellow bill
(which fades after death and cannot be
appreciated in museum specimens). Several
species, including those of the genus
Smithornis, also have on their backs one or
more white, yellow or orange flashes on a
dark background, exposed during flight, and
Silver-breasted broadbills have a bright
chestnut rump, often fluffed out when they
perch.

In most species the bill is both wide and
rounded along its sides, perhaps to aid the
aerial capture of large arthropods by rather
slow-moving birds. It is also variously
hooked, almost hawklike in the Dusky
broadbill which has been seen snatching big
orthopterans in an upward leap from the
perch. This bill-form is otherwise found only
in trogons and frogmouths, which share the
broadbill habitat and feed similarly. Other
foraging modes include "flutter-snatching"
from foliage and bark, and a Banded broadbill is recorded capturing a lizard. Most species forage at mid levels of the forest but the
Dusky broadbill is a high canopy bird. Two
others, the Black-capped in Africa and
Black-and-red in Asia, inhabit forest edge
and thickets, and will go to the ground to
feed. Besides taking insects in their waterside habitat, Black-and-red broadbills sometimes also capture aquatic organisms.

The African green broadbill and *Calyptomena* species alone have bills that are
straight-sided but still very wide at the base.
The latter feed largely on fruit and while

▲ **The considerable nests** of broadbills are usually constructed so that they hang over rivers or streams. They are made of fibrous material, drawn down underneath to provide disguise. This is the Black-capped broadbill.

◄ **Plumage gives disguise** in the case of Green broadbills. It is difficult to see them in the dense foliage of forests in Thailand and peninsular Malaysia.

(1,200m) in montane forest where fruit supplies may be more stable.

Insect-eating broadbills are more sedentary. Banded and Black-and-yellow broadbills space themselves through the forest. Their presence is advertised with loud, explosive trilling calls, invariably answered by neighbors. Most others are less vociferous. *Smithornis* species are peculiar in producing a nonvocal croaking noise, apparently during short, circular flights. This sound is produced by vibrating wings. These flights are thought to have a courtship function but the noise produced by the Black-capped broadbill carries up to 200ft (about 60m) and could also be a territorial signal. Most species give a clear two-syllable whistle, most often when foraging groups assemble after breeding. These groups are usually small but as many as 20 Silver-breasted broadbills may gather and up to 26 Long-tailed broadbills have been counted progressing together through mountain forest in North Sumatra. Only the Dusky broadbill is permanently gregarious, and occurs in noisy parties of up to 10 strong.

Broadbill nests are large, pear-shaped bags with a crudely overhung side entrance, slung by a long woven cord of nest material from an isolated branch, creeper or frond-tip. They are roughly made, of all kinds of vegetation, drawn out below into a wispy beard. Leafy creeper, lichen and moss and leafy liverworts are often included and it is common for the nest chamber to be lined with fresh green leaves. Usual nest-sites are well off the ground but the Green broadbill, whose nest is broadly strapped over its support, invariably builds low, as do *Smithornis* species. Black-and-red broadbills often use a dead stump or snag in a stream, and will sometimes take advantage of a service wire over a stream or road. There are no records of helpers attending broadbill nestlings, but the Dusky broadbill flock cooperates in nest construction. In Malaya Black-and-yellow broadbills have been seen feeding fledglings of the Indian cuckoo (*Cuculus micropterus*) and are presumed to be a brood host of this cuckoo. The one definitely identified egg of the local subspecies of the Indian cuckoo is a fairly close match for the broadbill egg in color and size.

Though only casually studied, most broadbills are frequently seen and even the least known, the Philippine and African green, are unlikely to prove rare once their habitats have been explored. With the rest of their communities, most nevertheless face the threat of habitat destruction.

DRW

these two genera are not necessarily closely related there is evidence that the African green broadbill also takes much plant material.

Green broadbills often advertise their presence by cooing rattles, and pairs will drive members of the same species off small, defendable fruit sources. At larger sources several may gather, as will Hose's broadbills. These two live mainly in lowland forests where fruit is scattered and like other fruit-eating birds they must wander over a sizable area if they are to find sufficient food. Green broadbills even disperse at night. Their much larger relative, Whitehead's broadbill, lives exclusively above 4,000ft

LYREBIRDS AND SCRUB-BIRDS

Families: Menuridae, Atrichornithidae
Order: Passeriformes (suborder Menurae).
Four species in 2 genera.
Distribution: see map and table.

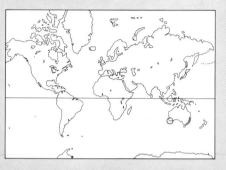

Lyrebirds   Scrub-birds

▶ **Front view of a glittering cascade,** a male Superb lyrebird in full courtship display.

▼ **The side view** of the same species reveals the contrast between the fowl-size body and the enormous tail. Male Superb lyrebirds occupy territories of 2–10 acres (0.8–4ha) in which they construct the mounds on which they sing and display. Each territory can contain up to six mounds.

THE existence of **lyrebirds** became known to Europeans in Australia in 1797 through the reports of an ex-convict who had lived for some years with, and fomented trouble among, aborigines in the bush. Surrendering to the authorities clad only in a kangaroo-skin apron, he told suspicious officials of the existence of "pheasants" near the Hawkesbury River. He was pardoned and the following year his bush-craft put to practical use on two arduous official expeditions on foot into the hinterland west of Sydney, on the first of which the first Superb lyrebird specimen was collected.

The affinities of the bird were controversial from the outset. It was variously claimed in early accounts to be a pheasant, a close relative of the domestic fowl, a bird of paradise and even a thrush. It was not until 1875 that a relationship with the scrubbirds was recognized, but even now the affinities of these two families with other groups are controversial.

The Superb lyrebird occurs from south Victoria to extreme southeast Queensland from sea level to above the snow line in dense temperate and subtropical rainforest and also in drier, open woodland in southern Queensland. It was introduced to temperate rainforest in Tasmania in 1934. The Albert lyrebird is restricted to subtropical and temperate rain forest in a narrow belt of northeast New South Wales and south Queensland (in some instances co-occurring with the Superb lyrebird).

The Superb lyrebird is a pheasant-sized bird, dark brown above, gray-brown below, with long legs and powerful feet, both dark gray. The Albert lyrebird is smaller, more rufous above and buff below and the male's tail resembles the Superb's, but lacks the lyre-shaped outer tail feathers.

Lyrebirds are mainly adapted for running and fly weakly, mostly by gliding. Nevertheless they roost high in the forest canopy, and are "shy" and hard to observe. They feed principally on soil invertebrates which they expose by digging with their powerful, long-clawed feet. Superb lyrebirds catch about 13–17 prey per minute spent foraging, dig to about 5in (12cm) deep and walk or run a few to several paces between excavations during steady foraging. They also obtain invertebrates living under the bark of rotting logs by ripping it away with their claws. Prey seem to be taken unselectively, the main ones in the nestling diet and probably

also in the adult diet being earthworms, amphipods, beetles and their larvae, spiders, millipedes, centipedes, slaters (sow bugs), fly larvae, ants, hemipterans and scorpions.

In both species females undertake all parental duties unaided. Female Superb lyrebirds spend about 160 hours on average collecting material for and building nests in fall and early winter. The female incubates the single egg for only 45 percent of daylight hours and the egg is deserted for 3–6 hours continuously each morning, during which embryonic temperature falls to ambient levels of less than 50°F (10°C) and development is interrupted. Consequently the incubation period is exceptionally long for a passerine bird.

The chick is brooded until it is able to maintain its own temperature at about ten days old. Thereafter it is fed on average every 23 minutes during daylight and its fecal sacs are deposited away from the nest by its mother. At fledging in October or November it weighs about 63 percent of its mother's weight and is accompanied and partly fed by her for up to eight months. Eighty percent of nest failures are attributable to predation by mammals and birds. The breeding biology of the Albert lyrebird is broadly similar.

Male Superb lyrebirds live up to 15 years and acquire the typical adult tail over the first 5–7 years. In early life they range widely in small groups, but at maturity they establish large, partly overlapping territories averaging 6–8.6 acres (2.5–3.5ha) which they defend especially strongly in winter by singing, displaying and chasing intruders. They are therefore fairly even spaced throughout suitable habitat, although some local clustering results from neighbors often having adjacent preferred display areas within their territories. Males scratch up many earth mounds 3–5ft (1–1.5m) across, up to 20 of which they use extensively for display and copulation in a season. In the peak mating season up to 50 percent of daylight hours are spent singing.

Males are polygamous. They exhibit no parental behavior and associate with females only briefly for courtship and mating. Although some female nesting territories lie entirely within a male territory, many overlap more than one and some females visit at least two males immediately prior to mating. While some females do mate with the same male in successive seasons, there is little sign of pair-bonding and males appear to be promiscuous.

Females probably breed at an earlier age than males. The evolution of single-parent

The Song of the Superb Lyrebird

Standing in full courtship display on his mound, the male Superb lyrebird presents a beautiful and bizarre spectacle. His specialized tail feathers are held horizontally over his back and droop forward over his head, forming a silvery-white fan. Periodically they are relaxed and then thrust forward once again.

The bird emits a continuous stream of loud, melodious song and turns slowly. When a female visits the mound, the tail feathers are held forwards but unfanned and are quivered rapidly as the male utters a curious clicking call. At the climax of his display, he prescribes several semicircles around the female with such rapid, short paces that he seems to glide and then leaps forward and back repeatedly in time with a rhythmical call ending in two, far-carrying, bell-like notes.

The song contains a component typical of the species lasting 5–6 seconds, audible from 0.6mi (1km) away when there is little wind and exhibiting marked local dialects. To this

is added a stream of accurately mimicked calls of cohabiting bird species, including such subtle imitations as the precisely timed duetting of whipbirds (*Psophodes olivaceus*) and kookaburras (*Dacelo gigas*) and the multiple wingbeats and calls of flying parrot flocks. Males also mimic the barking of dogs and, reputedly, occasionally even sounds made by inanimate objects such as car horns, although some of these latter claims are probably exaggerations. Up to 16 bird species may be mimicked in a local population, the particular models and their relative importance in the repertoire varying according to locality. Young males may partly learn their repertoires from older males rather than entirely acquiring them directly from the mimicked species.

Singing seems to be important in repelling rival males and attracting prospective mates, but why mimicry should be particularly effective in doing so is puzzling and controversial.   AL

brood-care, a crucial step in the evolution of bird promiscuity, was probably facilitated particularly by the small clutch size and hence low costs of egg production and feeding young; the embryo's ability to withstand cooling when it has to be deserted daily by its mother when she goes foraging, and the roofed nest which prevents wetting and probable death of eggs and nestlings at low temperatures.

Emancipated from parental duties, males can increase their reproductive success by copulating with several mates because females commence breeding at different times over a seven-week period. The regular, territorial spacing of males is probably the best way for them to meet and court several potential mates given that females and their territories are also evenly dispersed.

Although lyrebirds were slaughtered indiscriminately for their tail plumage in the 19th century, they are now fully protected and common in suitable habitat. The main threat to both species is further extensive habitat alteration and destruction.   AL

Scrub-birds are small, solidly built birds with strong pointed bills, long powerful legs, long tapered tails, short rounded wings and brown plumage: ideal attributes for birds that live close to the ground in dense vegetation. They are fast and alert, but have limited powers of flight. The Noisy scrub-bird is Australia's rarest passerine and the Rufous scrub-bird, although more numerous, is also rare. The Noisy scrub-bird is only found at Two Peoples Bay, 25mi (40km) east of Albany in Western Australia,

while the Rufous scrub-bird occurs in a number of isolated mountain localities in northern New South Wales and southern Queensland. Both species are terrestrial, eat insects and mainly occupy forest edges where the light and moisture allow the growth of a dense ground layer of shrubs and rushes. In their dense habitat the most conspicuous character of scrub-birds is the loud territorial song of the male.

Scrub-birds are closely related to lyre-

birds, but their relationship with other passerine groups is uncertain. Arguments have been put forward suggesting relationships with bowerbirds and birds of paradise and with the tapaculos of South America. Their disjunct distribution suggests that they were once distributed across Australia; their present relict status is the result of climatic and vegetation changes since the Miocene era (26–7 million years ago) and in particular the severe climatic oscillations in the

---

The 2 Families of Lyrebirds and Scrub-birds   ⒠ Endangered.   ⒭ Rare

Lyrebirds
Family: Menuridae.
Two species of the genus *Menura*.
E Australia. Temperate and subtropical rain forest. Size: males 35–39in (89–100cm) long, up to 2.5lb (1.15kg); females 30–34in (76–86cm), up to 2lb (950g). Plumage: brown above, buff to gray-brown below. The male's tail is very long, train-like and comprised of highly modified feathers; the female's is shorter and simpler. Voice: loud carrying song; much mimicry of other birds and mammals; also high-pitched alarm whistles, display calls. Nests: bulky, domed chambers of twigs, bark, moss and fern fronds, lined with rootlets and body feathers, having a side entrance. Located on the ground, earth banks, rock faces,

boulders, tree buttresses and exposed roots, logs, wire-grass clumps and in dead and living trees to a height of about 72ft (22m). Eggs: usually 1, light gray to deep khaki or purplish brown with blackish brown or deep gray spots and streaks; weight: 1.7–2.5oz (49–72g). Incubation period: about 50 days. Nestling period: about 47 days; from fledging to independence maximum 8 months. Diet: invertebrates in soil and rotting wood.

Species: **Albert's lyrebird** (*Menura alberti*), **Superb lyrebird** (*M. novaehollandiae*).

Scrub-birds
Family: Atrichornithidae.
Two species of the genus *Atrichornis*.
Noisy scrub-bird ⒠ (*Atrichornis clamosus*): Australia at Two Peoples Bay near Albany in Western Australia. Forest edges. Size: 6–8.5in (16–21cm) long, weight 1–1.8oz (30–50g); females smaller than males. Plumage: upper parts brown with darker fine cross bars; underparts range from white on throat to rufous around the anus; male has black bar on the upper breast. Voice: two alarm notes and a three-note call; loud variable song of 10–20 notes; another shorter and variable song that uses modified songs of other birds. Nest: domed with small side entrance. Eggs: 1, buff with irregular patches of brown, mainly at

the larger end; 1.1 × 0.8in (2.9 × 2cm). Incubation period: 36–38 days; nestling period: 21–28 days. Diet: invertebrates with occasional small lizard, gecko or frog.

Rufous scrub-bird ⒭ (*A. rufescens*): Australia in New South Wales and southern Queensland. Forest edges. Length 6–7in (16–18cm); females smaller than males. Plumage: upper parts rufous brown with fine black cross bars; underparts white on throat, remainder rufous brown; male has black bar across the upper breast which extends down the breast and belly. Voice: loud repeated chip; two alarm notes; also mimics other birds. Eggs: 2, pink buff with blotches of brown, mainly at larger end. Incubation and nestling periods: unknown. Diet: invertebrates.

▲ **Longsome maternal care** is a feature of the lyrebird social cycle. The female feeds her single offspring for up to 8 months. Here a female Superb lyrebird feeds a young male.

▼ **One of the world's rarest birds,** a male Rufous scrub-bird. In 1949, several decades after it had last been seen, a memorial to the species was erected near where it had originally been discovered.

Pleistocene era (2 million–10,000 years ago).

The diet of scrub-birds consists of a wide variety of invertebrates with the occasional small lizard, gecko or frog. Nestling Noisy scrub-birds eat species from at least 18 orders of invertebrates, the most common being spiders, grasshoppers, cockroaches and various larvae. Adults forage mainly in leaf litter, rushes and small shrubs where they move slowly while looking and listening and occasionally turning over leaves with a quick flick of the head. The smaller Rufous scrub-bird may even move under the litter layer while foraging. Prey may also be flushed out when the bird stands still and rapidly drums one foot on the litter.

Male Noisy scrub-birds occupy well-dispersed territories of 15–22 acres (6–9ha) within which they spend at least 80 percent of their time in a core area of 2.5–5 acres (1–2ha) which is usually centered on the best feeding area. The males roost in tall shrubs or trees away from the core area. There is normally one female within the male's territory who occupies a nesting area of 2.5–5 acres (1–2ha) outside the core area or on the periphery of the territory. There is little contact between the sexes, and as well as mating with the female in his territory a male may mate with females in adjacent areas not occupied by males or with young females on the periphery of his territory.

Male Noisy scrub-birds defend their territories throughout the year, with song. During the breeding season they sing throughout the day. Their singing begins in the breeding season of their second year and they develop their territorial song during the year. In addition the male Noisy scrub-bird has a short, more variable song, incorporating modified elements from the songs of other species, which it uses when interacting with other males or with females. The male Rufous scrub-bird sings only during the mating season. It is an excellent mimic.

Rufous scrub-birds breed in spring and summer while Noisy scrub-birds breed in winter. Female Noisy scrub-birds breed in their first year, males from the age of three onwards, perhaps living until they are nine years old. The female Noisy scrub-bird builds a domed nest with a small side entrance and lines the bottom of the cavity with decayed nest material or decayed wood which dries to a hard papier-mâché-like material. (Female Rufous scrub-birds line the nest cavity completely.) The nest takes up to three weeks to build and the single egg is laid a week later. Eggs are laid from May to October with the main peak in June (mid-winter). The female incubates the egg, which hatches after 36–38 days, an exceptionally long period but, as in the lyrebird, the egg is usually left unincubated for part of the day. As well as feeding the chick, she maintains hygiene in the nest by removing fecal sacs and placing them in a creek or under a bush away from the nest. After the chick leaves the nest it stays with its mother, probably until after it has finished its first molt when two to three months old. If the egg is lost the female may build another nest and lay again, but if the chick dies a second clutch is not attempted.

The Noisy scrub-bird was originally found in six isolated coastal localities between Perth and Albany between 1842 and 1889. Then nothing more was heard until 1961 when a small population was discovered. A battle by conservationists resulted in the bird's locality being set aside as a reserve for the species. The near extinction of the Noisy scrub-bird was caused by the changed fire regime initiated by Europeans and by destruction of habitat. The conservation area has been managed so as to prevent outbreaks of wildfires, and the population has grown, the number of singing males (the only measure of population) rising from 45 in 1970 to 138 in 1983. A second population has been established to the northeast of the original one, and the species could now be bred in captivity if necessary.

The distribution and abundance of the Rufous scrub-bird have also been affected by habitat destruction and fire and the species is now confined to a small number of National Parks. Although rare it is not considered endangered.   GTS

OVENBIRDS AND THEIR ALLIES

Families: Furnariidae, Dendrocolaptidae, Formicariidae
Order: Passeriformes (suborder Tyranni, part).
Four hundred and ninety-seven species in 121 genera.
Distribution: see maps and table.

Ovenbirds

Woodcreepers

Antbirds

THE **ovenbirds** take their name from the remarkable nest of the Rufous hornero. Made of mud, strengthened with hair or fiber, it has the shape of an old-fashioned baker's oven, rounded with a dome-shaped top. A narrow entrance leads to a chamber about 8in (20cm) wide which is lined with soft grass. One penalty of building this curious cave is that the ovenbird has become host to a bed-bug (family Cimiccidae). Only a few of these blood-feeders occur on birds, most of them on swifts and swallows.

Based on the number of species ovenbirds form the fourth largest, the most diverse and yet the most drab of South American bird families. They are found in a variety of habitats, some occupying niches that elsewhere would belong to such groups as larks, wheatears, dippers and nuthatches. On the basis of ecology and behavior three subfamilies have been recognized: Furnariinae, Synallaxinae, Phylidorinae.

The subfamily Furnariinae includes terrestrial birds of open land of mainly South America. Miners occupy arid land, where they walk or run but rarely fly. They resemble drab wheatears. Earthcreepers are similar but have longer tails, longer more downcurved bills and are even duller in color. Unlike the miners they may be closely associated with water. Dipper-like cinclodes are much more strictly associated with water; a few are even partly marine: Surf cinclodes rarely leave the water's edge where they feed. All these species nest in holes in the ground, either digging their own burrow or using the holes of other birds or rodents, or nesting between rocks. Nests can be as much as 4ft (1.2cm) from the entrance.

The true ovenbirds are also birds of the open land but penetrate further into the tropical belt, even close to forest, although in general they keep to open valleys and floodplains. At least the best-known species, the Rufous hornero, has adapted well to humans and is welcomed around settlements.

The subfamily Synallaxinae includes the spinetails, canasteros and thornbirds. They are usually rather small with longish, more or less graduated and often forked tails. The tails show great variation. The remarkable Des Murs's wiretail has only six main feathers in the tail, the short outer pair hidden in the tail coverts, the middle and inner pair very long but reduced to little more than the central shaft.

Members of the Synallaxinae mostly inhabit dense vegetation in or on the edge of forest, in reed beds, scrubland, grassland or even mangrove, while a few species are found in barren areas and a few others live in trees. The ovenbird family in particular is famous for its unusual nests and it is in this subfamily that they show the greatest diversity.

The Wren-like rushbird weaves a sphere of clay-daubed grass around growing reeds. An entrance near the top is protected by a woven awning and sometimes even by a hinged woven trapdoor. Often a depressed clay platform on top acts as a singing perch. Other ball-like nests of grass, etc, are built near or on the ground. The nest of Red-faced spinetails is also globular, but hung from the tip of a slender hanging branch. Some species nest on a branch and enter from below onto a platform lined with feathers; others build a nest 12in (30cm) in diameter with a side entrance into a small chamber leading by a tortuous tunnel to near the top of the nest where the tunnel opens directly into a nest chamber.

There are also various forms of nests of thorns with tunnels to the nest-chamber. That of Rufous-breasted spinetails is roughly oblong or retort-shaped and as much as 30in long by 50in high (75 × 50cm). A large dorsal platform leads via a tunnel through a tangle of thorns to a thatched nest-chamber lined with downy leaves. Cordilleran canasteros build large exposed vertical cylindrical baskets of thorny twigs; where there are no thorns available the nest is built into cactus plants. Rufous-throated thornbirds build a large unkempt-looking double-chambered nest of thorny twigs. In subsequent seasons other chambers are added to produce an apparently colonial nest. It is unlikely that more than one pair occupy a nest at any one time, but surplus chambers may be used by non-breeding members of a previous brood, other ovenbirds or even birds of other families. The Firewood gatherer also builds a voluminous thorny nest and often incorporates oddments of debris, eg bones, metal, colored rag. The lining of the neatly arched tunnel may include bits of bark, snake skin, snails and crab shell.

Members of the subfamily Phylidorinae generally live in trees and make simpler nests. (Cachalotes are the only members that build huge thorny nests, that of the White-throated cachalote being up to 5ft (1.5m) in diameter.) Many nest in banks at the end of tunnels up to 6ft (1.8m) long which are quite tortuous. Nest-chambers contain well-woven nests or small collections of loose leaves or rootlets. The bird may dig its own tunnel or improve an already existing one. Many use rock or tree fissures or holes, usually with a simple nest or using only wood chips.

Perhaps the only standard feature of ovenbirds is that their nests are always well enclosed—well, nearly always! Bay-capped wren-spinetails usually build flat open nests of grass lined with feathers a few centimeters above the water in a reed bed. Sometimes a rim is built and occasionally the rim is so well developed that there is only a small hole at the top. Some canasteros lay in what is virtually a well-concealed scrape on the ground, sometimes lined with a few bits of bone and fur from owl pellets. Rusty-backed spinetails make a crude chamber in a tangle of drift vegetation trapped by a branch during flood levels, or use the abandoned nest of another ovenbird. Tit-spinetails will also take over abandoned nests, but will use a variety of other sites, including holes in cacti.   AMH

The **woodcreepers**, sometimes known as woodhewers, are tree-climbing birds of Central and South America. Most are medium-sized, slender birds, brown to rufous with a variety of spots or streaks on the head, mantle and underparts. The tail is rufous with very stiff-tipped woodpecker- or treecreeper-like feathers. The main variation is in the bill which ranges from short, thick and slightly upturned to very long, thin and strongly downcurved. For a long time woodcreepers were considered a part of the ovenbird family, but while a few spe-

cies have characters intermediate between the typical woodcreepers and the ovenbirds, they are now regarded as sufficiently distinct to warrant inclusion in a separate family.

They are usually found alone or in pairs but occasionally in small groups that are often family parties. Some species will join flocks of mixed-species. Most spend much time in trees, using their tail as well as their strong legs and feet to work their way spirally up trees and out onto branches, then flying in the fashion of a treecreeper down to the base of another tree and starting their way upwards again. Some species spend a considerable amount of time feeding on or very close to the ground.

The Spot-crowned woodcreeper is a fairly typical species with a slightly downcurved bill of medium length, 1in out of a total length of 8in (2.5cm of 20cm). It occurs on wooded slopes to an altitude of 10,000ft (3,000m), ie higher than most of its relatives. Solitarily or in pairs woodcreepers hunt around the forest, poking among epiphytes, such as ferns and bromeliads, and under bark which may be levered off with the bill; it takes mainly small prey. This is one of the first species active in the morning and last to roost. Hence their roosts are difficult to find; but they roost alone in a crevice or hole in a tree. The eggs are laid in a concealed hole or crevice that is often enlarged. The nest hole is lined with wood chippings collected by both parents and added to throughout the nesting period. Both parents attend the eggs and young. The young hatch blind and almost naked; they tend to be rather noisy.

The Buff-throated woodcreeper has a fairly heavy and straight bill, enabling it to take quite large prey, including small

▲ **Work in progress.** Two partly built Rufous horneros' nests. Each completed nest will consist of between 1,500 and 2,500 lumps of clay.

▼ **Holding tight to branch and prey** a Gray-throated leafscraper (*Sclerurus albigularis*), a species of ovenbird from northern South America.

lizards. Although generally birds of thick forest, they will frequent clearings and open woodland and will often feed on the ground or on fallen logs. More solitary than the Spot-crowned woodcreeper, they rarely join flocks of mixed species and are rarely to be seen in pairs. Their clear melodious notes can be heard at all times of day, but unlike the Spot-crowned and other members of its genus, which form lasting pair-bonds, no such pair-bonds exist in this genus. In this genus the female takes entire responsibility for the nest and will frequently attack an intruding male. She may spend up to 80 percent of the daylight hours incubating and will return with extra bits of bark for the nest after her periods off the nest. Similarly she rears the young alone, bringing single food items at intervals of about half an hour. A further contrast to the Spot-crowned group is that the young of these single-parent families remain silent until they leave the nest. Having once left the nest they do not return, even to roost. Both groups lay the same number of eggs, and in spite of their different social organization incubation and fledging periods are the same.

The Plain-brown woodcreeper and its relatives lack the spots and streaks but are otherwise typical woodcreepers. They tend to spend much more time close to the ground and are common ant-followers.

They will often feed around the periphery of ant-swarms or in the absence of larger antbirds can be the dominant bird, feeding on vertical trunks with occasional sorties to pick insects off vegetation or from the air. Members of this genus and the Olivaceous woodcreeper are also one-parent families.

The Wedge-billed woodcreeper is by far the smallest member of the family and its short stout upturned bill is unlike that of any other woodcreeper. It lives mostly in trees and feeds actively on small invertebrates. Its nest is usually in a crevice or rot-hole close to the ground, but occasionally as high as 20ft (about 6m) above. This is another species in which both parents care for the nest and young. The young are fed with insects which are carried one at a time in the adult's bill.

The largest woodcreepers have the largest bills: the Great rufous woodcreeper, the size of a small crow, has a particularly heavy bill, the Long-billed woodcreeper has a long straight bill about one-fifth of its total length, while the curved bill of scythebills can be a quarter of the total length. With this bill the scythebills probe around trunks and logs and investigate cracks and crevices that are beyond the reach of other woodcreepers. They also take small vertebrates. Although it might seem essential that such a bill should be in good condition, a Black-billed scythebill trapped in southeast Brazil had

The 3 Families of Ovenbirds, Woodcreepers and Antbirds

Ovenbirds
Family: Furnariidae
Two hundred and seventeen species in 56 genera.
C Mexico, C America, S America, Trinidad and Tobago, Falkland and Juan Fernandez Islands. Deep forest to open arid land; sea level to snow line. Size: 4–10in (10–26cm) long, weight 0.3–1.6oz (9–46g). Plumage: generally somber browns, often rufous on head, wings or tail; underside streaked, spotted or plain, sometimes very pale. Voice: very varied, generally resonant; harsh rattles and creaks, screams, clear harmonious notes, whistling trills, etc. Nests: vary from mud chambers to huge bundles of twigs; burrows also used. Eggs: white, occasionally off-white or blue; incubation: about 15 days. Diet: mainly insects and other invertebrates.

Species and genera include: **Bay-capped wren-spinetail** (*Spartanoica maluroides*), **cachalotes** (genus *Pseudoseisura*), **canasteros** (genus *Asthenes*), **cinclodes** (genus *Cinclodes*), **Cordilleran canasteros** (*Asthenes modesta*), **Des Murs's wiretail** (*Sylviorthorhynchus desmursii*), **earthcreepers** (genus *Upucerthia*), **Firewood gatherer** (*Anumbius annumbi*), **miners** (genera *Geobates, Geositta*), **Red-faced spinetail** (*Cranioleuca erythrops*), **Rufous-breasted spinetail** (*Synallaxis erythrothorax*), **Rufous hornero** or **Rufous ovenbird** (*Furnarius rufus*), **Rusty-backed spinetail** (*Cranioleuca vulpina*), **Surf cinclodes** (*Cinclodes taczanowskii*), **thornbirds** (genus *Phacellodomus*), **tit-spinetails** (genus *Leptasthenura*), **White-chinned thistletail** (*Schizoeaca fuliginosa*), **White-throated cachalote** (*Pseudoseisura gutturalis*), **Wren-like rushbird** (*Phleocryptes melanops*).

Woodcreepers
Family: Dendrocolaptidae
Fifty species in 13 genera.
N Mexico S to C Argentina. Forest, forest edge, open woodland. Size: 5.5–14in (13.5–35cm) long, weight 0.4–4.2oz (12–120g). Plumage: brown to rufous, often streaked or spotted; stiff spiny tails. Voice: trills and repetitive notes, often loud but generally not unmusical. Nest: tree holes or hollows, sometimes behind loose bark. Eggs: 2–3; plain white to greenish white. Incubation: 15–20 days. Diet: insects, other invertebrates, small vertebrates.

Species and genera include: **Black-billed scythebill** (*Campylorhamphus falcularius*), **Buff-throated woodcreeper** (*Xiphorhynchus guttatus*), **Great rufous woodcreeper** (*Xiphocolaptes major*), **Long-billed woodcreeper** (*Nasica longirostris*), **Olivaceous woodcreeper** (*Sittasomus griseicapillus*), **Plain brown woodcreeper** (*Dendrocincla fuliginosa*), **scythebills** (genus *Campylorhamphus*), **Spot-crowned woodcreeper** (*Lepidocolaptes affinis*), **Wedge-billed woodcreeper** (*Glyphorynchus spirurus*).

Antbirds
Family: Formicariidae
Two hundred and thirty species in 52 genera.
C Mexico S to C Argentina. Forest; sometimes open woodland or brushland. Size: 3–14in (8–35cm) long, weight 0.3–2.6oz (9–75g). Plumage: males usually gray to black with varying amounts of white spots or bars, sometimes with rufous; females usually duller or browner. Voice: most species unmusical; many produce harsh churring alarm or contact calls; some species have attractive songs and melodious calls. Nests: open cup in forks; occasionally tree cavity or on ground. Eggs: usually 2; white, usually with dark spots. Incubation: about 14 days. Diet: mainly insects, some small fruit, vertebrates.

Species include: **Bicolored antbird** (*Gymnopithys leucaspis*), **Black-crowned antpitta** (*Pittasoma michleri*), **Bluish-slate antshrike** (*Thamnomanes schistogynus*), **Ocellated antbird** (*Phaenostictus mcleannani*), **Spotted antbird** (*Hylophylax naevioides*), **White-plumed antbird** (*Pithys albifrons*). Total threatened species: 6

the front third of the upper mandible broken off; its weight was normal, but its plumage was in poor condition and it seemed inefficient at controlling the level of parasites on its body.   AMH

Antbirds comprise a very large family restricted to the forested areas of Central and South America. Most species occur in the lower levels of forest or on the ground and prefer fairly close undergrowth, but a few occur in quite open areas or in the forest canopy. They are usually smallish birds.

The antbirds form a very diverse family, this diversity being reflected (not always accurately) in their names: antshrike, antvireo, antwren, antthrush and antpitta. In most species there is a strong difference between sexes: males are mainly dark gray to black with various amounts of white spots or bars; females tend to have more rufous or olive plumage. Some of the ground-dwelling species are more distinctively patterned and the sexes look alike in some of the most striking species, such as the White-plumed antbird. Many species have a concealed white patch on the back.

Antwrens and antthrushes are not especially wren- or thrush-like, but the former are small active birds of forest undergrowth, the latter are ground-dwellers, some with boldly streaked underparts (although mostly with very short upturned tails). Antpittas bear a strong resemblance to the Old World pittas, but are by no means so colorful. One group of large antpittas hops on the ground in dense cover, while the other group of small species lives in the undergrowth just above ground. The antvireos do not look especially like their northern counterparts, but resemble them in color, behavior and, to some extent, in breeding habits and song. Antshrikes have the robust, predaceous appearance of Old World shrikes, but little other similarity. The species of these groups make up a little more than half the family, most of the rest being simply called "antbirds."

Antbirds feed on insects and other invertebrates and some species take small vertebrates or fruit. Many species associate with or lead the mixed-species flocks that roam the forests (see box).

The feature of antbirds that is presumably responsible for their name is the habit of some species of following swarming army ants. Ants of the subfamily Dorylinae are well known for their frequent swarming through forests, either to move their colony or in raids for feeding. In Central and South America grossly exaggerated tales are told

of the ants' activities, but certainly several army ants (eg *Eciton burchelli*) swarm very frequently and a variety of birds takes advantage of the mass movement of the ants to feed on the other insects, etc, that are disturbed by the passage of the column of ants. So do a number of predatory and parasitic insects, and reptiles. The main bird families involved are cuckoos, woodcreepers, antbirds and tanagers. About 50 species are regular ant-followers, but many other birds will occasionally join in. Large colonies of regularly nomadic ants can attract at a time up to 25 birds of one or two species plus scattered individuals of up to 30 other species. Many "professional" ant-followers obtain up to 50 percent of their food from antswarms, keeping a regular eye on the colonies to take advantage the moment the swarm starts to move. There is often a strict

▲ **Courtship feeding** is an important stage in the formation of the monogamous pair-bond in antbirds. In the Ocellated antbird much singing is involved. (1) A female (left) screams at her mate who bobs his head ritually. Having brought food the male sings faintly while holding the item in his mouth (2). The male then feeds the female (3), who takes a low posture while eating the food (4). When the feeding session is over the female pecks at the male's bill while he bobs his head (5).

Feeding Flocks in Tropical Forests

Although European observers will be used to seeing mixed flocks of birds (eg tits, kinglets, nuthatches, creepers, finches) moving through woodland it is in the tropical forests that this activity is most manifest. In such forests it is often difficult to see birds at all, but a mixed-species flock gives the opportunity to study a number of species and compare their differing feeding behavior.

The function of such flocks is not fully understood, but the various suggestions fall into two categories: either to enhance feeding or to reduce the risk of predation by being with other birds, as in this case each individual is less likely to be caught unawares by a predator.

Whatever the reason, a mixed flock of insectivorous and omnivorous species in the tropics works through the forest at about 0.2mi (a third of a kilometer) per hour, occupying feeding levels from the ground to close to the canopy. The path followed may be very erratic and frequently crosses itself.

There is usually one bird or species that

maintains the cohesion and impetus of the flock. In Central America this is often one of the parulid warblers, eg the Three-striped warbler (*Basileuterus tristriatus*); in South America it is more frequently an antbird, eg the Bluish-slate antshrike. As these core birds move through changing forest habitats, calling frequently, other birds are attracted to the flock while it is within their home range. Thus there may be only one pair (perhaps together with its fledged young) of each highly territorial species involved in the flock at any one time. In this way a single antbird has been seen to involve about 80 species in two days and, of course, a large but unquantifiable number of individuals.

Nevertheless birds do not always join a flock that moves through their territory; they are more likely to do so if a trespassing member of their own species is present and are less likely to do so during the breeding season, during the early morning or late afternoon and during inclement weather.

AMH

hierarchy in the attendant birds, with the larger antbirds, such as the Ocellated antbird, holding a central "territory" just ahead of the ant column while smaller species, such as the Bicolored antbird and the Spotted antbird, hold increasingly peripheral territories. Some small species, such as the White-plumed antbird, are able to utilize the whole area by making raids from the periphery, at the expense of being frequently attacked. Large and potentially dominant ground birds, such as Black-crowned antpittas, have to occupy peripheral zones. Territories exist vertically as well as horizontally and many of the non-professional ant-followers feed in the outer or upper reaches or even between the territories of the professionals. Many of the less regular drop out as the ant-swarm moves out of their territory, while the professionals are prepared to share the resource to some extent, although individuals of a species only remain dominant over others of their own species while they are in their own ter-

ritory. These antbirds have learnt to utilize the movements of the ant-swarms.

Antbirds pair for life and the parents share nest building, incubation and care of the young. Nests are usually fairly frail, deep structures of loosely interwoven plant strands slung between the fork of a twig near the ground. Usually the nest is lined with leaves and sometimes with finer material. A few species nest on the ground and others in tree fissures, among epiphytes such as ferns well above the ground or in the crown of low tree ferns. The eggs are incubated by the female during the night and part of the middle of the day, with the male brooding for the morning and late afternoon. Young are fed on insects brought singly, but they fledge quickly, and sometimes before they are able to fly strongly, in about two weeks. The young birds often stay with the parents for a long time and young males may even bring a female into the family group prior to establishing their own breeding territory.   AMH

TYRANT FLYCATCHERS AND PITTAS

Families: Tyrannidae, Pittidae
Order: Passeriformes (suborder Tyranni—part).
Four hundred and two species in 89 genera.
Distribution: see map and table.

Tyrant flycatchers　　**Pittas**

▶ **The nest of the Dusky flycatcher**
(*Empidonax oberholseri*) is made of grasses and
fibers and lined with grass and feathers. The
young fledge 18 days after hatching. This
species breeds in western North America.

▶ **The Pied water tyrant** BELOW (*Fluvicola pica*)
loves water. Its range is Central America and
the West Indies.

▼ **Open country near water appeals** to the
Boat-billed flycatcher (*Megarhynchus pitangua*),
which is found from Panama south to Uruguay.
It occupies a variety of habitats, from sea level
to 6,200ft (1,900m), where it is an active
forager. Access to water, however, enables it to
dine on frogs.

THE **tyrant flycatchers** comprise the largest and most diverse family of birds in the New World. No other bird family contains species that breed from the spruce forests of northern Canada to the rugged, treeless hillsides of Tierra del Fuego. Flycatchers occupy every habitat in between, from tropical forests and seacoasts up to the snow line on the highest mountains. In South America, the center of diversity of the family, more than one-tenth of all land bird species are tyrant flycatchers.

By no means do all flycatchers make their living "catching flies." Rather, the widespread diversity of the flycatchers in the New World results largely from a tremendous diversity of ecological roles and associated body forms found within the family. True "fly-catchers," ie species that perch motionless and make aerial sallies after passing insects, are actually in the minority within the family. In South America flycatcher equivalents exist for numerous other types of birds found on other continents.

The largest flycatchers are the drab, grayish or brownish shrike-tyrants of the high-altitude grasslands in the Andes. These jay-sized birds search for prey by scanning the ground from elevated perches, and they tear apart large insects and small lizards with their strong, hooked bills. The related ground-tyrants, mostly grayish, run along the rocky slopes of the high mountaintops on long legs, looking very much like pipits. They pick insects from the ground, and on long, pointed wings they can rapidly dart after any escaping prey. Among the larger flycatchers is a large group of species that shares a similar, conspicuous plumage pattern of bright yellow underparts and black-and-white striped crowns. Best known of these is the Great kiskadee, widespread from North America south to central Argentina. This species eats almost anything, but is especially fond of catching small fish or tadpoles from shallow lakeshores. At the opposite size extreme are the tiny, greenish tody-tyrants and pygmy-tyrants, which live in dense foliage in the moist, tropical lowlands. Some of these species are smaller than most hummingbirds, and the Short-tailed pygmy-tyrant (Costa Rica through to Amazonian South America) is the smallest species in this enormous order.

Many pygmy-tyrants have wide, spoon-shaped bills with which they scoop insects from the undersides of leaves during rapid darts through the vegetation. Related to these are the spadebills, named for their weird, oversized bills that are shaped like wide shovels or spoons.

The most common type of flycatcher is of medium size, dull olive in color, and lives in the treetops or scrubby forest edges. Many of these species have relatively wide bills bordered with well-developed rictal bristles. These apparently aid in snagging insects that are captured on the wing, although some evidence now indicates that bristles also serve to protect the eyes from damage during active foraging through dense vegetation; they probably also have a sensory function. A few flycatchers, such as the Scissor-tailed flycatcher, possess extraordinarily long, forked tails. Typically these belong to species that sally out into mid-air to capture flying insects. The long outer tail-feathers aid in the rapid aerial maneuvering required to capture wary insects in the open.

Only a few flycatchers are brightly colored. The male Vermilion flycatcher is entirely scarlet on the crown and underparts. He displays these colors to other males and the drab brown females, during a conspicuous aerial flight display over open meadows, accompanied by a melodious, warbled song. The Many-colored rush tyrant, perhaps the strangest flycatcher, is a wren-like inhabitant of tall, dense reed beds in the high Andes and in Argentina. This species is a patchwork pattern of blue, green, black, white, yellow and red. The Royal flycatcher occasionally displays its wide, vivid red crest by holding it erect across its crown while it opens its bill to display a bright orange mouth.

The size and colors of males and females are usually similar but there are a few exceptions. The female Strange-tailed tyrant is straw-brown above and whitish below, with slightly elongated tail feathers. The male, however, is boldly marked with black and white, with a huge, streamer-like tail and a bright yellow, bare throat patch during the breeding season. This species belongs to a group of closely related forms, nearly all of which have black or black and white males and drab-colored females. These species inhabit open country, especially grasslands and marshes. The conspicuous, flashy patterns of the males are associated with aerial displays that are visible over great distances across these habitats. The females perform most nesting duties, and their brownish color serves to camouflage their activity around the nest.

Most flycatchers eat insects, captured after brief, almost motionless searches from exposed perches near vegetation or above the ground. Many of the variations in size and body shape found within the family are associated with slight differences in the exact manner of searching or prey capture. For example, those that frequently sally to or along the ground have long legs, for strength and stability on the ground. Those that sally into the air have long, forked tails, relatively long wings and short legs. Species that pick their insect prey from tiny crevices in leaves and twigs have narrow, tweezer-like bills, usually with few or no rictal bristles. Those that snatch prey from leaf surfaces during a quick flight off the perch have rather broad bills and long bristles. Nearly all flycatchers eat some fruit, usually small berries found while foraging for insects. A few species actually specialize on fruit taken from large trees.

Virtually all flycatchers are monogamous. Some species, especially migratory ones, pair anew each year as the breeding season begins. Many nonmigratory tropical species remain paired the year round, dwelling on permanent territories. In many smaller species only the female constructs the nest, usually with the male close by. With few exceptions only the female incubates eggs and broods young. The male defends the territory and the nest-site, frequently perching within a few feet of the nest for hours on end while the female incubates. Typically both sexes feed the young, but again females of some smaller species perform this role exclusively. In a few small, fruit-eating species, such as the Ochre-bellied flycatcher, the male has no role in the nesting process whatsoever. In these species males display in traditional arenas or "leks," separate from the nest sites, and females visit these sites to mate.

In most species the young reach independence within a few months of leaving the nest, and are breeding on their own territories the following year. In many tropical species the young remain with their parents during this intervening year, the family foraging together as a group. The White-bearded flycatcher carries this association one step further: the young remain with their parents for up to several years and help raise subsequent broods of siblings.

Virtually all flycatchers live on defended territories. Those breeding in North America abandon the territory in late summer and migrate to Central or South America. In some cases migration is accompanied by dramatic shifts in habits. The pugnacious Eastern kingbird is a monogamous breeder on vigorously defended territories in open country throughout much of North America. However, while wintering in the Amazon basin it travels in huge, nomadic flocks, prefers forest habitats, eats mostly fruit instead of insects, and is subordinate to resident birds in the region. Other migratory flycatchers, including some that move northwards out of Patagonia during the southern winter, join mixed species flocks in the treetops. These flocks usually contain various species of resident flycatchers as well, and can include up to 30 species or more when swelled with migrants. Such flocks of mixed species jointly defend their giant territories against other flocks, just as pairs defend smaller territories against other pairs in nonflocking species.   JWF

The brightly colored **pittas** form a compact and remarkable family of primarily terrestrial forest birds centered in the Southeast Asian tropics. Like precious jewels, their brilliant hues, combined with their rarity and mysterious origins, have given them a popularity amongst songbirds that may only be surpassed by the birds of paradise.

All pittas are stocky, long-legged, short-tailed birds with strong bills, well adapted to life on or near the forest floor, where most of their time is spent. Their bright plumage is often intensely vivid scarlet, turquoise blue, rich and delicate greens, velvety black or porcelain white. As the brightest colors are usually found on the undersides of pittas they can be very difficult to see in the dense understory of the forest, particularly with their characteristic habit of standing motionless with their backs toward any

source of alarm; otherwise they flee by rapid, bounding hops or short flights close to the ground. Larger species, such as the Rusty-naped pitta, possess disproportionately large eyes, an adaptation to their preference for gloomy forest areas that seldom receive any sunlight, even at midday; they are also known to forage at night. Evolution has provided some pittas with white wing patches (specula) and iridescent patches of light blue on the shoulders and primaries to facilitate visual contact in dim light.

Pittas range widely throughout tropical Asia, extending to Japan (Fairy pitta), Australia and the Solomon Islands (six species), and tropical Africa (African pitta), occurring from sea level up to 8,200ft (2,500m). All species are found in forested regions, especially the remaining tracts of extensive lowland to mid-montane evergreen rain forest. These forests are inhabited by the rarest and least known species (including the very distinctive Eared pitta, Blue pitta, Giant pitta), and confined to a few Philippine islands are the red-bellied Koch's pitta and the black and sky-blue Steere's pitta. The striking blue, yellow and black Gurney's pitta is unique in having a limited

---

Elusive Flycatchers

In the humid forests of the eastern Andes and the Amazon basin up to 70 flycatcher species may occur together at a single locality. The distributions of many of these species are very restricted. With so many flycatcher species occupying small ranges, scientists still occasionally discover new ones, but the process is not easy. Some recently discovered species, which have escaped detection through 200 years of scientific exploration, had special reasons for being so elusive.

In 1976 a team of ornithologists became the first scientists to explore the cloud-enshrouded summit of a mountain ridge in extreme northern Peru. Here they discovered a tiny flycatcher new to science, later described as the Cinnamon-breasted tody-tyrant. This species is restricted to the mossy, stunted cloud-forests atop a few isolated peaks in this region. Because it evolved on these high, remote mountain "islands" it remained undiscovered until scientists were able to work their way up to those peaks.

In 1981 another new flycatcher was discovered in the rainy tropical forests at the base of the eastern Andes in southern Peru. This new "bristle-tyrant" (still unnamed) lives high in the treetops, where it joins flocks of tanagers and other flycatchers. It is in its locality quite common, but escaped detection because of its tiny size (weighing just 0.24oz, 7g), its treetop habits and its restriction to remote foothills of the Andes.

Many scientists suspect that more of these startling new flycatchers remain hidden and unknown, awaiting future generations of explorers of the remote tropical corners of South America. **JWF**

distribution in continental Asia between two faunal zones (about 310mi, 500km) of peninsular Thailand and adjacent Burma). The shy and secretive habits of many pittas have also been a source of anomalies in distribution and this is illustrated by an example from the Malay Peninsula. For 30 years sightings were reported of an unknown and elusive large pitta from Fraser's Hill in the highlands of Central Malaysia. The mystery was solved in 1977 when one was caught and identified as a new form of the Rusty-naped pitta.

Apart from some minor dispersion according to season and altitude only eight pittas (including the Indian pitta and Blue-winged pitta) are known to undertake regular migration. These pittas are nocturnal migrants and many unusual records have resulted from their attraction to lights. The African pitta was thought to be sedentary until 50 years ago when an ornithologist living in Tanzania found that over several years records of birds flying into lighted houses at night developed a seasonal pattern. Further study has shown that regular migration occurs in East Africa where a long-winged form is found, but records of night movements from West and Central Africa suggest that the picture is still incomplete. A survey of nocturnal migration in Malaysia has not only established the dates of movements, but revealed that pittas are unusual among song birds in that the peaks of migration are during the new moon, not the full moon as with other song birds.

Pittas spend much of their time searching for their food, particularly worms, snails and insects, in the leaf litter and humus soil of the forest floor. Leaves and other debris are flicked over with their strong bills, or small openings are made in the litter in the manner of a chicken. Occasionally prey is located by sound with the pitta's head turned sideways, or flushed by wing-flicking movements. Some pittas are attracted to sites favored for snails, eg Banded pittas at limestone cliffs, and will readily use a rock or log as an anvil when breaking open the shells. Pittas also have the most highly developed sense of smell among song birds, a useful adaptation in dimly lit habitats or at night. A study of the food habits of a captive Hooded pitta revealed a strong preference for earthworms: it would dig for them with its bill completely immersed in the damp soil, where a sense of smell would enable it to locate the prey more easily. This bird ate approximately its own weight in food each day.

Pittas' large bulky nests may be found up to 26ft (8m) above ground (but usually less than 10ft, 3m) or on the ground, in stumps, root buttresses, fallen trees, tangled clumps of vegetation, in banks or rock clefts. If disturbed at the nest the entrance may be concealed with a leafy twig, and the parent bird may attempt to draw the intruder away from the nest by calling.

▲ **Cleaning up,** a Hooded pitta in New Guinea removes a fecal sac. Such sacs are produced by the nestlings of many passerines and a few close relatives. It is an adaptation that enables nests made of delicate materials to be kept clean. Sacs and such nests must have evolved in parallel.

▶ **From Thailand to Bali** lives the Banded pitta. The word "pitta" comes from the Madras area of South India where it merely signifies "bird."

The 2 Families of Tyrant Flycatchers and Pittas

⬚ Threatened, but status indeterminate.

Tyrant flycatchers
Family: Tyrannidae
Three hundred and seventy-six species in 88 genera.
N (except extreme N), C and S America, West Indies, Galapagos Islands. Forest, woodland, savanna, temperate grassland, alpine zones, cultivated land. Size: 2.5–19.7in (6–50cm) long, weight 0.16–2.8oz (4.5–80g). Plumage: dull olive-green above, pale yellowish below; also black, brown, rusty or white; one species is bright scarlet; many have brightly colored crown patches. Voice: generally weak, whistled or warbled notes, sometimes in simple phrases or trills. Nests: highly variable, including woven cups, globular nests with side holes, pendant- and purse-shaped nests, simple cups on the ground or in natural or excavated cavities. Eggs. 2–8, usually 3 or 4; white or whitish, sometimes lightly to heavily mottled with reddish brown. Incubation: 14–20 days. Nestling period: 14–23 days. Diet: chiefly insects; fruits of tropical trees and vines; occasionally small fish, lizards, snakes and tadpoles.

Species and genera include:
Cinnamon-breasted tody-tyrant (*Hemitriccus cinnamomeipectus*), **Eastern kingbird** (*Tyrannus tyrannus*), **Great kiskadee** (*Pitangus sulphuratus*), **ground-tyrants** (genus *Muscisaxicola*), **Many-colored rush tyrant** (*Tachuris rubigastra*), **Ochre-bellied flycatcher** (*Mionectes oleagineus*), **Piratic flycatcher** (*Legatus leucophaius*), **pygmy-tyrants** (genera *Atalotriccus, Colopteryx, Hemitriccus, Lophotriccus, Myiornis, Pseudotriccus*), **Royal flycatcher** (*Onychorhynchus coronatus*), **Scissor-tailed flycatcher** (*Tyrannus muscivora*), **Short-tailed pygmy-flycatcher** (*Myiornis ecaudatus*), **shrike-tyrants** (genus *Agriornis*), **spadebills** (genus *Platyrinchus*), **Strange-tailed tyrant** (*Yetapa risora*), **Vermilion flycatcher** (*Pyrocephalus rubinus*), **White-bearded flycatcher** (*Conopias inornatus*), **White-cheeked tody flycatcher** (*Poecilotriccus albifacies*).

Pittas
Family: Pittidae
Twenty-six species of the genus *Pitta*.
Africa, E and S Asia to New Guinea, the Solomon Islands and Australia. Evergreen and deciduous forest, bamboo jungle, mangroves, wooded ravines; secondary forest, plantations, overgrown gardens. Size: 5.9–11in (15–28cm) long, weight 1.5–7.7oz (42–218g) (some heavier weights known). Plumage: very colorful with brightly contrasting blues, greens, reds, yellows and intermediate shades with the brightest parts on the head and underparts; little or no difference between sexes (four species have drab females). Young birds are more brownish and mottled or spotted. Voice: short series of variably pitched whistles, often of two syllables; range of trilling, rolling sounds and loud barking notes when alarmed. Nests: huge, untidy globular or elliptical structures, built of twigs and rootlets, often decorated with moss and lined with finer materials; all have low side entrance, also a small platform in front. Eggs: 1–7, usually 3–5; varying from broad blunt oval to spheroidal in shape, some with much gloss; white or buffish with reddish or purplish spots or speckles and fine gray or lilac undermarkings; weight about 0.18–0.35oz (5–10g). Incubation: 15–17 days. Nestling period: 2–3 weeks.

Species include: **African pitta** (*Pitta angolensis*), **Banded pitta** (*P. guajana*), **Blue-banded pitta** (*P. arcuata*), **Blue Pitta** (*P. cyanea*), **Blue-rumped pitta** (*P. soror*), **Blue-winged pitta** (*P. moluccensis*), **Eared pitta** (*P. phayrei*), **Fairy pitta** (*P. nympha*), **Giant pitta** (*P. caerulea*), **Gurney's pitta** ⬚ (*P. gurneyi*), **Hooded pitta** (*P. sordida*), **Indian pitta** (*P. brachyura*), **Koch's pitta** (*P. kochi*), **Noisy pitta** (*P. versicolor*), **Rusty-napped pitta** (*P. oatesi*), **Steere's pitta** (*P. steerii*).

The breeding season in the summer at higher latitudes may cover most months near the equator, except at the height of the monsoon period. The male initiates courtship by confronting the female with erect posturing, vertical movements of the body, and wing spreading, accompanied by loud calls. If the female responds in kind, mating takes place and the male starts nest-building with some assistance from the female. Both sexes share incubation and the care and feeding of the young, but they may drive away the young shortly after they have fledged. Pittas may be long-lived birds as a pair of Giant pittas first bred after 10 years in captivity.

When calling pittas will perch in trees up to 33ft (10m) above ground, and may throw back their heads when repeating their loud, penetrating whistles, usually at dawn and dusk, before rainstorms and on moonlit nights, and often in chorus with one or several others. They readily respond to imitations of their calls. Outside the breeding season pittas are usually solitary and occupy foraging territories. They quickly respond to intruders and a threat display recorded for some species, such as the Noisy pitta, involves a crouching posture with feathers fluffed, the wings outspread and the bill pointing upward. The Blue-rumped pitta has a similar display, but the head is bent low over the back to expose a triangular, white-spotted patch below the throat.

In 1979–81 the World Wildlife Fund supported a fauna survey of Sabah, North Borneo. It found pittas, regarded as strictly forest-dwelling birds, to be one of only a few families (and the only one of the song birds) of special value in studying the dynamics of change in bird communities after the effects of logging. It was found that pittas are adversely affected, but will return to lightly disturbed or partially regenerated forest. So far only Gurney's pitta is considered threatened by habitat destruction and this survey provides the first evidence of the adaptability of pittas to habitat changes.

The word "pitta" comes from the Madras area of South India where it merely signifies "bird" and was first applied to the Indian pitta in 1713. In parts of Indonesia the local names, based on the call, are likened to variations of the Malay word for "grandfather" and have given rise to a favorite story of a child walking with its grandfather in the forest but who loses its way only to be transformed into a bird that must now always call for its grandfather. In Borneo some inland tribes dry the skins of pittas for use as children's toys.   MDB

MANAKINS AND COTINGAS

Families: Pipridae, Cotingidae
Order: Passeriformes (suborder Tyranni, part)
One hundred and eighteen species in 42 genera
Distribution: see map and table.

Manakins   Cotingas

THE manakins and cotingas are closely related to each other and quite closely related to the huge American family of tyrant flycatchers (Tyrannidae). They are distinguished from the tyrant flycatchers by some anatomical characters and, more obviously, by the fact that they are mainly fruit-eaters rather than insect-eaters, and in most species there are considerable differences between the sexes with males brilliantly colored. Courtship behavior is very elaborate.

Typical **manakins** (*Pipra*, *Manacus*, *Chiroxiphia* and some smaller genera) are small, compact, highly active birds with short bills and large heads. They live in the understory of forest, feeding on small fruits and insects which they take in rapid flight sallies. Although semisocial in feeding and other routine activities they do not form pairs. The males spend a great deal of their time at traditional display sites, some species at "leks" or communal display areas, others singly but usually within ear-shot of other males. A large lek of the White-bearded manakin, one of the best known species, is an extraordinary sight when in full activity. Each male clears a small "court" on the ground, within a few meters of its neighbors, and on and round it performs an astonishing range of rapid maneuvers accompanied by sharp calls and loud snaps made by the modified wing-feathers (see box). The females visit the leks solely for the purpose of mating, carrying out all nesting duties single-handed, as is the rule in all manakins studied. They sling their delicate cup nests between two parallel or diverging twigs of some low plant, often beside a forest stream, and after an unusually long incubation period for a small bird (about 19 days) feed the young by regurgitation on a mixed diet of insects and fruits.

Manakins of the largest genus, *Pipra*, display on higher perches, usually 3–10m (10–33ft) above ground, on which they perform rapid slides, "about-faces," "twists" and other maneuvers. The details vary according to species, but a swift flight to the display perch, ending in a conspicuous landing, is a feature of all of them. A unique feature of the display of the Wire-tailed manakin brings into play the elongated wire-like filaments which project from the tips of its tail-feathers. Backing towards the female, the male raises its posterior and rapidly twists its tail from side to side, so that the filaments brush the female's chin. The third main genus, *Chiroxiphia*, is supreme in the complexity of its displays. In the initial stages two or more males perform a vocal duet followed by a synchronized joint dance before the female, while the final phase of the courtship, leading to mating, is carried out by the dominant male of the group alone (see box).

The **cotingas** are such a diverse family that practically no generalization applies to all species. At one extreme of size is the Kinglet calyptura, about 8cm (3in) long, and at the other the huge umbrellabirds, the size of a crow. In proportion they range from short-winged heavily built birds, for example the Guianan red cotinga, to the long-winged, almost swallow-like purpletufts. In color form they range from the most highly dimorphic species, with brilliantly ornamented males, to species in which both sexes are uniform gray or brown. In behavior they are equally varied, with social systems ranging from conventional monogamy to extreme polygamy. It is by no means certain that they are monophyletic,

The Catherine Wheel Courtship of the Blue-backed Manakin

Probably no other birds have courtship displays as complex as those of some manakins. The Blue-backed manakin's is among the most spectacular. Males display in pairs, and the whole courtship sequence is in three distinct phases.

Phase one, two males perch side by side in a tree, facing the same way and almost in contact, and utter long series of almost perfectly synchronized calls. Although the calls are so well synchronized that they seem to come from a single bird, in fact one bird, the dominant member of the pair, begins each note about one-twentieth of a second before the other. The function of this duet is to attract a female.

hovering, to land behind the second male, who hitches forward and in turn jumps up and moves back in hovering flight. The two males thus form a revolving Catherine wheel in front of the female. As it proceeds, the Catherine wheel dance becomes more and more rapid and the twanging calls more frenzied, until the dance is brought to a sudden end by the dominant male, who utters one or two very sharp calls, whereupon the subordinate male leaves the perch.

Phase two, when a female approaches, the two males fly down to a special display perch near the forest floor. Perching side by side they begin to jump up alternately, rising a few inches in the air and accompanying each jump with a nasal twanging call. The female may then come to the display perch, in which case the two males turn to face her and continue their coordinated dance in a different form. The male nearer the female jumps up, facing her, and then moves back in the air,

Phase three, the dominant male performs an aerial display around the female, crisscrossing the display perch, every now and then perching, crouching to present his red head-shield, then flying on to continue his butterfly flights. Occasionally he flies to an outlying perch, crouches and with a snap of his wings flies back towards the display perch. If the female remains on the display perch, showing that she is ready to mate, the male eventually lands beside her and mounts.

▷ **Jungle jewels,** OVERLEAF a pair of Peruvian cock-of-the-rock (*Rupicola peruviana*). The male is on the right. The two species of cocks-of-the-rock live on rock cliffs and rocky outcrops in South American forests.

◄ **A bird of striking contrast,** the Red-capped manakin (*Pipra mentalis*).

▼ **The call of the male bellbird** may be the loudest of any bird. This is the Three-wattled bellbird (*Procnias tricarunculata*).

The 2 Families of Manakins and Cotingas

① Threatened, but status indeterminate.

Manakins

Family: Pipridae

Fifty-three species in 17 genera.

C and S America. Forest at tropical levels. Size: 3.5–7.5in (9–19cm) long, weight 0.35–0.88oz (10–25g). Plumage: males of most species brightly colored, black with patches of red, orange, yellow, blue or white; females olive-green. (A few species are mainly olive-green or brown with no difference between sexes.) Voice: variety of sharp whistles, trills, buzzing notes; no true songs; some species also make loud mechanical sounds with modified wing feathers. Nests: open cups, usually in low vegetation. Eggs: almost always 2;

dull white or buff with brown markings (blackish markings in the Thrush-like manakin). Incubation: 17–21 days. Nestling period: almost always 13–15 days.

Species include: **Blue-backed manakin** (*Chiroxiphia pareola*), **Thrush-like manakin** (*Schiffornis turdinus*), **White-bearded manakin** (*Manacus manacus*), **Wire-tailed manakin** (*Pipra filicauda*).

Cotingas

Cotingidae

Sixty-five species in 25 genera.

Mexico, C and S America. Forest, at all levels from tropical to temperate montane. Size 3–20in (8–50cm)

long, weight 0.21–14oz (6–400g). Plumage: extremely varied; males of many species brilliantly colored with reds, purples, blues, etc, and unusually modified display plumage; females usually duller without ornamentation. Voice: very varied, ranging from sharp whistles and rapid trills to booming sounds and hammer- or bell-like clangs; some species make mechanical sounds with modified wing-feathers. Nests: mainly open cup- or saucer-shaped nests, in some cases very small and frail for the size of the bird. (Cocks-of-the-rock are exceptional in building bracket-shaped nests attached to rock faces.) Eggs: 1–3, usually buff or olive in ground color with spots and blotches

of darker browns and grays. Incubation: 19–28 days. Nestling period: 21–44 days. Diet: fruits and insects.

Species and genera include: **bellbirds** (genus *Procnias*), **blue cotingas** (genus *Cotinga*), **calfbird** (*Perissocephalus tricolor*), **cock-of-the-rock** (genus *Rupicola*), **Guianan cock-of-the-rock** (*Rupicola rupicola*), **Guianan red cotinga** ① (*Phoenicircus carnifex*), **Kinglet calyptura** (*Calyptura cristata*), **purpletufts** (genus *Iodopleura*), **umbrellabirds** (genus *Cephalopterus*), **White-cheeked cotinga** (*Ampelion stresemanni*), **White-winged cotinga** (*Xipholena atropurpurea*), white-winged cotingas (genus *Xipholena*). Total threatened species: 4.

that is, more closely related to one another than any of them are to other groups of birds, and it may be that they are descended from a number of different lines that evolved from primitive tyrant flycatchers and became specialized for fruit-eating. Only a few of the diverse types can be mentioned.

One group, the "typical" cotingas, includes the blue cotingas, the white-winged cotingas and some other genera of medium-sized, sexually highly dimorphic birds with short wide bills. They are preeminently birds of the forest treetops and for this reason the details of their behavior are not well known, but in some species, and perhaps in all, the conspicuously colored males—clad in blue, purple or white—display aerially above the forest canopy, while the cryptically colored females (to judge from the few species whose nests are known) build tiny nests which they tend single-handed, laying a single egg.

Yet more highly dimorphic and with even wider, shorter bills that give the head an almost frog-like appearance are the four species of bellbirds. They are among the most specialized of fruit-eaters, their very wide gape enabling them to swallow comparatively huge fruits for their size. Bellbirds are notable for the males' extraordinarily loud calls, perhaps the loudest made by any bird, the main element of which is an explosive clang or "bock," reminiscent of a hammer striking an anvil. The call advertises the male on his display perch and is audible for a half a mile (1km) or more. When a female ready for mating visits a male, a complex courtship ritual follows, which varies according to the species and culminates in a leap by the male, accompanied by a deafening "bock," onto the female's back. Male bellbirds display in loose groups, occupying perches within earshot but not very close to each other.

The same type of display organization is found in some other cotingas, for instance the umbrellabirds, in which each male occupies a separate display tree and attracts females by uttering deep booming calls accompanied by visual displays. In a few species the males display at much closer quarters. Thus in the calfbird the males display in groups, occupying adjacent perches in the same tree. This species acquired its name from the strange lowing or "mooing" calls that accompany the males' grotesque display movements.

The cocks-of-the-rock have developed communal display to an extreme degree. In the Guianan cock-of-the-rock the males display in groups, each bird maintaining a cleared "court" on the forest floor, a system similar to that of the White-bearded manakin. The main display is static: the male crouches in the middle of his court with the brilliant plumage spread and the head turned sideways so that the semi-circular topknot is fully displayed to the females who come into the trees above. As in so many of the manakins and cotingas, the details of the different phases of the courtship display are so complex that no brief description is adequate. The two cocks-of-the-rock are unique in their nesting habits: the female fixes her bracket-shaped nest of mud and rootlets, hardened with saliva, to a vertical rock face. Since suitable nest-sites are limited, several females may nest in close proximity. Unlike the other large cotingas, whose relatively tiny nests can hold only one egg and nestling, the cock-of-the-rock lays a two-egg clutch.

The brilliantly colored cotingas are mainly birds of tropical and subtropical forest. At temperate levels in the Andes are found a number of species with sober plumage, similar in both sexes, which live conventionally in pairs. These too are primarily fruit-eaters, feeding on the berries of montane shrubs and epiphytes. Some are highly specialized for particular fruits. Thus the White-cheeked cotinga of the Peruvian Andes is reported to feed solely on the fruits of two kinds of mistletoes, and it undoubtedly serves as their main dispersal agent because it wipes regurgitated seeds onto suitable tree branches and no other fruit-eating birds occur in its bleak montane habitat. These high-altitude cotingas build substantial cup nests, doubtless as an adaptation to the cold climate, and lay two or three eggs, with both parents attending the nest.

Among the more aberrant cotingas the four species of purpletufts are outstanding. These very small cotingas are long-winged and superficially martin-like. They take mistletoe fruits, but also hawk for flying insects from treetop perches above the forest canopy. The only purpletuft nest ever found is of a type unique in the cotingas, a tiny cup reminiscent of a hummingbird's nest. The Kinglet calyptura is also very different from other cotingas. A tiny, very short-tailed bird about the size of a goldcrest and much like a goldcrest in color, it is known from a handful of specimens collected in the mountains of southeastern Brazil and ranks as one of the least known of birds, unrecorded in this century although there is no obvious reason why it should have become extinct.   DWS

GNATEATERS AND OTHER NOISEMAKERS

Families: Conopophagidae, Rhinocryptidae, Oxyruncidae, Phytotomidae, Xenicidae, Philepittidae
Order Passeriformes (suborder Tyranni, part).
Forty-eight species in 19 genera.
Distribution: see maps and table.

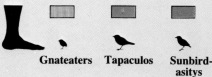

**Gnateaters   Tapaculos   Sunbird-
asitys**

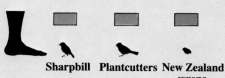

**Sharpbill   Plantcutters   New Zealand
wrens**

► **Representative species of gnateaters and other noisemakers.** (1) A Crested gallito (a tapaculo; *Rhinocrypta lanceolata*). (2) A Rufous gnateater (*Conopophaga lineata*). (3) A False sunbird (a sunbird-asity; *Neodrepanis coruscans*). (4) Two riflemen (New Zealand wrens; *Acanthisitta chloris*), male above, female below. (5) A Rufous-tailed plantcutter (*Phytotoma rara*). (6) A sharpbill (*Oxyruncus cristatus*).

WITH their long legs, very short neck and tail and short rounded wings, **gnateaters** have the appearance of a dumpy, tailless robin. The males of most species have a distinctive tuft of often very long white or silvery-white feathers behind their eyes; the females sometimes have a similar but less conspicuous tuft.

The eight species of gnateaters are distributed across most of Brazil and adjacent countries, but few species overlap. Even where the ranges of two species do overlap, they often occupy different habitats. They are mainly ground-dwelling forest birds and although it is relatively easy to call them into view, they normally skulk in dense undergrowth.

When approached Rufous gnateaters give sharp alarm calls very different from their melodious, if simple, song: a series of short whistles gradually increasing in pitch and volume. Other species have similar vocalizations and males of some species can produce a harsh sound with their wings.

Alone or in pairs they work through leaf litter or low vegetation feeding on relatively small insects. The nest is placed close to the ground and made mainly of large leaves and lined with softer plant fibers. Both sexes incubate and will feign injury if disturbed at the nest.

The two species of antpipit (*Corythopis*) used to be included in the gnateater family, but they have little general resemblance to the gnateaters and are now placed with the tyrant flycatchers.   AMH

The **tapaculos** occur mainly in the cooler humid parts of South America at altitudes above 3,300ft (1,000m). Only in the south do they occupy lowland habitats. Although seven genera are restricted to the tropical belt, the greater number of species are in the temperate southern Andes. Only *Scytalopus*, by far the largest genus with 11 species, spans almost the entire range of the family.

Perhaps the most distinctive feature of tapaculos is a large movable flap covering the nostrils. They are rather compact with short rounded wings and large strong feet and legs. The most distinctive species is the Ocellated tapaculo of the northern Andes; it is strikingly patterned, has a very heavy bill, which is markedly flattened on top, and a very long straight hind claw. Most other

species are rather drab and wren-like, particularly in that the tail is usually raised, often lying almost along the bird's back. The tail is usually short, but is long in genera such as the bristlefronts of eastern Brazil.

Tapaculos skulk in thick vegetation. Rarely leaving the ground, they walk (or run rapidly) scratching among ground litter in search of invertebrates and occasional plant material. The difficulty of seeing them is compensated for by their loud and often weird songs. Some species (eg the two bristlefronts and the two huet-huets) are quite musical, but others (especially many of the *Scytalopus* species) produce characteristic monotonous repetitions of one or two unmusical notes.

Nests are usually on or close to the ground, sometimes several feet up in the undergrowth or in tree-hollows, while some (eg the two *Scelorchilus* species) dig nest burrows. Most nests are domes with a small side entrance, although some of the hidden nests are cup-shaped. Eggs are relatively large and round and are incubated by both parents.   AMH

The **sharpbill** has a wide but curiously discontinuous distribution from southern Brazil to Costa Rica, with some variation in plumage and voice. Despite being widely distributed and reasonably common in some areas, its tendency to be a solitary bird of rain and cloud forest (from 1,300–6,000ft, 400–1,800m) keeps it poorly known. Even its status as a one-species family is uncertain.

It is a strong direct flier. The male has a serrated edge on his outer primary feathers which may be used to produce sound, but no sound has been associated with the bird's curious display flight. In parts of south Brazil its long thin whistle, smoothly descending from a very high pitch, can be frequently heard in good, usually montane forest, but it generally stays high in the canopy. It will move around in a tit-like fashion in the outermost leaves of the canopy, often hanging upside-down to pick invertebrates from leaf clusters or rolled leaves. It will also hang on bunches of small fruits to feed, rejecting many of the hard stones. Its peculiar sharp bill and short strong legs are well adapted to these feeding techniques.

So far only one nest has been described. It was saddled onto a small horizontal branch near the top of the canopy of one of the tallest trees (100ft, 30m) in the area. It was a shallow cup of roughly interwoven leaf stalks with a few leaves. The outer surface had a thin coat of mosses, liverworts and spiders' webs secured with a dried saliva-like substance. Young were fed by regurgitation of small fruit and invertebrates. Only one parent was ever in attendance and was thought to be female; certainly birds singing in the breeding season show no interest in nesting activities.
                                    AMH

Plantcutters are a small group of South American species of uncertain affinities. Their bill, which earns them their name, has finely serrated edges and is used to pluck and cut buds and tender leaves as well as fruits and seeds. With short rounded wings and relatively long tail they have a heavy undulating flight, usually keeping close to the ground. Although usually occurring singly or in pairs, numbers may accumulate in orchards and small parties of up to six or more occur in winter.

Away from any conflict with man, they live in wooded mountain valleys to an altitude of 10,000ft (3,000m) and on prairie interspersed with bush (especially thorns) and trees. The southern populations of the White-tipped plantcutter, the smallest and brightest species, migrate to winter in bushy pastures of northeast Argentina and Uruguay. The Peruvian plantcutter, the dullest and most tropical species, is more sedentary.

From high in bushes and trees, the males

sing an unmusical song, that of the White-tipped being likened to tree branches rubbing together, to sheep bleating, or to frogs croaking, with other discordant squeaks. Sometimes they make a slow display flight with very rapid wing beats. The Rufous-tailed plantcutter produces a rasping trill. The White-tipped nests inside thick, thorny bushes, or even cacti, but the Rufous-tailed normally nests in tree-forks (often in fruit trees). At least in the White-tipped plantcutter most of the care of the nest and the young is performed by the female, who may raise two broods. Plantcutters have been recorded as hosts to the parasitic Shiny cowbird.   AMH

New Zealand wrens are a small, obscure family of three species with no known affinity to other groups of birds. There was once a fourth species, the Stephen Island wren, which may have been flightless. It was discovered in 1894 when a lighthouse keeper's cat carried in 15 specimens. The cat is assumed to have destroyed the entire remaining population.

The three living species are the Rock wren, the Bush wren and the rifleman; none is a strong flier. Having lived for so long in

The 6 Families of Gnateaters and Other Noisemakers

E Endangered.   I Threatened, but status indeterminate.

Gnateaters
Family: Conopophagidae
Eight species of the genus *Conopophaga.*

S America. Forest undergrowth. Size: 4.5–6in (11–14cm) long, weight 0.7–0.8oz (20–23g). Plumage: pale brown above, very pale below, head variously patterned (usually including a tuft of long white plumes behind the eye in the male). Voice: simple, melodious whistling. Nest: bowl-shaped near ground. Eggs: 2; yellowish with spots or smudges. Diet: insects.

Tapaculos
Family: Rhinocryptidae
Twenty-nine species in 12 genera.

S and C America. Dense forest, brushland undergrowth. Length: 4.5–10in (11–25cm). Plumage: mostly dark gray or brown with rufous or black and white bars on underparts. Voice: usually loud and repetitive. Nests: grass, twigs, moss, etc, in burrows, tree hollows, thickets. Eggs: 2–4; white. Diet: insects, spiders, some vegetable matter.

Species include: **Black-throated huet-huet** (*Pteroptochos tarnii*), **Brasilia tapaculo** I (*Scytalopus novacapitalis*), **Chestnut-throated huet-huet**

(*Pteroptochos castaneus*), **Ocellated tapaculo** (*Acropternis orthonyx*), **Slaty bristle-front** (*Merulaxis ater*), **Stresemann's bristle-front** I (*M. stresemanni*).

Sharpbill
Family: Oxyruncidae
Oxyruncus cristatus

C and northern S America. Forest canopy. Length: 7in (17cm). Plumage: green above, heavily blotched white below; yellow to scarlet crest bordered with black; cheeks and throat narrowly barred. Voice: long, smoothly descending whistle. Nest: cup straddling branch. Eggs: 2? Diet: small fruits and invertebrates.

Plantcutters
Family: Phytotomidae
Three species of the genus *Phytotoma*.

W and southern S America. Bushland, low woodland, open cultivation. Length: 7–8in (17–20cm). Plumage: upper parts gray-brown, streaked in male; forehead and underparts rufous (male) or light ocher (female). Nest: shallow untidy structure of twigs in horizontal fork, lined with fine roots, etc. Eggs: 2–4; greenish blue with sparse dark

spotting. Diet: fruit, buds, tender leaves, seeds.

Species include: **Peruvian plantcutter** (*Phytotoma raimondii*), **White-tipped plantcutter** (*P. rutila*).

New Zealand wrens
Family: Xenicidae (or Acanthisittidae)
Three species in 2 genera.

New Zealand. Forest or woodland. Size: 3–4in (8–10cm), weight 0.2–0.3oz (6.3–9g). Plumage: upperparts greenish, underparts whitish with yellow wash on the sides; females are generally duller and are striped brown (blackish above in the rifleman). Voice: Bush wren produces a succession of merging cheeps or subued trill; Rock wren produces a whirring call of three notes and piping sound; rifleman produces a rapidly repeated *zsit–zsit* sound. Nests: built in holes in tree trunks, banks, walls, and posts, of roots, leaves, moss and ferns; lined with feathers. Eggs: 2–5; white; incubation period: 19–21 days in the rifleman; nestling period 23–25 days in the rifleman. Diet: arthropods.

Species: **Bush wren** E (*Xenicus longipes*), **rifleman** (*Acanthisitta chloris*), **Rock wren** (*X. gilviventris*). Now extinct: **Stephen Island wren** (*Xenicus lyalli*).

Sunbird-asitys
Family: Philepittidae
Four species in 2 genera.
Madagascar. Forest. Diet: insects, fruit.

Asitys (genus *Philepitta*), two species. Length: about 6in (15cm). Plumage: male is dark black with yellow fringes on feathers after molting; yellow fringes wear off and greenish wattle develops over the eye; Schlegel's asity has larger extent of yellow with black head and wattle surrounding the eye; females have greenish plumage; bill is black, short and broad. Voice: thrush-like whistle. Eggs: white. Other breeding characteristics unknown. Species: **Schlegel's asity** (*Philepitta schlegeli*), **Velvet asity** (*P. castanea*).

False sunbirds (genus *Neodrepanis*), two species. Length: about 4in (10cm). Plumage: males have metallic blue plumage above, canary yellow below; in the Small-billed wattle sunbird the undersides of both sexes are yellower; females are dark green above, yellowish below; bill is brown, long, tapering and curved. Voice and breeding characteristics unknown. Species: **False sunbird** (*Neodrepanis coruscans*), **Small-billed wattle sunbird** I (*N. hypoxantha*).

◀▲ **The rifleman lives on insects and spiders,** spending much of its time foraging for them on large branches and trunks. It is often to be seen working its way up and around tree trunks, taking a spiral route to a height of 20–30ft (6–9m). Having mounted one tree it flies off to the foot of another.

the absence of predators they have been ill able to cope with new predators introduced by man and with modification of their habitat. They have a stocky appearance, with large shanks and toes, and almost no tail. Their bill is slender, about the same length as the head; in the rifleman it is slightly upturned. They have soft plumage and short, rounded wings.

The Bush wren and the Rock wren are thought to be examples of an indigenous genus that developed two forms, the former inhabiting vegetation at low altitudes, the latter living in alpine vegetation.

The Rock wren occurs on the mountainous divide of South Island at altitudes between 3,000 and 8,000ft (900–2,500m), preferring sparsely vegetated rock and bolder screes and moraines. It eats mainly insects, foraging for them in cracks and crevices, under bolders and in short, tight plant swards, even when these are covered with snow (in which case the bird moves through air spaces between the snow and the ground surface). It also uses crevices and holes for nest-sites and for caching food. Rock wrens occupy well-defined territories, using three-note calls to advertise the location of their boundaries.

The Bush wren, of which there are three subspecies, could now be extinct in the North and South Islands. As a weak flier, nesting in holes near the ground, it was particularly vulnerable to habitat changes wrought by man and mammal predators introduced by man.

Under modern conditions it is the rifleman that has fared best of all the New Zealand wrens. One of its main habitats, beech forest, remains abundant on both main islands and it has begun to enter cultivated areas. It is slightly more secure than the Bush wren because it nests in holes with tiny openings high in tree trunks.

The rifleman is one of the smallest birds in New Zealand. But a female's egg weighs about 20 percent of her body weight, and since she lays every other day and a complete clutch is five eggs a female produces, in nine days, her own body weight in eggs. This combination probably explains some of the factors influencing the rifleman's breeding characteristics.

Most of the nest building is undertaken by the male rifleman who also increases his mate's intake of food during the 10 days before and during egg-laying by bringing her up to nine food items an hour. Between the laying of each egg there is an interval of two days. The young hatch in an undeveloped condition and then take longer than usual to develop: the breeding cycle for one clutch may take up to 60 days. After the clutch has been laid the male undertakes most of the daytime incubation and is also more active than the female in feeding the young, though this may be done with the assistance of other adults (see box). The young birds put on a lot of weight; prior to fledging they may be considerably heavier than their parents.

Before the young of the first clutch have left the nest their parents have usually started building a nest for a second clutch. This time the breeding pattern differs slightly from the first one, due to the continuing demands of the first brood on the parents. The nest is smaller, loosely built, often unlined. In the period of egg production and during incubation the male does not bring extra food to the female. The size of the second clutch is on average one egg smaller than the first. After all eggs have been laid there is sometimes a pause of several days before incubation begins, probably because the parents are still feeding dependent young from the first clutch.   GHS

Sunbird-asitys have two well-known features: differences between the two genera and similarities of False sunbirds with true sunbirds. Their ecology and behavior however are little known. The asitys have been described as "quiet" and "sluggish" with an apparently limited vocal repertoire. They are thought to eat fruit but probably take insects as well. It has been suggested that the False sunbirds' conspicuous long, curved and tapered bill is an adaptation for feeding on nectar and has evolved in the virtual absence of competitors that exploit flowers for nectar and possibly pollen. False sunbirds have a specialized tongue similar to that of other nectar feeders which supports this view. However, few field data exist indicating the feeding preferences of False sunbirds.

The radically different bills and dissimilar plumage of the sunbird asity genera illustrate the wide radiation that has occurred in the family and suggest that intermediate genera may have existed in the past. Indeed Madagascar is well known for the relatively recent extinction of both birds and other animals. The development of obvious differences between false sunbirds and asitys has been paralleled with the evolution of striking similarities with the true sunbirds. These similarities include their tubular tongue, bill shape and biannual molt.

GHS

SWALLOWS

Family: Hirundinidae
Order: Passeriformes (suborder Oscines, part).
Seventy-four species in 17 genera.
Distribution: worldwide except Arctic,
Antarctic and some remote islands.

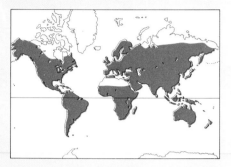

Habitat: open areas along rivers, above forests, etc.

Size: 4.5–8.5in (11.5–21.5cm)
long, weight 0.4–1.9oz
(10–55g).

Plumage: upperparts chiefly metallic blue-
black, green-black or brown; underparts often
white, buff or chestnut; some species have
white or buff rumps. Little or no difference
between sexes (males are sometimes brighter
with longer tails than females). Juveniles are
often duller and have shorter tails than adults.

Voice: simple rapid twittering or buzzing song.

Nests: hole, burrow or open or enclosed mud
nest.

Eggs: usually 3–8 (Southern martin 1 or 2);
white or white with red-brown spots;
incubation: 13–16 days; nestling period:
16–24 days (New World martins 24–28 days).

Diet: chiefly insects.

Species and genera include: **African river
martin** (*Pseudochelidon eurystomina*), **American
rough-winged swallow** (*Stelgidopteryx ruficollis*),
Barn swallow or **swallow** (*Hirundo rustica*), **Blue
swallow** (*H. atrocaerulea*), **Brown-chested martin**
(*Progne tapera*), **Cliff swallow** (*Petrochelidon
pyrrhonota*), **House martin** (*Delichon urbica*),
New World martins (genus *Progne*), **Purple
martin** (*Progne subis*), **Rough-winged swallows**
(genus *Psalidoprocne*), **Sand martin** or **Bank
swallow** (*Riparia riparia*), **Southern martin**
(*Progne modesta*), **Tree swallow** (*Tachycineta
bicolor*), **White-eyed river martin** ⒤
(*Pseudochelidon sirintarae*).

⒤ Threatened, but status indeterminate.

▶ **A multitude of hungry birds,** ABOVE the first
annual brood of a Barn swallow. While young
are in the nest each parent will make between
11 and 50 visits per hour to the nest, the exact
number depending on the size of the nestlings
and the weather.

▶ **Drinking in flight,** BELOW a fast-moving
Barn swallow.

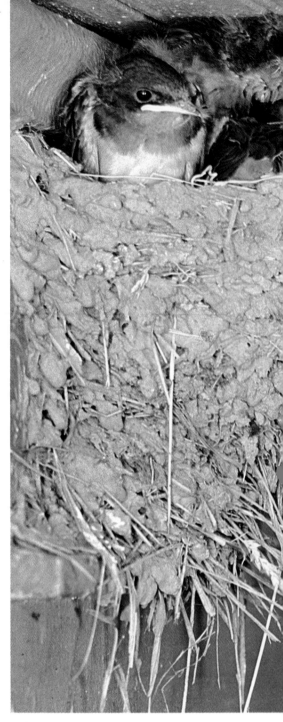

SWALLOWS have for long enjoyed a
harmonious association with man, often
nesting in and on his homes and other buildings, whether they be mud huts or concrete
skyscrapers. Because swallows eat insects
they are usually popular birds. In temperate
lands, returning swallows are welcomed as
the symbolic ending to the long, cold winter.

The family is almost cosmopolitan, occurring in open habitats from sea level to high
mountains, from small forest clearings to
extensive grasslands. Twenty-nine species,
including 19 members of the largest genus
Hirundo, are confined to Africa south of the
Sahara; it is likely that the family originated
here. Twenty-five species are found only in
the New World, 5 in Australasia and 4 in
Asia. The rest are widespread in the Old
World. Sand martins and Barn swallows
(the latter known in Europe as the swallow)
have the most extensive ranges, breeding in
both North America and Eurasia.

There are no taxonomic differences
between "swallows" and "martins," the
names being interchangeable. European
Sand martins, for example, are known as
Bank swallows in North America. Although
superficially similar to swifts, swallows and
martins form a distinct family. They are
streamlined in appearance with a short
neck; long, pointed wings with nine primary feathers; a short, broad, flat bill with
wide gape; small, weak feet; and, usually,
a forked tail which makes them very
maneuverable in flight. African and White-
eyed river martins, however, have large,
robust bills and feet and are placed in a
separate subfamily (Pseudochelidoninae)
from other swallows (Hirundininae). The
distribution of the river martins is unusual,
since the ranges of the two species lie
6,000mi (10,000km) apart. African and
American rough-winged swallows are also
distinctive; they have a hook-like thicken-
ing on the outer margin of the first primary
feather, the function of which is unknown.

All swallows are insect-eaters, feeding
almost exclusively while in flight. Tree swallows, however, also eat some seeds and berries (in particular the bayberry), especially
in cold weather when insects are scarce.
Swallows eat a wide variety of insects but
some specialize on a particular size or type.
The largest of the swallows, the New World
martins, for example, consume moths, but-
terflies and dragonflies. Different species of
swallows living in the same area often have
different diets so competition between them
is avoided. Thus in Britain Barn swallows
eat mainly very large flies such as blue-
bottles and hoverflies; Sand martins eat

smaller flies and mayflies; while House
martins feed on small flies and greenfly.
Swallows in the tropics differ from their
temperate counterparts in eating more flying ants and parasitic wasps but fewer flies
and aphids. Similarly, when in their winter
quarters Barn swallows also feed on ants
rather than flies.

The feeding behavior of swallows changes
with the weather. In cold, wet weather,
when flying insects are scarce, swallows find
it more difficult to find enough insects and
have to spend longer feeding. The few
insects which fly in bad weather occur
mainly near ground level and over water,
so this is where swallows concentrate their
hunting. There is a saying that the weather
will be fair when swallows fly high and wet
when they fly low. This is true of House

martins which feed high up in warm weather, but not of Barn swallows which feed low over the ground whatever the weather. When swallows are flying in bad weather they often use a combination of flapping and gliding instead of flapping their wings all the time, since gliding uses up less energy.

Occasionally swallows catch nonaerial prey, especially in bad weather. They may pick up spiders, ants and other insects from vegetation or from the ground. Barn swallows also take certain moth caterpillars.

Swallows usually carry several insects at a time to their nestlings, compressing the insects into a ball which is carried in the throat. Barn swallows may bring some 400 meals a day to a rapidly growing brood of five, about 8,000 insects in all!

Since insects are scarce in winter at high latitudes, swallows of temperate zones have to migrate, whereas tropical species are resident all year. Swallows are unusual among birds in postponing their post-breeding molt until they have reached their winter quarters. Once there, they often form flocks: many hundreds or even thousands of individuals may roost together in reed-beds or, sometimes, on overhead wires in cities. However, they do not breed in their wintering areas.

Swallows usually return each year to their old nesting site, the oldest individuals arriving first. Birds in their first year, how-ever, usually disperse though they remain within a few miles of their parents' nest-site. Old nests are often reused; mud nests may be strengthened with fresh mud. Temperate-zone swallows normally only live for about four years, rarely seven or eight, but a nest made of mud may outlast the occupants and subsequently may be used by a different pair. Burrowing swal-lows, however, such as the Sand martin, usually make new nests because of the presence of parasites in the old one and because old burrows sometimes collapse.

Swallows do not hold exclusive feeding territories but they will defend a small area around the nest from other swallows. The radius of this area varies from a few inches in the colonial Cliff swallow to about 18ft (6m) in the solitary Tree swallow. Most spe-cies are solitary or nest in small groups, although where suitable nesting sites are scarce large numbers may nest together. Only a few species are truly colonial: colonies of House and Sand martins, may number hundreds, and Cliff swallows thousands of pairs, with nests built very close to each other. Nesting in colonies may enable these swallows to detect and deter predators more quickly; individuals may also find distant or scarce sources of food by following successful foragers.

All swallows are monogamous, although promiscuous matings do occur, especially in colonial species. However, the roles of the sexes vary. Usually only the female incubates and broods the young nestlings, but in a few species, mainly those living in colonies, the male shares these duties. Both sexes feed the nestlings. Individuals from the first broods of Barn swallows and House martins have also been known to help their parents feed the second brood.

Swallows start to breed each year when their insect food has become sufficiently abundant in the spring, in temperate areas, or before the period of peak rainfall in the

▲ **A wide gape** is a particular feature of swallows. It provides a large trap for catching insects in flight and a trowel for scooping up mud when nest-building. These are Pearl-breasted swallows (*Hirundo dimidiata*).

◄ **Miners among swallows.** Sand martins nest in chambers at the ends of tunnels, usually about 39in (1m) deep. The locations they select include sand or clay walls, steep river banks and brick factories. Both members of a pair excavate, requiring only three or four days to bore their tunnel. They nest in colonies: their holes en masse can make a bank look like an Emmenthal cheese.

▼ **Examples of swallows' nests** built of mud. (1) A Barn swallow's cup nest built on a pole. (2) A nest of a Red-rumped swallow (*Hirundo daurica*) and (3) a House martin's nest, both built in roof structures.

The growth of nestling swallows is strongly influenced by the prevailing weather and food abundance. Bad weather sometimes leads to nestlings starving to death, although they can survive a few days of adverse weather.

Most swallow populations have probably benefited from their close association with man, as more artificial nesting sites and more open spaces have extended suitable habitat for them. However, intensification of agriculture, the use of pesticides, and industrial pollution have probably contributed to a decline in some areas. In Britain air pollution in towns and cities has decreased since the Clean Air Act of 1956 and numbers of House martins have since increased in urban areas, although the presence of suitable nesting and feeding sites remains crucial. No species of swallow is considered to be a serious pest, although large flocks of roosting swallows, especially the Brown-chested martin in South America, may create local cleaning, health and safety problems. Indeed, swallows are usually welcomed as they eat many insect pests such as greenfly and midges.

The biology of many swallows is still poorly known; the nests and eggs of some species have never been found. One swallow, the White-eyed river martin, was only discovered in 1968 but may already be close to extinction. Ten individuals were originally found at Lake Boraphet in Thailand in a reedbed roost among other swallows. The breeding sites, however, are unknown. Since 1968 a few individuals have been seen but none were found during an intensive search in 1980–81. This species is protected in Thailand and is listed in the *Red Data Book*.   AKT

tropics since very wet weather prevents swallows collecting enough food to raise a brood successfully. Eggs are laid at daily intervals but bad weather may delay laying for a day or more.

Clutches of temperate species are larger than those of tropical swallows. Island species lay the smallest clutches: the Southern martin of the Galapagos Islands has only one or two eggs whereas its close relative, the Purple martin of North America, lays up to eight. Clutch size declines during the breeding season perhaps because the time or good weather available for feeding the nestlings also becomes reduced. Old females also usually have larger clutches than do young birds. There are one or two broods a year depending on the species and locality, occasionally three in a favorable season. Some individuals, especially first-year birds, only have one brood; female House martins rearing one brood have a lower risk of mortality than double-brooded birds.

Varieties of Nest-sites and Nests in Swallows

Swallows are traditionally birds of open habitat: coasts, rivers, grassland and forest clearings, nesting opportunistically in or on any available surface. As a nest-site, many species just use a hole or crevice in a tree, rock, cave or cliff. Blue swallows will nest in the burrows of antbears; Brown-chested martins in the nests of ovenbirds and tree termites; and American rough-winged swallows in the burrows of kingfishers. A few species, such as the Sand martin, excavate their own burrows in sandy banks. Other swallows, particularly *Hirundo* species, construct a mud nest on a vertical or horizontal surface. The mud nest may be open at the top (Barn swallows) or closed (House martins and Cliff swallows). Within the nest cavity the swallow makes a nest of dry grass and twigs, often lined with feathers.

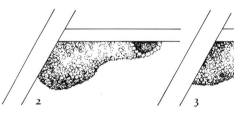

The advent of man and his buildings has increased the number of suitable nesting sites. Houses, barns, bridges, fence posts and nest boxes are all used, as well as some less likely sites, including chimneys, lampshades, old hats left on pegs, the shafts of tin mines, pipes, piles of sawdust, and even moving objects such as boats and trains. Some species now only rarely use natural sites. Purple martins nest mainly in multiple nest boxes ("villages"), Barn swallows and House martins nearly all on buildings and bridges.

Both sexes take part in building a mud nest or burrow, although only the female makes the grass lining. Barn swallows take a week to build a new nest, longer in bad or very dry weather. Over a thousand mouthfuls of mud, as well as dry grass or straw, are needed for a nest. Sand martins spend 5–10 days excavating a burrow, which is 20–40in (50–100cm) long with an enlarged nest chamber at the far end. The burrow usually slopes upward to prevent rain entering.

AKT

LARKS, WAGTAILS AND PIPITS

Families: Alaudidae, Motacillidae
Order: Passeriformes (suborder Oscines—part).
One hundred and thirty species in 18 genera.
Distribution: see map and table.

Larks   Wagtails and pipits

▶ **Representative species of larks, wagtails and pipits.** (1) A Yellow wagtail (*Motacilla flava*) holding an insect. This is the black-headed form of E Europe and Russia. (2) A skylark (*Alauda arvensis*). (3) A Richard's pipit (*Anthus novaeseelandiae*). (4) A Yellow-throated longclaw (a wagtail; *Macronyx croceus*). (5) A Singing bush-lark (*Mirafra javanica*). (6) A Horned lark (*Eremophila alpestris*). (7) A Fischer's finch-lark (*Eremopterix leucopareia*).

▼ **Striking display flights** are a prominent feature of the behavior of the male Bifasciated lark (of North Africa and the Middle East). In these the male takes an upward spiral course and then glides downwards.

Larks are a familiar feature of the bird communities of most open areas within the Old World. They are particularly varied and plentiful in the arid areas of Africa. Many species have evolved elaborate songs which are often given in flight.

Although many species of larks are associated with very arid desert or semidesert areas, this does not mean that they necessarily need hot climates. In the arctic tundras and high on mountain ranges (as well as through much of North America) the Horned lark breeds while a survey found the skylark of Britain to be that country's most widespread breeding bird. Most species are basically brown birds although some have dark markings and white patches on their plumage—in some cases only readily visible when the birds are in flight. For the most part their plumage serves to conceal the birds when they are on the ground and, particularly, when they are incubating. Most species have fairly strong bills although one, the Thick-billed lark, has a monstrous beak similar in size to that of a hawfinch and others, like the Bifasciated lark, have rather long and down-curved bills. Many species have been seen to dig in the ground when feeding—either searching for insects or, more often, for seeds.

In common with many other predominantly ground-dwelling birds larks generally have fairly long legs with long hind claws: these give them additional stability on the ground. Although some species fly at the slightest sign of danger many prefer to escape by walking or running. These species are often masters at using the contours of the ground and any vegetation for concealment during their retreat. Many species have no need of trees or bushes within their area but others regularly perch on posts, bushes or trees. These are often birds of open scrubland and include the varied genus of bush-larks.

Although most species are predominantly seed-eating all take some invertebrate food at times. For example when they are feeding young birds animal protein seems to be essential. In natural habitats the availability of seeds may be severely limited—for instance in desert conditions—and so birds may only be found singly or in pairs. However, where there has been a particularly productive set of seeds, for instance immediately after the rains in a normally arid area or where crops are being cultivated, flocks of dozens or even hundreds of larks may be found. These will normally be of a single species, but flocks of mixed species are not uncommon.

Many species are highly territorial and defend their territories and advertise for their mates, by singing in flight. Many have songs that are very pleasing to man, for example the skylark, woodlark, Bifasciated and Calandra larks. The latter regularly sings from the ground and has often been kept as a songbird in the Mediterranean region. Recognition and warning call notes are also pleasing and more elaborate than those found in some other groups.

In many areas the breeding season of the larks is strongly related to rainy seasons. Breeding starts in time for the young to be in the nest as the weed seed stocks reach their peak. In such circumstances only a single brood may be raised but temperate species often raise two and even three. Almost all species nest on the ground, sometimes in the open but usually at least partly concealed in some vegetation. A few species, mostly from the hottest desert areas, build nests just off the ground in bushes where the circulation of the air may cool the nest slightly. Some incubating birds have been observed spending long periods on the nests standing up and shading the eggs from the sun at its height. Clutch sizes are often low in very hot and dry areas—Fischer's finch-lark generally has a clutch of two and nests in equatorial East Africa. Other temperate species regularly lay four, five or even six

eggs—for example the skylark and Crested larks breeding in Europe. A number of desert-dwelling species have been described as building a buttress of stones below the lower edge of their nest which is generally built on a slope. This has been postulated as a method of allowing the nest to drain quickly in the event of a flash flood.

The young always receive some insect food in their first days but many species revert to a vegetable diet well before the chicks move away from the nest, still flightless, within two weeks of hatching. It is thought that this immediate change to vegetable food may lead to the fledglings having rather poor-quality feathers and certainly all lark species so far studied undergo a complete post-juvenile molt. Most other passerines only molt the body plumage at this stage and retain the wing and tail feathers grown in the nest for most of a year.

Modern agricultural techniques within areas where crops are being maximized are probably affecting populations adversely, in some cases through direct poisoning due to misuse of chemicals and in others because weed seeds are gradually being eliminated from cultivated areas and so depriving the birds of their winter food. There is, however, certainly no reason to fear the loss of the familiar song of the skylark and for years to come it will remind people of Shelley's immortal words:

> Hail to thee, blithe Spirit!
> Bird thou never wert,
> That from Heaven or near it,
> Pourest thy full heart
> In profuse strains of unpremeditated art.

(From *To a Skylark*, 1819.)   CJM

Although they probably originated in natural grassland in Africa, the **wagtails and pipits** are now one of the most widespread bird families in the world. They must have benefited considerably from forest clearance carried out by man and are now commonly found in farmland of many types. A few species, notably the White wagtail, are strongly associated with man, being common around habitations, parks and golf courses. Several species live in close harmony with domestic livestock, using these animals as "beaters" to flush insect prey from the grassland they inhabit.

All members of this family are essentially birds of open country. Two genera, the longclaws and the Golden pipit, are still largely confined to savanna grasslands in Africa. Wagtails are essentially birds of wet grassland, lakesides and river margins. Several species are resident in Africa, but they are most widespread in Europe and Asia. One species, the Yellow wagtail, has managed to gain a small foothold in Alaska, but each

The 2 Families of Larks, Wagtails and Pipits   ℝ Rare.

Larks

Family: Alaudidae

Seventy-six species in 13 genera.

Europe, Asia, Africa, America, Australia. Open country. Size: 5–9in (12–24cm) long, weight 0.5–2.6oz (15–75g). Plumage: most are brown, some with black and white markings; the Black lark is completely black. Voice: melodious songs ranging from short songs to prolonged warbling. Nests: most species build cups of dead grass on the ground; some species build a more complex, partly domed structure. Eggs: 2–6, speckled in most species; incubation period: 11–16 days. Diet: seeds, insects.

Species and genera include:

Bifasciated or Hoopoe lark (*Alaemon alaudipes*), bush-larks (genus *Mirafra*), Calandra lark (*Melanocorypha calandra*), Crested lark (*Galerida cristata*), Fischer's finch-lark (*Eremopterix leucopareia*), Horned or Shore lark (*Eremophila alpestris*), Lesser short-toed lark (*Calandrella rufescens*), Razo lark ℝ (*C. razae*), Short-toed lark (*C. cinerea*), Singing bush-lark (*Mirafra javanica*), skylark (*Alauda arvensis*), Thick-billed lark (*Rhamphocoris clotbey*), woodlark (*Lullula arborea*).

Wagtails and pipits

Family: Motacillidae

Fifty-four species in 5 genera.

Worldwide except for very high latitudes and some oceanic islands.

Grassland and steppe. Size: 5–9in (12.5–22cm) long, weight 0.4–1.8oz (12–50g). Plumage: wagtails are either black and white or have gray, brown, greenish or bluish upperparts with whitish, yellow or yellowish underparts; in some species there is a boldly contrasting bib or chest band; longclaws and the Golden pipit are mostly brown above (usually heavily streaked) with bright yellow, yellowish or reddish underparts (often with a strikingly contrasting dark pectoral band). Pipits are mostly brown, often heavily streaked, paler below; all species have white or pale outer tail feathers. Voice: sharp call-notes (often repeated when in flight); simple and repetitive song, infrequent in wagtails, elaborate and musical in

pipits and longclaws. Eggs: 2–7, white, gray or brown, typically speckled with brown; incubation period: 12–20 days; nestling period: 12–18 days. Diet: almost entirely arthropods; some mollusks and vegetable matter.

Species and genera include: **Citrine wagtail** or **Yellow-headed wagtail** (*Motacilla citreola*), **Gray wagtail** (*M. cinerea*), **Golden pipit** (*Tmetothylacus tenellus*), **longclaws** (genus *Macronyx*), **Meadow pipit** (*Anthus pratensis*), **Mountain wagtail** (*Motacilla clara*), **pipits** (genus *Anthus*), **Sokoke pipit** ℝ (*A. sokokensis*), **wagtails** (genera *Dendronanthus, Motacilla*), **White** or **Pied wagtail** (*Motacilla alba*), **Yellow wagtail** (*M. flava*).

▶ **A wagtail associated with watercourses** OVERLEAF is the Gray wagtail (*Motacilla cinerea*). The numbers in wagtail broods vary with latitude. Species living in equatorial regions produce two or three young; the Gray wagtail inhabits most of Europe and the Middle East.

▲ **Bill types of larks.** Several larks inhabit the veld of southern Africa. They can be divided into two groups, those that are primarily grain-eaters (granivorous) and those that are primarily insect-eaters (insectivorous). Insect eaters have longish bills (**1**, **2**), grain-eaters have short, stubby bills (**3**, **4**). (**1**) Spike-heeled lark (*Certhilauda albofasciata*). (**2**) Fawn-colored lark (*Mirafra africanoides*). (**3**) Stark's lark (*Calandrella starki*). (**4**) Pink-billed lark (*Calandrella conirostris*).

◀ **A lark of the African savanna**, the Flappet lark (*Mirafra rufocinnamomea*).

▶ **One of the eight species of longclaws**, the Pangani longclaw (*Macronyx aurantigula*). They form a genus of wagtails and pipits.

▼ **Out on the water,** a juvenile White wagtail. The dark plumage will soon be lost.

autumn these birds return across the Bering Sea to winter in Southeast Asia, along with their fellows from the Old World. Members of the most widespread genus, the pipits, are almost worldwide in distribution and are most successful in areas of dry grassland, subdesert or open woodland. Many species are strongly migratory, moving from high latitudes towards or across the Equator in winter, or from hill and mountain tops down towards the coast.

Wagtails and pipits are mostly small, rather slender birds, with characteristically long tail and long legs. All species have long toes and often very elongate claws, particularly to the hind toe. In most species the bill is slim and rather long, but in longclaws it is rather more robust, so as to deal with the strong bodies of their mostly beetle prey.

The Golden pipit and the longclaws have mostly dull, cryptically colored upperparts. In contrast their underparts are strikingly colored, often yellow, and usually with a bold dark breast band. This is used to effect when in display, during which birds raise their bill to show off their chin and throat, and pout their chest.

The wagtails and the pipits have evolved opposite extremes of plumage patterning and coloration, which seems to relate to their reproductive behavior. Pipits are very inconspicuously colored, mostly brown and often heavily streaked, but they have usually a very conspicuous song flight and, though rather simple and repetitive, their song is often loud and carries far. In contrast, wagtails are brightly plumed with either striking patterns of black and white or combinations of bluish, greenish or olive upperparts and bright yellow or yellowish underparts. As their name implies, these birds often wag their tail in a prominent fashion which may well serve as an effective territorial signal, to maintain spacing between neighboring birds. Whilst they have piercing call notes, their songs are mostly rather quiet and used much less frequently than in the pipits. Several wagtail species exhibit very striking racial differences in plumage pattern. In the Yellow wagtail these differences have led some authorities to split the groups into as many as 14 separate subspecies on the basis of coloration, largely that of the head. However, at the boundaries between different races many birds with intermediate plumage characteristics occur, suggesting a considerable degree of interbreeding.

Wagtails and pipits are extremely adept at catching insects, since they form the bulk of the diet of most species. The most sedentary prey are merely picked from amongst vegetation or stones, but more mobile prey may be secured by a sudden lunge, a rapid running pursuit or by flycatching. The morphology of individual wagtail and pipit species seems to be closely related to the situation in which they most commonly find their prey, and hence to the feeding techniques they most often employ. For example, in wagtails the lengths of the tail and legs appear to be inversely related, associated with the proportions of picking or flycatching feeding activity. At one extreme the Citrine wagtail has very long legs and a short tail, and spends much of its time wading in the shallow margins of lakes and slow-flowing rivers, picking insects and perhaps mollusks from below or on the surface of the water. In contrast the Gray wagtail has a very long tail and rather short legs. It is found by fast-flowing mountain streams, often perching on prominent rocks from which it sallies forth to catch insects in flight above water. Here its long tail probably acts as an efficient rudder, enabling complicated aerial maneuvers to be readily accomplished. However, wagtails and pipits are less agile fliers than, for example, swallows, and hence prefer to feed on the least agile flying insects.

The breeding season of some species is closely linked with the times at which suitable prey emerge. Thus Meadow pipits may feed their young on only one or two species of cranefly which occur in great abundance in some upland grasslands and heaths. Similarly, Gray wagtails may concentrate on the clumsily flying mayflies that emerge seasonally from the waters of the rivers they live beside.

Naturally most wagtails and pipits nest on the ground, making a fairly deep nest, often at the base of a clump of concealing vegetation. Some pipits also use holes in the dry banks of temporary rivers or in small cliff faces, Gray and Mountain wagtails utilize tree roots, holes in riverbanks and bridges, and White wagtails use holes in screes, drystone walls, crevices in buildings and quite often the old discarded nest of another bird species.

Many wagtails and pipits are highly migratory and several species annually traverse the Sahara Desert during journeys between breeding and wintering areas. This may involve them in continuous nonstop flights of over two and a half days' duration and to achieve this they almost double their body weight by accumulating fat reserves (the fuel for the journey) before setting out. In winter many species associate in large flocks, particularly when roosting at night. This has enabled several species to be caught in large numbers for ringing and other scientific studies. Once they have located a suitable wintering area during their first year of life, most birds appear to be remarkably faithful to this in subsequent winters. Thus although their average annual mortality is about 50 percent, which is normal for small birds, at least one Yellow wagtail has been retrapped in its winter roost in West Africa over seven years after it was originally caught and ringed there. This particular bird must thus have successfully crossed the Sahara Desert at least 13 times in its lifetime.　BW

BULBULS

Family: Pycnonotidae
Order: Passeriformes (suborder Oscines, part).
One hundred and eighteen species in 16 genera.
Distribution: Africa, Asia Minor, Middle East, India, Southern Asia, Far East, Java, Borneo, etc; successfully introduced elsewhere.

Habitat: forest thickets, scrubland; many species have adapted to rural cultivated areas and suburban areas.

Size: length 6–11in (15–28cm), weight 0.7–2.3oz (20–65g). In some greenbul species females are much smaller than males.

Plumage: dull brown, gray or green, rarely black, often with bright contrasting patches of red, white or yellow, which is nearly always on the head or under tail coverts. Sexes are normally similar in appearance; females are sometimes a little duller.

Voice: wide range of single and double notes, whistles and chattering calls; many species are exceptionally noisy.

Nests: in the fork of a tree or bush, built of twigs, leaves, spiders' webs and other materials; often lined with fine roots or grass; shallow, usually substantial but some insubstantial.

Eggs: 2–5, pink or white, blotched with various shades of purple, brown or red; about 1 × 0.7in (2.5 × 1.8cm).

Incubation period: 11–14 days.

Nesting period: probably 14–18 days.

Diet: fruit, berries, buds; some species eat insects.

Species and genera include: **Black bulbul** (*Hypsipetes madagascariensis*), **Black-headed bulbul** (*Pycnonotus xanthopygos*), **Brown-eared bulbul** (*Hypsipetes amaurotis*), **Common bulbul** (*Pycnonotus barbatus*), **finch-billed bulbuls** (genus *Spizixos*), **Pale-olive greenbul** (*Phyllastrephus fulviventris*), **Red-vented bulbul** (*Pycnonotus cafer*), **Red-whiskered bulbul** (*P. jocosus*).

▶ **The Black-headed bulbul** of Southeast Asia produces lively, sharp musical chirps. It inhabits stream sides, second growth and coastal scrub.

BULBULS are basically forest dwellers but a number of species have adapted to a variety of other habitats; it is perhaps this adaptability that has made them so popular with man. They make pleasing cage birds and many of them are cheery songsters, which probably explains why they have been introduced to so many parts of the world, either intentionally or accidentally, and why so many of these introductions have been successful. Two species have adapted particularly well, the Red-whiskered bulbul, which has established itself in the USA, southern Malaya, Australia, Mauritius, Singapore, and the Nicobar and Hawaiian Island groups, and the Red-vented bulbul, which has been successfully introduced to several Pacific islands.

Bulbuls are a well-defined, somewhat primitive group of Old World birds. Their most notable feature is a group of hair-like feathers that spring from the nape. These are often long and in many species form a distinct crest.

Bulbuls have short wings, usually rather more curved from front to back than those of most birds, comprising 10 primary feathers, the first of which is very short. The tail, which is made up of 12 feathers, is medium to long and is either square, rounded or slightly forked. They have a short neck and very well-developed bristles around the gape. Almost all species have relatively slender, slightly downcurved bills with longish narrow or oval nostrils. (There are two exceptions: the finch-billed bulbuls.) In size bulbuls vary from that of a House sparrow to that of a large Mistle thrush. One species widespread in North Africa and the Middle East has now been reclassified as two, viz. the Common bulbul of North Africa and the Black-headed bulbul of the Middle East, the latter having yellow undertail covert feathers and a darker head.

Although bulbuls are now probably most familiar in Asia the family apparently originated in the Ethiopian region: it is in Africa and Madagascar where they have attained their greatest development. Here all but two of the 16 genera occur. As one would expect from birds with such short rounded wings they are feeble flyers and not very migratory—the majority of species do not migrate at all, while others only migrate from one altitude to another, especially in Asia, where they occur from 10,000ft (3,000m) up in the Himalayas down to sea level. Only one species appears to be a true migrant, that is the Brown-eared bulbul, which occurs in Japan, and even then it is only the more northern populations that are

migratory, wintering as far south as Korea. They migrate by day, often in large flocks of up to a thousand.

Nearly all bulbuls are active, alert, noisy, gregarious birds, full of character and movement. They often feed in flocks with other species and are almost always the first to give warning of a predator, whether it be a hawk in the air or a snake or cat on the ground, and they often attract the naturalist's attention to rarer birds such as owls which they discover roosting and then mob and torment with shrieks and screams.

The nesting of bulbuls is relatively straightforward. Many are hardly territorial or aggressive to others of their kind, even during the breeding season, though some, such as the Red-vented bulbul, are quite pugnacious. (In Asia they are even kept as fighting birds on which sums of money are placed, fights occasionally continuing until one bird has killed the other.) The nest is usually built in the fork of a tree or bush, often poorly concealed. Because of this many species are often taken by such predators as cats, crows and lizards and are often parasitized by various species of cuckoos. Most nest at a height of 5–30ft (1.5–9m) although the nest of the Black bulbul has been recorded at over 50ft (15m), while the Pale-olive greenbul nests between 2 and 4ft (0.5–1.6m) and conceals its nest in thick undergrowth such as brambles.

The incubation period is usually 11–14 days, with both sexes taking turns on the eggs, which in some species are extremely beautiful; many have unusually thick hard shells for birds of their size. Normally more than one brood is reared in a year, and the young are fed by both parents.

Although bulbuls are not noted for their nuptial displays, these can nevertheless be quite attractive and certainly make the most of what distinctive features they have. The male Red-vented bulbul, whose mating display is one of the best documented, depresses and spreads his tail laterally to show off his bright crimson undertail coverts while fluttering his spread wings up and down above his head. This is not only used to attract females but to warn off rivals when it is accompanied by a series of defiant calls. Many bulbuls are probably cooperative breeders but this is not documented.

Although bulbuls have been introduced to many different parts of the world it is debatable whether this was a wise policy. They damage valuable crops, especially fruit, and probably cause severe damage when liberated where their natural foods are in short supply.   cw

SHRIKES AND WAXWINGS

Families: Laniidae, Campephagidae, Irenidae, Prionopidae, Vangidae, Bombycillidae, Dulidae
Order: Passeriformes (suborder Oscines, part).
One hundred and eighty-seven species in 38 genera.
Distribution: see maps and table.

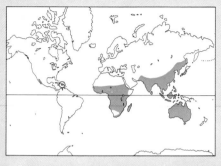

Cuckoo shrikes   **Palmchat**

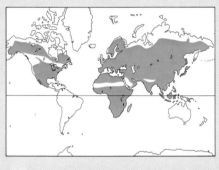

Shrikes   **Vanga shrikes**

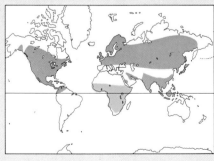

Leafbirds   Waxwings   Helmet shrikes

In many parts of the world **shrikes** are familiar birds of villages and large towns, being noisy and usually conspicuous because of their bright colors.

The majority of the family (77 percent of species) are endemic to Africa south of the Sahara, and many of these species are probably closely related. Some of the true shrikes occur throughout the northern temperate and Arctic region and some of these are closely related to the African *Lanius* species. The Northern or Great gray shrike is found in North Africa and throughout Europe and the USSR and also occurs in North America south to Mexico. In southern and eastern China the Northern shrike is replaced by the Long-tailed gray shrike. The Rufous-backed shrike also has an extensive range from India through Asia and onto New Guinea. In contrast, the Strong-billed shrike is endemic to the Philippines and the Bornean bristle-head to Borneo. Most African genera have species that either inhabit dense tropical forests, both lowland or montane, or else open deciduous woodland. Thus the puff-back and Sabine's puff-back occur throughout West and Central Africa, the former in savanna and the latter in forest. Some genera are, however, confined to savanna areas (eg the true shrikes, Western long-tailed shrike and the Brubru shrike). Outside Africa shrikes occur in open woodland, orchards and often in pine and oak forests. The African genus *Malaconotus* is remarkable in that pairs of species, one large and one small, that live in the same habitat are color replicas of each other. Thus the Orange-breasted bush-shrike is a small edition of the Gray-headed bush-shrike, both occurring in the savanna of West Africa. Forest species also show this replication and other examples occur elsewhere in Africa. The function of such duplication is uncertain, particularly as the species involved are ecologically separate.

All shrikes have a sharply hooked and notched bill, features that are more prominent in some genera than in others. The powerful beak is used for killing the prey. In the majority of species the legs and feet are strong and the claws sharp for holding prey. The tail is long in many species and often graduated or rounded. Many African shrikes are incredibly beautiful. The gonolek is crimson below and black above apart from a dull yellow crown and under-tail coverts, and other related species are similarly colored. In contrast, the Tropical boubou is black and white and the Sooty boubou is black. The sexes are alike in the first two species but in the case of the Sooty boubou the

female is dark olivaceous brown below.

All *Laniarius* species are skulkers in dense habitat and use a variety of contact calls, the sexes duetting, often alternately. The Gray-headed bush-shrike has a green back and yellow underparts and the Gorgeous bush-shrike is similarly colored but has, in addition, a bright red throat bordered by black (less prominent in the female than the male). Other African shrikes are not so brightly colored. Some bush-shrikes have rufous wings, brown backs, pale underparts, patterned heads and black and white tails and in the majority of these the sexes are alike. The Red-backed shrike is well known in Europe but is only one of several *Lanius* species which have rufous or chestnut backs. The male has a gray head and rump, a black eye stripe and a black and white tail; in the female the gray and black areas are replaced by mouse brown. Many *Lanius* species are a mixture of black, gray and white, some have long tails, and the sexes are alike in many. Any differences are confined to flank colors and the presence of some slight barring on the female breast in some species. Two African shrikes, although markedly different in color, are considered closely related, partly because of the social behavior and partly through their distribution. One, the Western long-tailed shrike, is essentially brown above, buff below and is profusely streaked black above and below. Its bill is yellow and on each wing there is a chestnut patch. The other occurs in southern Africa

▲ **The Rufous-backed shrike** (*Lanius schach*) frequents scrub and open country in South and Southeast Asia. Note the large grasshopper impaled in the larder.

◄ **The Red-backed shrike** (*L. collurio*) nests in Europe and western Asia and winters in tropical Africa and Southeast Asia. Its nests are built in bushes and hedges from stalks, roots and twigs. They are lined with grasses.

and is mainly black with white on the wings and flanks.

After breeding in northern latitudes, all populations of the Woodchat shrike and Lesser gray shrike migrate to Africa. Some populations of the Red-backed shrike do also but other populations migrate to Southeast Asia. North–south movements occur in other shrikes that breed at high latitudes but the more southern populations are sedentary. Local movements are suspected for some savanna shrikes in Africa but this has not been proved through ringing. While on migration the *Lanius* species are territorial

and some (Red-backed shrike) defend territories in their winter quarters. In Africa the migrant species are solitary and males return to breeding grounds before the females; in Woodchat shrikes, however, the sexes may arrive already paired.

The Boubou shrikes and smaller bush-shrikes are predominantly insect-eaters and feed near and on the ground. The larger species (*Malaconotus*) and puff-backs feed in trees, the former methodically searching the foliage for food, the latter feeding actively like warblers. Small vertebrates and bird eggs make up the diet of the larger species.

The true shrikes characteristically search the ground from a vantage point and pounce on their prey. They may, however, catch insects on the wing and search the ground for food from the air. Many of them store food by impaling their prey on thorns, barbs of wire or else hanging it from the fork of a branch, but not all African *Lanius* species do this. When in Africa the Red-backed shrike does not use such a "larder." The principal food of the Northern shrike is vertebrates, and when dealing with large prey which it could not tear up when frozen it tears the prey into smaller pieces before impaling them, and these may be eaten frozen.

The majority of shrikes breed in pairs; some resident species remain paired for a year or more and maintain their territories outside the breeding season (observed in Boubou shrikes, puff-backs, bush-shrikes). For the majority of species in Africa the breeding season overlaps the end of the dry season and the beginning of the rainy season but in some (Fiscal shrike, Western long-tailed shrike) it is prolonged and ceases during the molting period which is synchronized in a given population. Two or three successful broods are normal for these shrikes. Breeding in northern latitudes is confined to the short summer period (May–July) and one brood is the norm; replacement clutches are quickly laid.

The courtship display of the majority of species has not been described. Male puff-backs puff out their rump feathers and look like puff-balls in their display. Bush-shrikes of the genus *Tchagra* use a display flight accompanied with wing flapping and a duet. The male Woodchat shrike nods his head rapidly up and down while singing to the female and both partners join in a duet, and a similar display is used by the male Red-backed shrike. Courtship feeding of female by the male has been observed in several species of *Lanius* and *Corvinella* and the female's calls (resembling young) quickly reveal the nest location.

Both sexes help build the nest and feed the nestlings. The female alone incubates in *Lanius* and *Corvinella* species but in other genera the limited data available suggest that both sexes incubate. The nests of many of the endemic African shrikes are inconspicuous—neatly formed cups made from tendrils, fiber, grass and spider webs, either secured to a horizontal branch or placed in a fork of a tree. The larger species and the *Lanius* species have more bulky nests of twigs, lined with fibers, tendrils and grass or else (at higher latitudes) with wool,

hair and feathers; these may be placed in trees or thickets.

A good deal of attention has been given in recent years to the study of cooperative breeding, and this occurs in some African shrikes. In southern Ghana, the Western long-tailed shrike lives in groups (average 12 birds) throughout the year and various individuals defend the territory, feed the breeding female, nestlings and fledglings. Breeding in pairs did not occur during a five-year period of study, and two females in their sixth year were still helping in a group.

▲ **Common, intolerant and voracious** is the Fiscal shrike. Its range is Africa south of the Sahara (except for the Kalahari Desert) where it is common in savanna, open country and near human habitations. Birds that come near it are liable to be seized and impaled on thorns or barbed wire. It also frightens birds in cages, especially canaries: they flutter against the bars of their cages where they are seized by the head and killed.

THE 7 FAMILIES OF SHRIKES AND WAXWINGS

Shrikes

Family: Laniidae
Seventy species in 9 genera.

Africa, Europe, USSR, India, Asia, Philippines, Japan, Borneo, New Guinea, N America. Primary and secondary tropical forests, dry and moist savanna woodlands, cultivated orchards. Size: 5.8–15in (15–38cm) long, known weights 0.4–3oz (10–87g). Plumage: many are brightly colored crimson, yellow, green; others are mixtures of black, gray and white; no difference between sexes in most species, but in a few there are marked or slight differences. Voice: some have melodious songs, others have discordant and harsh calls; many species duet, some mimic. Nests: in trees or shrubs, usually supported by twigs, but some are secured to a horizontal branch. Eggs: 2 or 3 in bush shrikes, 4–7 in most other species, ground color ranges from white through blue to pale pink, with brown or purple brown streaks or blotches; incubation: 12–14 days, 15–18 days in some species; nestling period: 16–20 days, 12–15 days in some species. Diet: chiefly insects but some take a variety of invertebrates and the larger species take small vertebrates.

Species and genera include: **Black-headed bush-shrike** (*Tchagra senegala*), **Bornean bristle-head** (*Pityriasis gymnocephala*), **boubous** (genus *Laniarius*), **Brubru shrike** (*Nilaus afer*), **Fiscal shrike** (*Lanius collaris*), **gonolek** (*Laniarius barbarus*), **Gorgeous bush-shrike** (*Malaconotus quadricolor*), **Gray-headed bush-shrike** (*M. blanchoti*), **Lesser gray shrike** (*Lanius minor*), **Long-tailed gray shrike** (*L. sphenocercus*), **Northern** or **Great gray shrike** (*L. excubitor*), **Orange-breasted bush-shrike** (*Malaconotus sulfureopectus*), **puff-back** (*Dryoscopus gambensis*), **puff-backs** (genus *Dryoscopus*), **Rufous-backed shrike** (*Lanius schach*), **Sabine puff-back** (*D. sabini*), **Sooty boubou** (*Laniarius leucorhynchus*), **Strong-billed shrike** (*Lanius validirostris*), **Tropical boubou** (*Laniarius aethiopicus*), **true shrikes** (genus *Lanius*), **Western long-tailed shrike** (*Corvinella corvina*), **Woodchat shrike** (*Lanius senator*). Total threatened species: 2.

Cuckoo-shrikes

Family: Campephagidae
Seventy-two species in 9 genera.

Africa S of the Sahara, Madagascar, India, SE Asia, Philippines, Borneo, Celebes, New Guinea, Australia, some Polynesian and Indian Ocean islands, S and E China, Japan, SE USSR. Dense primary and secondary forest; some species prefer forest edge, cultivated areas and coastal scrub. Size 5.5–14in (14–36cm) long, known weights 0.7–3.9oz (20–111g). Plumage: many species are pale or dark gray, some black and white, others black and red; females of many species are paler than males; minivets are brightly colored, males being predominantly red and black, females yellow, orange and black. Voice: call notes range from high-pitched whistles (often loud, clear and musical), soft trills to harsh shrike-like notes; the songs of many species are more elaborate versions of the call notes; the Long-billed graybird or cicadabird sounds like a cicada. Nest: high in the fork of a tree or bonded to the top of a horizontal branch, always well concealed; constructed of twigs, roots, mosses, lichens, cobwebs; the nests of some Australian species are occasionally grouped together. Eggs: number varies, 1–5; white, grayish or pale green blotched brown, purple or gray; incubation: where known, 14 days (*Lalage* species), 20–23 days (*Coracina* and *Campephaga* species); fledgling periods: for these two groups, 12 and 20–25 days respectively. Diet: mainly insects, caterpillars, etc; some species take fruit, others take lizards and frogs.

Species and genera include: **Ashy minivet** (*Pericrocotus divaricatus*), **Black-breasted triller** (*Chlamydochaera jefferyi*), **Black cuckoo-shrike** (*Campephaga flava*), **Flame-colored minivet** (*Pericrocotus ethologus*), **flycatcher-shrikes** (genus *Hemipus*), **Ground cuckoo-shrike** (*Pteropodocys maxima*), **Large cuckoo-shrike** (*Coracina novaehollandiae*), **Long-billed graybird** or **cicadabird** (*C. tenuirostris*), **minivets** (genus *Pericrocotus*), **Orange cuckoo-shrike** (*Campochaera sloetii*), **Scarlet minivet** (*Pericrocotus flammeus*), **Small minivet** (*P. cinnamomeus*), **trillers** (genera *Chlamydochaera*, *Lalage*), **White-winged triller** (*Lalage suerii*), **wood shrikes** (genus *Tephrodornis*). Total threatened species: 2.

Leafbirds

Family: Irenidae
Fourteen species in 3 genera.

From Pakistan through India and SE Asia to the Philippines. Evergreen forest to dry scrub. Size: 5.5–11in (14–27cm) long, about 0.4–3.2oz (10–90g); slight to moderate differences between sexes. Plumage: blue and black or predominantly green; most ioras have white double wing-bars; juveniles resemble females. Voice: strident whistles and melodious mimicking songs. Nest: arboreal open cup. Eggs: 2–3; pinkish speckled and lined red and purple; in Asian fairy bluebird greenish white to stone, streaked brown, gray and purple. Diet: insects, fruit, nectar.

Species and genera include: **Asian fairy bluebird** (*Irena puella*), **Blue-masked leafbird** (*Chloropsis venusta*), **Blue-winged leafbird** (*C. cochinchinensis*), **Common iora** (*Aegithina tiphia*), **Golden-fronted leafbird** (*C. aurifrons*), **Great iora** (*A. lafresnayei*), **Green iora** (*A. viridissima*), **ioras** (genus *Aegithina*), **leafbirds** (genus *Chloropsis*), **Marshall's iora** (*A. nigrolutea*), **Orange-bellied leafbird** (*C. hardwickii*).

Helmet shrikes

Family: Prionopidae
Nine species in 2 genera.

Africa S of the Sahara. Wooded savanna (Red-billed shrike lives in dense lowland forest). Size: 7.5–10in (19–25cm) long, known weights 1.2–1.8oz (33–52g). Plumage: boldly marked black or brown and white, or black and brown with some species having patches of chestnut, gray or yellow; *Prionops* species have prominent crests; most species also have brightly colored wattles. Voice: characteristic sounds are rasping, nasal call notes and bill snapping; some have whistled call notes which sound like those of orioles in the Red-billed shrike. Nests: built on horizontal boughs or in forks high above ground. Eggs: usually 3–5, sometimes 2 or 6; wide range of ground colors (white, pale blue, olive green), blotched or spotted with brown, violet brown and chestnut; incubation and nestling periods: unknown. Diet: insects.

Species include: **Chestnut-fronted helmet shrike** (*Prionops scopifrons*), **Gray-crested helmet shrike** (*P. poliolopha*), **Long-crested helmet shrike** (*P. plumata*), **Retz's red-billed shrike** (*P. retzii*), **Rueppell's white-crowned shrike** (*Eurocephalus rueppelli*), **White-crowned shrike** (*E. anguitimens*), **Yellow-crested helmet shrike** (*P. alberti*).

Vanga shrikes

Family: Vangidae
Thirteen species in 9 genera.

Madagascar (with a subspecies of the Blue vanga occurring on Moheli in the Comoro Islands). Woodland and areas covered in shrubs. Length: 5–12.6in (13–32cm). Plumage: many are metallic black above, white below, some having additional chestnut and gray areas; two species are predominantly blue; sexes differ in some species. Voice: varies between species; loud, tremulous, beautiful whistles in the Rufous and Helmet vangas, drawn out in the Hook-billed vanga, often repeated in the Lafresnaye's vanga; the calls of the Sicklebill falculea are likened to the cry of a playing child. Eggs: 3 or 4; various ground colors (white, cream, pink, greenish blue), profusely marked with brown or gray blotches. Incubation and nestling periods: unknown. Diet: insects.

Species include: **Blue vanga** (*Leptopterus madagascarinus*), **Chabert vanga** (*L. chabert*), **Helmet bird** (*Euryceros prevostii*), **Hook-billed vanga** (*Vanga curvirostris*), **Lafresnaye's vanga** (*Xenopirostris xenopirostris*), **Madagascar nuthatch** (*Hypositta corallirostris*), **Red-tailed vanga** (*Calicalicus madagascariensis*), **Rufous vanga** (*Schetba rufa*), **Sicklebill falculea** (*Falculea palliata*). Total threatened species: 3.

Waxwings and their allies

Family: Bombycillidae
Eight species in 5 genera.

Europe, Asia, N and C America. Woodland and forest. Length: 7–9.5in (18–24cm). Plumage: soft; chiefly brown, gray and black with some red and yellow; sexes similar except in the phainopepla where the male is shiny black and the female olive-gray. Voice: can be noisy, especially when feeding, but songs are poorly developed and are often sung very quietly. The phainopepla sometimes sings in flight. Nests: in trees, built mainly from twigs. Eggs: 2–7; gray, blue or whitish green; incubation: 12–16 days; nestling period: 16–25 days. Diet: berries and insects.

Species: **Black-and-yellow silky flycatcher** (*Phainoptila melanoxantha*), **Bohemian waxwing** or **waxwing** (*Bombycilla garrulus*), **Cedar waxwing** (*B. cedrorum*), **Gray hypocolius** (*Hypocolius ampelinus*), **Gray silky flycatcher** (*Ptilogonys cinereus*), **Japanese waxwing** (*Bombycilla japonica*), **Long-tailed silky flycatcher** (*Ptilogonys caudatus*), **phainopepla** (*Phainopepla nitens*).

Palmchat

Family: Dulidae
Dulus dominicus.

W Indies. Open woodland. Length: 8in (20cm). Plumage: softer than waxwings; upperparts olive, underparts buffy white, boldly streaked with brown. Voice: has a variety of calls but no true song. Nests: large communal nest of twigs. Eggs: 2–4; heavily spotted. Diet: berries, flowers.

Many ideas have been put forward about the usefulness of such behavior and its evolution, and its study will continue to be profitable and worthwhile; the African shrikes are ideal subjects for investigating this behavior.   LGG

Although the majority of **cuckoo-shrikes** have shrike-like bills, and colors and plumage patterns resembling cuckoos, they are not related to either shrikes or cuckoos. They are a family of two distinct groups: the cuckoo-shrikes (8 genera, 62 species) which are drably colored in general and range in size from that of a sparrow to that of a dove, and the brightly colored minivets (10 species) which are much more active and gregarious, and wagtail-like in size and shape.

Two genera occur in Africa, one (*Campephaga*, 6 species) is endemic and the other (*Coracina* with a total of 40 species but only 4 in Africa) occurs from East Pakistan through Southeast Asia to New Guinea and Australia. The Ground cuckoo-shrike is endemic to Australia, another (Black-breasted triller) is endemic to Borneo and a third (Orange cuckoo-shrike) to New Guinea. The remainder are distributed throughout the Indian subcontinent, Southeast Asia, Malaysia, Indonesia and northwards to eastern China and Russia.

Cuckoo-shrikes have long pointed wings, moderately long tails (either graduated or rounded), and well-developed rictal bristles which in many species cover the nostrils. Many species (*Campephaga*, *Coracina*, minivets) have spine-like shafts to the feathers of the rump and lower back. These are not normally visible but are raised in defense display. The newly hatched young of some (eg *Campephaga*, *Hemipus*, *Tephrodornis*) are covered with white or gray down which blends in perfectly with the nest and environment. The fledglings are similar to females and differences between sexes are minimal except for *Campephaga* species. In this genus the males are predominantly black with little difference between them and some species have patches of bare yellowish skin at the sides of the gape which is unique in the family. The females are so different from the males that they might easily pass for another species.

In direct contrast the minivets are dainty and strikingly colored with slender narrow wings with a prominent wing bar, and a long strongly graduated tail. There is a marked difference between the sexes. The Scarlet minivet has the whole of the head, throat, back, most of the wings, and central tail feathers black, the rest of the plumage being red. The female is just as striking with yellow replacing the red and also the black on the chin, throat and forehead. In contrast the male Ashy minivet has a gray back and rump, black and white tail, a prominent black nape and crown, and white on the forehead and underparts. The female and juveniles are similarly colored and patterned but not so prominently.

All the family, particularly the minivets, are gregarious and are usually first located in parties of up to 20 or more birds as they move through the tops of trees in search of food. They invariably make up part of any mixed feeding flocks, which are a characteristic of the forests and open woodlands of India and the whole of Southeast Asia. Minivets move through the canopy in noisy parties as they follow each other searching for insects. Flycatcher-shrikes do the same but also catch insects on the wing, and their bills are proportionally shorter and wider at the gape than those of other members of the family. The wood-shrikes are a little more cumbersome and slow moving when feeding but will catch insects in flight and feed on the ground when necessary. The larger *Coracina* species also form loose feeding parties and eat fruit in addition to insects. Most trillers do this as well but the Black-breasted triller, a montane forest species, is thought to eat only fruit. Some trillers in Australia and the Ground cuckoo-shrike feed mainly on the ground. The latter has strong legs well adapted for walking and running. In flight it is much like a cuckoo with black wings and tail contrasting with a gray mantle and head and the finely barred white underparts. The White-winged

repeatedly for some seconds, while calling vigorously; this is then repeated at intervals. However, females also flick their wings (Black cuckoo-shrike) and wing flicking seems characteristic of the group as it is often observed after a bird perches. The male Black cuckoo-shrike performs a moth-like fluttering flight with tail fanned and depressed during his courtship display. In some species (White-winged triller, Large cuckoo-shrike, flycatcher shrikes) both sexes take part in nest building, incubation and feeding nestlings. In others (eg Scarlet minivet, Flame-colored minivet) males feed the nestlings and contribute a little to nest building, whereas in others (Black cuckoo-shrike) the male only helps feed the nestlings, although he may accompany the female while she builds.

Some species are single brooded but others (Small minivet) have two broods in rapid succession, and some (Large cuckoo-shrike in India) have two breeding seasons a year (February–April and August–October). Nest helpers have been recorded at nests of the Small minivet and the Ground cuckoo-shrike. The White-winged triller defends large territories in coastal areas of Australia but in the interior may breed in close proximity to each other.

The Ashy minivet is the only long-distant migrant of the family and leaves its breeding areas in China and USSR to winter in Southeast Asia. Prior to migrating, flocks of up to 150 birds form on the breeding grounds. The rest of the family are mainly sedentary or nomadic but Australian species move north–south over large distances and some Indian species undergo altitudinal migration.   LGG

▲ **Open forest and forest edge** provide a home for the Large cuckoo-shrike (*Coracina novaehollandiae*) across the enormous expanse of India, South China, Southeast Asia, Australia and New Zealand.

◄ **Parks, gardens and lightly timbered areas** are the preference of the White-winged triller (*Lalage suerii*), which is found in Java, Timor and New Guinea and throughout Australia. This is the female.

triller is a unique member of the family as the male molts from a black and white breeding dress into a nonbreeding dress resembling the female's which is brown above and white (lightly streaked brown) below.

The courtship and breeding behavior of the family have been little studied. The male Scarlet minivet pursues the female into the air from a perch and seizes her tail in his bill. They then spiral down together to the perch and just before landing he releases her tail. Such flights above the tree tops seem to be a feature of all minivets, but some of these may well be territorial in function as a similar spiraling descent has been recorded for a male White-winged triller when defending his territory. In the courtship display of some larger cuckoo-shrikes the male lifts each wing alternately and

The three genera in the **leafbirds** family differ considerably and may not form a natural assemblage. Fairy bluebirds, in particular, need further taxonomic study. Their combination of brilliant blue and black is, nevertheless, repeated in the throat pattern of most male leafbirds (*Chloropsis* species). These two genera also have similar short, thick tarsi with small toes and both shed body feathers profusely when handled—as do bulbuls. It may have escape value in that it may confuse the predator. The intense red eye of adult fairy bluebirds is not shared with others of the family. Leafbirds are otherwise smaller and, as their name implies, green with or without blue on the wing-coverts and tail, and blue, yellow and/or orange on the head and underparts.

Ioras are smaller again, with proportionately long bills and slender legs. They too are basically green or green and yellow with slight to marked plumage differences between the sexes, Great and Common ioras varying in the extent to which males develop a black dorsal breeding plumage. Fairy bluebirds and leafbirds differ significantly in plumage between the sexes, except in the Philippines. There only one species per genus occurs per island. In isolation females of the endemic Philippine fairy bluebird have evolved plumage similar to that of the males and the males of the endemic species of leafbirds have lost their dark head pattern.

Ioras cover the full range of family habitats, from dry acacia scrub (Marshall's iora) through forest edge and cultivation (Common iora) to closed canopy forests (Great and Green). Golden-fronted leafbirds inhabit deciduous monsoon forest; all other species, and the two fairy bluebirds, live in evergreen forest and therefore are of restricted (and shrinking) distribution west of Burma. The Asian fairy bluebird is now extinct in Sri Lanka. Three leafbirds are mountain dwellers: Orange-bellied on the Asian continent, a possible form of the Blue-winged in Borneo and the Blue-masked (with an isolated subspecies of the Golden-fronted in secondary vegetation) in Sumatra.

All species are confined to trees and in forest feed at canopy level. Ioras search foliage for insects, and the Green iora is a regular core member of foraging flocks of mixed species. Fairy bluebirds are fruit-eaters, roaming the forest between scattered sources of food which they may visit in some

numbers, advertising themselves with loud, liquid whistles. Leafbirds take both insects and fruit (papped in the bill and the contents sucked out). They also take nectar and may help to pollinate some forest trees. Fairy bluebird songs are inadequately recorded but leafbirds, especially Orange-bellied and Golden-fronted, are fine singers (the latter is also a notorious mimic). Common ioras are conspicuous by their loud, varied calls and the males of at least Common and Great ioras also perform a parachute display flight.

Ioras build compact cup nests felted to branches with cobweb. The few leafbird nests that have been described also incorporate cobweb but are suspended by the rim from twin twigs. Asian fairy bluebirds form a cup of rootlets and moss and liverworts on a platform of twigs in a sapling or small forest tree; only the female builds and incubates but both sexes feed the young. Common ioras may separate their two fledglings, the parents tending one each.

DRW

Many species of tropical birds are gregarious in both breeding and nonbreeding seasons. Such sociability is one of the most important field characteristics of **helmet shrikes**. They always are found in parties of up to 12 or more birds, often with other species.

Although the savanna helmet shrikes have a wide distribution, the ranges of the different species usually do not overlap and when they do overlap are ecologically separate. Thus the Long-crested helmet shrike has several subspecies in its wide range of latitude (15°N–25°S) but is replaced in

Kenya by the Gray-crested helmet shrike, and in the highlands of the eastern Congo by the Yellow-crested helmet shrike. In areas where it occurs together with both Retz's red-billed shrike and the Chestnut-fronted helmet shrike, the Long-crested helmet shrike searches low down on or near the ground while Retz's searches for insects high up in the canopy; the Chestnut-fronted helmet shrike being smaller than the other two is thought to feed on different prey from the others. The insect diet of helmet shrikes is varied (beetles, caterpillars, grasshoppers, mantises) and small geckos are occasionally

▲ **The nest of the Common iora** (a leafbird) is usually built between 6.5 and 13ft (2–4m) up a tree and consists of fine grasses of fibers plastered with cobwebs. The breeding season is mainly July and August when two or three eggs are laid. This species is common in India, southwest China, the Greater Sundas and Palawan.

◄ **The Chabert vanga** (a vanga shrike) is restricted to Madagascar where it often forms small flocks. They fly from tree to tree, in undulating flight, looking out for small and medium-sized insects.

taken by the Long-crested helmet shrike. The *Eurocephalus* species feed mainly on ground-living prey, pouncing on them from a vantage point.

The bill of helmet shrikes is strong, sharply hooked at the tip, and either black or red. The tail is long and rounded and the feet are strong. As a family they are distinctive in having scales (scutellations) on both the side and front of the tarsus. The Long-crested helmet shrike has a black back, white underparts, gray head and white crest. Most red-billed species are mainly dark slate gray-brown with black head and

breast, the exception being the Chestnut-fronted helmet shrike which has a black back, throat and tail, a white head and chestnut and white underparts. The Yellow-crested helmet shrike is wholly black other than its crest, although this is dull grayish white in young birds. The two white-headed species are distinguished by their brown and white plumage, one (White-crowned shrike) having a brown rump, the other (Rueppell's white-crowned shrike) a white one.

Additional birds, other than the breeding pair, have been recorded as helping in nest construction and/or in feeding nestlings of

the Long-crested helmet shrike, the Gray-crested helmet shrike and the Chestnut-fronted shrike. This cooperative breeding may occur in others but not, apparently, in Retz's red-billed shrike. However, several pairs of this and the other three helmet shrikes may build nests close together, forming a loose colony. Breeding occurs mainly in the dry season, but extends into the wet season, at least for some species. In central East Africa several of the helmet shrikes occur in the same area.   LGG

The **vanga shrikes** or vangas are a good example of what happens when a unique stock of birds (possibly belonging to the helmet shrikes) becomes established on a large isolated island containing only a few other groups of birds. On Madagascar they have filled the ecological niches that, in other parts of the world, are occupied by woodpeckers, shrikes, tits and nuthatches. As a result they differ markedly in size and color, and even more in the shape of the bill: to describe one would draw a picture atypical of the group. But similarity of the skull's shape and of the structure of the bony palate are the basis for placing them in one family. They are found in wet forests (Rufous vanga, Helmet vanga, Madagascar nuthatch), dry forests and open savanna (Sicklebill falculea) and in semidesert

(Lafresnaye's vanga). The size and shape of their bills reflect the size of insect prey taken, their location and the mode of capture. The larger species have shrike-like bills with a characteristic hook at the tip, the bill of the Helmet vanga having a relatively large casque (enlargement) which is bright blue. These search the foliage for large insects and also capture small vertebrates, chameleons and amphibians in the manner of small birds of prey. The three species of *Xenopirostris* have horizontally compressed bills and sit immobile on a twig and catch passing insects like a flycatcher. The bills of the Red-tailed vanga and Madagascar nuthatch are much finer, the former hunting small insects along branches like tits, the latter searching trunks and major branches in the same way as true nuthatches but always moving upwards while searching. The Sicklebill falculea's long curved bill is well adapted for locating prey in crevices in the bark of trees, and this species takes the place of woodpeckers.

In those species studied both sexes help in nest construction, incubation and feeding young; an extra member of the same species has been seen at a nest of a Chabert vanga that was being built. The nests of the majority are neat cups made from small leaves, roots, fibers and bark all bound to the support with spider web but, in marked con-

▲ ▶ **Representative species of shrikes and waxwings.** (1) A Large cuckoo-shrike (*Coracina novaehollandiae*). (2) A Northern shrike (*Lanius excubitor*). (3) A Red-shouldered cuckoo-shrike (*Campephaga phoenicea*). (4) A Golden-fronted leafbird (*Chloropsis aurifrons*). (5) A Bohemian waxwing (*Bombycilla garrulus*). (6) A Long-crested helmet shrike (*Prionops plumata*). (7) A Helmet brid (a vanga shrike; *Euryceros prevostii*) holding prey. (8) A palmchat (*Dulus dominicus*). (9) A Burchell's gonolek or Crimson-breasted shrike (*Laniarius atrococcineus*).

trast, that of the Sicklebill falculea is made from twigs and is like that of a crow.

Most of the vanga shrikes are gregarious in the nonbreeding season, feeding and moving in loose flocks of 4–12 individuals (Chabert vanga, Rufous vanga), but as high as 25 or more in the Sicklebill falculea; others join flocks of mixed species which may include other vangas (eg Blue vanga, Red-tailed vanga). In contrast the Hook-billed vanga and Lafresnaye's vanga are usually solitary.

Of all the endemic groups on Madagascar the Vanga shrikes are the most successful, both in number of species and abundance, but their survival is threatened by the destruction of their forest and wooded habitats.   LGG

The eight species of **waxwings** all depend to a large extent on fruit and are gregarious at some times of year. Although the biology of the true waxwings is quite well known that of their tropical relatives is poorly understood.

The three species of true waxwings are

widely distributed across the coniferous forests of northern Asia, Europe and America. All are similar in ecology and appearance. The name waxwing refers to sealing-wax-like red drops at the tips of the adults' secondary feathers (and more rarely on the tail). The function of these drops is not known. In many other ways too, waxwings are mysterious birds; unpredictable in the timing, numbers and location of their occurrence. They were once thought to be bad omens, which earned them the name "pest-bird" in some parts of Europe.

Waxwings have soft silky plumage, drab colors, short stout bills and legs, long claws and prominent crests. They have relatively long wings which allow them to fly fast. Speeds of up to 29mph (46kh) have been measured for Cedar waxwings. Their flight is characteristically strong and undulating.

All species rely on berries for much of their food, although in spring and summer petals and insects are eaten. Insects are caught on the wing, by fly-catching from high exposed branches, and include such agile prey as dragonflies. Captured insects are brought to a perch to be eaten. The Bohemian waxwing turns to fruits as soon as they appear and will take raspberries, hawthorn, rowan, cedar, juniper, mistletoe and many domestic fruits. These birds will gorge themselves on berries in one place until they seem hardly able to fly, stripping the bushes clean before moving on. An occasional consequence of eating fermenting berries is that waxwings can sometimes be found showing signs of intoxication! Their reliance on fruit and their nomadic habits in winter may make them important dispersers of seeds. However, since seeds can pass through the digestive tract in as little as 16 minutes most seeds will presumably be voided near to where they were eaten.

Waxwings feed mainly in trees, though they will sometimes pluck at groups of berries while hovering at the edge of a bush or tree. They visit the ground to feed, but more often to drink. They are catholic in their tastes and will be attracted to bird tables (feeding stations) by the provision of currants, raisins, dates or prunes. In the wild they will feed on flowing sap. Waxwings are often very tame and will enter cities and feed near the feet of people.

All waxwings are monogamous. Pairing occurs in the winter flocks. A courtship ritual takes place in which a male and female pass an object back and forth between them several times. In Bohemian waxwings the object is sometimes inedible and is not swallowed but in Cedar waxwings the display ends when one bird eats the berry which the pair have used. It is apparently not known whether it is always one sex or the other that thus terminates the sequence. This display may have its evolutionary origin in courtship feeding of females by males, but has now become highly ritualized.

Pairs do not defend territories, except for the area immediately around the nest. In some areas loose colonies are formed. The nest is built by both parents but the female does most of this work. Nest sites are well away from the main trunk of a tree on a horizontal limb. The height of the nest may be up to 50ft (17m) above the ground. The nest itself is loose and bulky, made of twigs, grass and lichens, and lined with fine grasses, mosses and pine needles. They can often look very similar to loose piles of moss and

◄ **Quick passage.** Waxwings process food at great speed, though it is only half digested when excreted. This feature makes the waxwings important as distributors of the seeds of trees and shrubs. This is the Bohemian waxwing.

► **Annual passage.** BELOW Cedar waxwings of North America breed in southern Canada and the northern USA and migrate to the southern USA and Mexico for winter.

▼ **Head of a phainopepla.** This relative of the waxwing is found in desert scrub from the southwest USA to central Mexico.

twigs that have collected by chance on a branch. Females do all or nearly all of the incubation but are fed on the nest by their mates. Both parents feed the young. Most waxwings are single-brooded but Cedar waxwings are occasionally double-brooded.

Out of the breeding season waxwings are found in flocks which roam widely in search of food. In some years they spread much further south—traveling by day—and in larger numbers than usual. The causes of these invasions are not fully understood but implicated as important factors are food scarcity and population levels. There is some evidence that waxwing numbers grow and fall following a 10-year cycle, independent of food availability, though it is difficult to suggest what other factor could drive such cycles. Waxwings do not seem to return to the same areas to nest every year so it seems that they lead a nomadic existence, probably governed by the availability of berries.

The Gray hypocolius has a restricted distribution in the Tigris-Euphrates Valley. Its biology is little known although it shows some of the characteristics of waxwings (such as flocking outside the breeding season and fruit-eating). It feeds on dates, figs, nightshade and mulberry fruits. A quiet bird with no known song, it spends much of its time hidden in foliage.

The best known silky-flycatcher is the phainopepla whose scientific name means "shining robes". The male is black, with a red eye and white wing-patches. The female is olive-gray. Both sexes have long tails and are crested. Their open cup nest, held together by spider silk, is built largely by the male, who also does much of the incubation during the day.

The biology of the other three silky-flycatchers is less well known. All four species feed on berries, petals and insects. Insects are caught in spectacular flights from high perches. Several insects may be captured on each sortie. All species are loosely colonial. MA

The **palmchat** is sometimes assigned to the waxwing family. It is similar to them in being a gregarious fruit-eater. It differs from them in having rougher plumage and a heavier bill.

The most striking aspect of palmchat life, as least as we know it at present, is the communal nesting habit. Large nests, over 3ft (1m) in diameter and 10ft (about 3m) high, are built communally by up to 30 pairs (though most nests are probably built by many fewer birds, and some just by pairs). In the lowlands the usual nest-site is in the frond bases of a Royal palm, but conifers are used at higher altitudes. Each pair has its own compartment and entrance to the nest and as far as is known each pair lives independently of the rest. However, it is difficult to observe any interactions which might occur within the nest. The nest is used communally for roosting outside the breeding season. The advantages (and disadvantages) of this communal life-style are not known for this species.

Palmchats live wholly in trees, feeding on berries and flowers. They are common and conspicuous but the details of their biology remain unknown. MA

DIPPERS AND WRENS

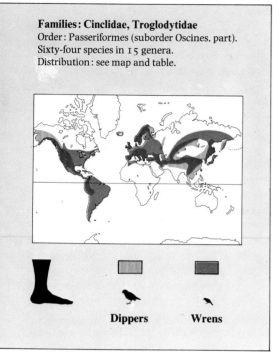

Families: Cinclidae, Troglodytidae
Order: Passeriformes (suborder Oscines, part).
Sixty-four species in 15 genera.
Distribution: see map and table.

Dippers **Wrens**

▶ **Desert bird.** ABOVE The spotty Cactus wren has adapted to desert conditions so successfully that in the desert areas of SW USA and N and C Mexico it is often seen and frequently heard (its song being a distinctive unmusical monotone of low-pitched notes). It has learnt to build its nests among the spines of cactus plants but is famed for its ability to lift and overturn stones and rocks when out foraging for insects.

▶ **Water bird.** BELOW Like all dippers the American dipper lives along fast-flowing streams. Its range stretches from Alaska down the western flank of North America and through Central America to Panama; it is often found in hilly country. The precise locations and population levels of dippers tend to be determined by the availability of nest-sites near rivers and streams.

IPPERS have the remarkable ability to walk underwater seemingly oblivious of the current: they are the only truly aquatic members of the passeriformes. One's first view of a dipper is often that of a dark bird flying fast and low, following the twists and turns of a stream. The Reverend Cotes, author of Thomas Bewick's *History of British Birds*, coined the name dipper in 1804: "It may be seen perched on the top of a stone in the midst of the torrent, in a continual dipping motion or short courtsey oft repeated." The whole body moves up and down vertically during the dipping motion and the blinking membrane moves giving the appearance of a white eye.

Dippers are dark rotund birds like giant wrens (to which they may be related) with a thrush-like bill, stumpy tail and brown legs with strong claws. The five species are very similar, differing only in range and plumage color. Species only overlap in Central Asia; here the White-breasted dipper occupies the higher streams and rivers while the Brown dipper occurs at lower altitudes. Dippers swim, dive and walk into shallow water to obtain their food; they can remain underwater for 30 seconds but most dives are much shorter. They have extra thick body feathers to aid waterproofing and insulation and can survive winter temperatures down to $-49°F$ ($-45°C$) if the river is not completely frozen; they can even feed under ice.

They are highly territorial in summer and winter, using a neck-stretching display and chasing to maintain territorial boundaries. Territory size is mainly determined by the extent of stream bed available for feeding.

Dippers breed in early spring when food

is most abundant, and are usually monogamous. Both sexes build the nest (in 14–21 days) although females do most of the building. Nests are placed among tree roots, on small cliffs, under bridges and in walls and sometimes behind waterfalls where the adult must fly through water to the nest. The bulky nests are often inconspicuous, either because they are built in crevices or because the mossy shell closely resembles the surroundings. The nestling period is relatively long but nesting success is usually high (70 percent). If disturbed, nestlings may explode from the nest after 14 days (when full body weight is attained); remarkably they can swim and dive expertly before they can fly. When dippers have second broods they are perhaps unusual in often using the same nest (relined); they frequently use the same nest in successive years, often for three or four years. Dippers become very secretive during molt, which is rapid, and the American dipper can become flightless. Most populations of dippers are sedentary although some populations move more than 625mi (1,000km) between summer and winter areas.

Post-fledging mortality is high (over 80 percent in the first six months) but thereafter annual mortality is between 25 and 35 percent. In suitable breeding areas the habitat is continuously occupied and a non-breeding surplus of birds either does not exist or is small and frequents areas unsuitable for breeding. Hence replacement of an adult which dies in the breeding season is unusual.   DRL

The Latin word *troglodytes*, from which the wren family name is derived, means "cave-

The 2 Families of Dippers and Wrens   ⒱ Vulnerable.   ⒭ Rare.   ⒤ Threatened, but status indeterminate.

Dippers
Family: Cinclidae
Five species of the genus *Cinclus*.
Western N and S America, Europe, N Africa, Asia. Clear running water, usually among hills and mountains. Size: 6–7in (15–17.5cm) long, weight 2.1–2.8oz (60–80g). Plumage: chiefly black, brown or gray, sometimes with a white "bib", back or cap; no difference between sexes. Voice: all species produce a harsh *zit* call and a rich warbling song. Nests: large globular structures, about 8 × 8 × 6in (20 × 20 × 15cm) deep with an opening 2.5in (6cm) in diameter, usually over running water; constructed of mosses and lined with grasses and old leaves. Eggs: 4–6, usually 5, white;

incubation period: 16–17 days; nestling period 17–25 days, usually 22–23 if undisturbed. Diet: chiefly aquatic larvae, especially of stoneflies, mayflies, caddisflies; also crustaceans, mollusks; occasionally eat small fish, tadpoles.

Species: **American dipper** (*Cinclus mexicanus*), **Brown dipper** (*C. pallasii*), **Rufous-throated dipper** ⒤ (*C. schultzi*), **White-breasted dipper** or **dipper** (*C. cinclus*), **White-capped dipper** (*C. leucocephalus*).

Wrens
Family: Troglodytidae
Fifty-nine species in 14 genera.
N, C, S America, Common wren in Eurasia and just into N Africa. Dense, low undergrowth in forest or by

watercourses; rocky and semidesert localities. Size: most 3–5in (7.5–12.5cm) long, weight 0.3–0.5oz (8–15g), the largest is the Cactus wren, 6.5–9in (16–22cm) long; females are sometimes slightly smaller than males. Plumage: brown, cinnamon or rufous with dark barring above; paler and sometimes spotted below; no striking differences between sexes. Voice: varies from long single whistles to songs containing hundreds of notes and melodious and intricate alternating duets. Nests: suspended in vegetation, holes or under overhangs; always roofed with a side entrance and sometimes with an access tunnel; typically 3–5in (8–12cm) high, 2.5–4in (6–10cm) wide; Cactus wrens, however, build structures up to 24in (60cm) by 18in (45cm). Eggs:

maximum of 10 in northern temperate species; 2–4 in the tropics; white with red or reddish flecking; 0.5 × 0.7in (1.3 × 1.8cm) by 0.7–0.9in (1.8–2.4cm). Incubation period: 12–20 days; nestling period: 12–18 days. Diet: exclusively invertebrates, mainly insects, spiders, etc; also butterfly and moth larvae and adults.

Species include: **Apolinar's marsh-wren** ⒱ (*Cistothorus apolinari*), **Cactus wren** (*Campylorhynchus brunneicapillus*), **Common, European** or **Winter wren** (*Troglodytes troglodytes*), **Flutist wren** (*Microcerculus ustulatus*), **House wren** (*Troglodytes aedon*), **Long-billed marsh wren** (*Cistothorus palustris*), **Musician** or **Song wren** (*Cyphorhinus aradus*), **Zapata wren** ⒭ (*Ferminia cerverai*).

dweller"—a reference to the habit of all **wrens** of building elaborate roofed nests which they use not only to house eggs and nestlings but also as communal roosts and as aids to male courtship. In several species prodigious nest-building is matched with fine energetic singing by the males. Field studies of the polygynous wrens of Europe and North America suggest that the form and extent of both these activities may be extreme, perhaps a result of strong sexual selection through female mate choice. Many of the Central American species are thought to be monogamous, while those in the Cactus wren group (genus *Campylorhynchus*) live in family parties and have evolved a cooperative breeding system: independent young help their parents to raise further broods of young. Thus in the wrens we have a passeriform family of exceptional social diversity, despite the fact that virtually nothing is known about the habits of most of its tropical species.

Members of all 14 genera occur in the area between Mexico and the equator in South America. The broad, blunt wings, evident poor flying ability and small size of most wrens have not, however, prevented them from invading some offshore islands. For instance Cuba has an endemic species in the Zapata wren, and distinct subspecies of the Common wren are found, for example on Taiwan and on St Kilda (off northwest Scotland). This species, known as the Winter wren in North America, is the sole representative of the family in the Old World. It is therefore thought to have migrated west from Alaska to Siberia, and its range now stretches from the eastern USA to Iceland. Another species with a transcontinental distribution is the House wren, which occurs from the eastern USA to Patagonia. These two forms must obviously be very flexible in their habitat preferences and diet, although they and other species breeding at temperate latitudes, such as the Long-billed marsh wren, undertake seasonal migrations to and from wintering grounds with more equable climates. Other wrens, and especially the numerous forms endemic to Central America, occupy much narrower ecological niches and may be very restricted in distribution.

On the basis of behavior and form wrens fall into two distinct groups. The majority are small, cryptically colored, secretive and rather solitary inhabitants of dense forest understory. They flutter and climb among tangled vegetation in search of tiny insects and other animals that make up their diet.

▶ **Adaptable bird.** Wrens originated in the New World tropics, but 8,000–9,000 years ago the Common or Winter wren managed to cross the Bering Strait. Since then it has colonized northern Asia, Europe and northwest Africa. It can cope with every kind of habitat except extensive open moorland and dense urban areas.

▼ **Courtship in the Common wren.** A male Common wren's courtship is energetic and involved. The mating sequence begins as a male, sitting on an exposed perch (**1**) or foraging on the ground, sees a female in his territory. He reacts by flying fast and low straight towards her (**2**). As the male approaches, the female often flies off and a chase ensues, the male pursuing the female in a twisting, rapid flight (**3**). These chases often end in a "pounce," in which the male attempts, usually without success, to make physical contact (or possibly to mate) with the female (**4**).

After this episode the male sings his soft and abbreviated courtship songs to the female and then attempts to lead her towards one of his nests (**5**). When the female is within a few feet of the nest the male sometimes motions her to enter the nest by repeatedly inserting and withdrawing his head (**6**). The female may then go inside (**7**), the male singing meanwhile from a nearby perch. She will not usually emerge for at least 10 seconds, and sometimes not for several minutes (**8**). Some time later the female brings material for lining the nest (**9**). Copulation takes place outside the nest during or after this elaborate ritual.

In a minority are the much bigger Cactus wren and its allies, living in the more open semidesert habitats of Central America. Although they have a diet similar to that of their smaller relatives, they move much more boldly, perhaps because they are often in small family flocks which should afford them some protection from predators.

All wrens studied in detail seem to be territorial, at least during the breeding season. The role of song in the defense of space is uncertain, but as a family the wrens are renowned as songsters. Several of the monogamous forest-dwelling species live in pairs all year round and some, including the Musician wren, produce melodic and beautifully coordinated alternating duets.

There seems to be little doubt that the song of the males in polygynous species, such as the Common and Long-billed marsh wrens, serves two roles: in defending territory and attracting several mates— trigamy is not uncommon. Neighboring males spend a large proportion of their time each morning answering each other across well-defined territory boundaries. When a female enters a territory she is courted vigorously by the occupant who sings and leads her to a nest he has already built. Common and House wrens may have three or four nests ready simultaneously for use both in these displays and by females making breeding attempts, which they commence promptly after courtship and the collection of some lining materials for the nest cup— their token gesture towards nest construction. Males of these species may build 6–12 nests in the course of a three-month breeding season, but their efforts are paltry beside those of male Long-billed marsh wrens, who construct as many as 25–35 nests over a similar period. They are built in clusters, some even being semidetached, and appear to have a primarily ceremonial role. Males sing vigorously from these collections of nests and lead any female that appears to several of them in succession. Subsequently the male builds yet another nest, in which the female attempts to breed, usually away from his conspicuous courtship center.

Observations suggest that females in these species have a free choice of where to breed, subject to the availability of usable nests. Consequently one can predict that any trait in males that enhances their ability to attract females will be subject to intense sexual selection. Thus it is no surprise to find that males of polygynous species build more nests, have more elaborate courtship displays and songs, and spend more time singing in the breeding season than do those of monogamous species. These adaptations may be seen as the results of an evolutionary

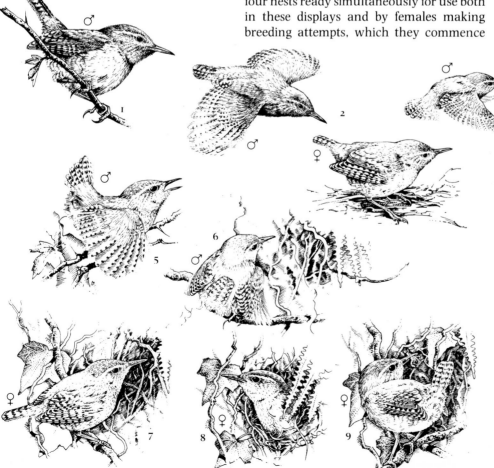

"arms race" driven over the millennia by a combination of male salesmanship and female sales-resistance. Because they spend so much time attempting to obtain mates male Common and Long-billed marsh wrens never incubate and only help feed their nestlings at the end of the season when, presumably, chances of achieving further productive matings are negligible.

In complete contrast, the Cactus wren is monogamous and uses a cooperative system. Parents produce up to four broods a year, later ones being fed in the nest by both the parents and their independent young from earlier broods. All members of these family groups assist the breeding male in territorial defense against other families, but rather paradoxically all but recently fledged juveniles sleep alone in one of the many large nests dotted about in the cacti on their territory.   PJG

MOCKINGBIRDS

Family: Mimidae
Order: Passeriformes (suborder Oscines, part).
Thirty species in 9 genera.
Distribution: New World, from S Canada to
Tierra del Fuego.

Habitat: scrub (often arid), keeping mainly
close to the ground.

Size: 8–12in (20–30cm),
including a fairly long tail in
most species.

Plumage: most are primarily brown or gray
above, usually with pale or white underparts—
often heavily streaked or spotted. A few are
brighter, either rich brown (Black-capped
mockingthrush) or bright gray blue (Blue
mockingbird). Many have strikingly colored
eyes: red, yellow or white. Sexes are similar.

Voice: powerful, complex songs which in some
species include many noises copied from other
birds or animals.

Nest: largish, untidy cup-nest of grass and
twigs, usually fairly close to (or on) the ground,
but sometimes high up in a tree.

Eggs: usually 2–5; color varies from pale,
whitish to dark greenish-blue, often heavily
streaked or spotted with darker markings.

Incubation: 12–13 days.

Fledging period: 12–13 days; may be longer in
some tropical species.

Species include: **Black-capped mockingthrush**
(*Donacobius atricapillus*), **Black catbird**
(*Dumetella glabrirostris*), **Blue mockingbird**
(*Melanotis caerulescens*), **Brown thrasher**
(*Toxostoma rufum*), **Brown trembler**
(*Cinclocerthia ruficauda*), **Curve-billed thrasher**
(*Toxostoma curvirostre*), **Galapagos mockingbird**
(*Nesomimus trifasciatus*), **Gray catbird**
(*Dumetella carolinensis*), **Northern mockingbird**
or **mockingbird** (*Mimus polyglottos*), **Patagonian
mockingbird** (*M. patagonicus*), **Sage thrasher**
(*Toxostoma montanus*).

► **The Curve-billed thrasher** ABOVE usually
builds its nest in the fork of a cholla cactus. It
is made of twigs and lined with fine grasses,
rootlets and feathers.

► **Master mimic.** The Northern mockingbird,
widespread in the southern USA, is the chief
mimic in the mockingbird family. Mimicry,
however, constitutes little more than 10
percent of total song output.

THE mockingbird family's name is derived
from the ability of several members of the
family, especially the Northern mockingbird, to copy the noises made by other
animals. Although birds of other species are
the main source for their mimicry, mockingbirds have also been recorded mimicking
frogs, pianos and even human voices. Their
songs are clear, powerful and far-carrying.

The mockingbirds (also known as mimic-
thrushes) are a fairly distinct group of New
World birds, thought to be closely related to
thrushes and wrens. They are mostly
thrush-sized, though they tend to have
longer tails and longish beaks, the latter
often strongly downcurved as in the Curve-
billed thrasher. Many are marked rather like
a "standard" thrush, brown above and
paler below with heavy streaking. A number of others are darker and more uniformly
gray. The brightest is probably the Blue
mockingbird which is a bright, grayish-blue
all over except for a black mask. The Gray
catbird is one of the smaller members of the
family and is somewhat aberrantly colored:
it is a uniform gray all over (darker above
than below) with a black cap and bright
chestnut undertail feathers. Many mockingbirds cock their long tail in a conspicuous
manner.

The family occurs over much of North,
South and Central America except for the
northern parts of Canada; only the Patagonian mockingbird occurs in the southern
third of South America. Mockingbirds are
also found in many Caribbean islands and
in the Galapagos and have been introduced
to Bermuda and Hawaii. Many of the birds
in the northern parts of this range move
southwards for the northern winter; for
example, most Gray and Black catbirds and
Brown thrashers leave Canada during the
winter and the large majority of the Sage
thrashers that breed in the USA probably
spend the winter in Mexico or farther south.
However, some Northern mockingbirds
spend the winter in Canada.

The main habitat of the family is scrub or
forest understory; many species inhabit dry,
near-desert habitats. All use the low, often
dense vegetation as cover and most forage
on the ground. Two exceptions are the
Brown trembler of Dominica and nearby
islands which lives in rainforest and the
Black-capped mockingthrush which lives in
dense vegetation in marshes.

Most mockingbirds take a wide variety of
foods; they spend most of their time hopping
through the undergrowth on their long,
powerful legs. Through much of the season
they will eat ground-living arthropods, but,
in season, they will also take many fruits
and berries. The Galapagos mockingbird
also takes small crabs along the shoreline
and, in addition on some islands, especially
Hood (Española) this species has acquired a
reputation for pecking open unattended
eggs of a wide variety of seabird species and
of stealing eggs of the Galapagos dove and
both the Land and Marine iguanas. Most of
their prey is taken from the ground using
their powerful beak which serves either as
a probe or (as in the case of the eggs) for
breaking into a potential food item.

The resident species spend most of the year in their territory which they defend strongly against other members of their species. Usually they live alone or in pairs, but in some species, such as the Galapagos mockingbird, the birds may live in groups of 4–10 individuals, several of which may help in raising the young. While it is not known for certain what the relationships of the birds in a group are, in some cases the extra members helping to raise a second or subsequent brood in a season are known to be young from an earlier brood of the same pair.

As far as is known all species build rather bulky, untidy nests of twigs in dense vegetation. In most cases the nest is either on the ground or within about 6ft (2m) of the ground, though sometimes pairs may build at heights of 50ft (15m) or more. Two to five (rarely six) eggs are laid and these hatch in about 12–13 days and are raised to the point of leaving the nest in about the same length of time. Breeding commences in the spring or, in some arid areas such as the Galapagos, shortly after the start of the rainy season. The breeding season can be prolonged with two or even three broods being raised. Pairs will often remain together in successive seasons, though in the Gray catbird it has been shown that birds are more likely to separate and/or leave the territory and move to another if they fail to raise young than if they succeed. This is thought to be an adaptation against predators; since most nests that fail do so because they are taken by predators, moving after a nest is lost might result in the parent birds being able to find a safer place to nest.

The Brown trembler of Dominica and other islands of the Lesser Antilles is an aberrant species of mockingbird. It is easily recognized by its habit of trembling its wings (which is probably a social signal to others of its species). It also spends much of its time up in the trees of the rainforest where it forages while clinging to the trunk on its rather short legs. It is thought possible that it has taken over the woodcreeper niche of hunting for insect prey on tree-trunks (woodcreepers are absent from these islands).

The Galapagos mockingbird is particularly interesting in that, as with the Galapagos finches (see p108), it influenced Charles Darwin's thinking on evolution by means of natural selection. The mockingbirds in the Galapagos have differentiated strongly on different islands; four well-marked forms are present and some consider them to be four separate species.　CMP

ACCENTORS

Family: Prunellidae
Order: Passeriformes (suborder Oscines, part).
Thirteen species of the genus *Prunella*.
Distribution: Europe, Africa N of the Sahara,
Asia except southern peninsulas.

Habitat: mountainous regions, especially
scrub.

 Size: length 5–7in (13–
18cm), weight 0.6–0.9oz
(18–26g).

Plumage: upperparts rufous or brownish gray,
streaked or striped in most species; underparts
grayish usually with rufous markings. Sexes
are similar.

Voice: little known; the dunnock has a high-
pitched *tseep* call and a complex song structure.

Nest: open cup of plant fragments and feathers,
on the ground or in low scrubs or in a rock
crevice.

Eggs: 3–6; ranging from light bluish green to
blue; unmarked.

Incubation period: 11–15 days.

Nestling period: 12–14 days.

Diet: mainly insects in summer; seeds and
berries in winter.

Species include: **Alpine accentor** (*Prunella
collaris*), **Black-throated accentor**
(*P. atrogularis*), **dunnock** (*P. modularis*), **Himalayan
accentor** (*P. himalayana*), **Maroon-backed
accentor** (*P. immaculata*), **Robin accentor**
(*P. rubeculoides*), **Siberian accentor** (*P. montanella*).

▶ **Hardy mountain bird.** Most accentor species
are mountain-dwellers. This species, the Alpine
accentor, is found in the mountains of
Northwest Africa, southern and central Europe
and Asia. Here one is seen in Nepal, at 14,000ft
(4,300m), though it is capable of breeding at
16,500ft (5,000m).

Accentors are small plainly colored
birds, usually confined to mountainous
regions. They are sparrow-like in appearance but with a more slender and pointed
bill. The sexes are similar in plumage but
males are larger (with longer wings and
heavier) and a little brighter. Until recently
they were thought to be most closely related
to the thrushes. However, recent biological
studies suggest that their nearest relatives
are wagtails, pipits, sunbirds, sparrows (*Passer* species) and the cardueline and fringilline finches.

The accentors have the rare distinction of
being almost exclusive to the Palearctic
region (ie Europe, Africa north of the Sahara
and Asia north of the Himalayas). Fairly
ubiquitous in this region is the Alpine accentor but it occurs only at high altitudes
(probably 3,300–16,500ft, about 1,000–
5,000m). This may have resulted in the
evolution of many races or subspecies: eight
or nine subspecies have been described. All
species of accentor except the dunnock
breed in mountains: the Himalayan accentor can be found breeding at 16,500ft
(5,000m) above sea level; the Robin accentor is also found at high altitudes though it
prefers to live in dwarf rhododendron and
other scrub, or in willows and sedge in damp
meadow. The range of the Siberian accentor
reaches northwards beyond the taiga
region, whereas one subspecies of the Black-
throated accentor (*P. atrogularis fagani*),
although native to Central Asia, is found
further south in winter. The Maroon-backed
accentor is found from Nepal to western
China and shows a preference for damp

areas deep in coniferous forest. Some of the
accentors are migratory, others move only
to lower altitudes in winter. The dunnock,
however, is known to do both.

Unfortunately information about the
behavior and breeding biology of the accentors is rare, except for the dunnock, and
even this common species has only recently
been studied.

During the breeding season (late March
to August) members of this species establish
several different types of territory: solitary
males, pairs of male and female, or male and
female plus an additional male. Bigamy and
bigamy plus extra males have also been
recorded. It is unclear why some territories
contain extra males, and suggesting a function for them is made more difficult by the
fact that a pair of accentors with an additional male do not seem to produce more offspring than a solitary pair. However, an
extra male sometimes feeds the young,
mates with the female, and with the other
male defends the territory. Pairs with an
extra male have significantly larger territories than do solitary pairs.

In all dunnock populations so far
examined there has been an excess of males.
This may be because fewer females survive
the winter because they have a lower place
in the dominance hierarchies.

Another fascinating aspect of the
behavior of the dunnock is its unusual pre-
copulatory display. During this display the
female stands with her body horizontal to
the ground, her head slightly raised, her
body feathers partly erected, her wings
drooped (which she flicks occasionally), and

her tail raised at an angle of 30 degrees which she vibrates rapidly from side to side. In response to the female's display the male makes tentative hopping movements from side to side at the rear of the female. At the same time he also makes pecking movements towards the female's cloaca. The display lasts about 40 seconds and ends with the male jumping at a slight angle towards the female and the pair making contact with their cloacas for a fraction of a second.

The probable reason for such an elaborate display has recently become clear. Because the female can often be mated by either of two males with whom she shares a territory her mate has to be certain that his mating has been successful. The elaborate pre-copulatory display may be a method whereby he can safeguard the paternity of the offspring. The male's pecking behavior appears to stimulate the female to eject any material she has in her cloaca. This material can contain sperm, ie the female's mate can stimulate her to eject sperm from the extra male. (To prevent the extra male from remating the male guards the female during the critical period.) It has been observed that the intensity of the male's display increases with the likelihood of another male having just mated the female.   MEB

▼ **Named for its drabness.** The dunnock's common name is derived from *dunn*, the Old English word for dark or dull. Modern research has revealed that its behavior is exceptionally interesting: it is one of the few temperate species with a cooperative breeding system.

THRUSHES AND THEIR ALLIES

Family: Muscicapidae
Order: Passeriformes (suborder Oscines, part).
One thousand three hundred and ninety-four
species in 255 genera belonging to 11
subfamilies.
Distribution: worldwide.

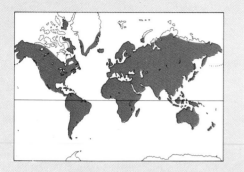

THE **thrushes** are a large and widespread group of birds with few characters that clearly distinguish them from related groups such as the babblers, flycatchers and warblers. There is thus no easy definition of a thrush, but most of them show the following features: they have 10 primary feathers, of which the outer one is much reduced in length; the tarsus (shank) is "booted" (not divided into separate scales on the leading edge); the juvenile plumage is spotted; they build cup-shaped nests; and they typically forage on the ground for animal food, supplemented with fruits taken from trees and shrubs.

Most of the thrushes that have been well-studied are basically similar in their social systems. Monogamous pairs defend nesting territories in the breeding season; in resident species pairs may remain together all year. In the nonbreeding season thrushes tend to be highly social, feeding in flocks and, especially in cold weather, roosting communally; but some migratory wheatears defend feeding territories in their winter quarters. The larger thrushes may defend their nests pugnaciously, and one among them is apparently unique in the way in which it does so. Fieldfares nest semi-colonially (an unusual habit in the subfamily) and attack predators which approach their nests by flying at them and "bombarding" them with their feces. Hawks have been known to become so plastered with feces in this way that they have been unable to fly and eventually have succumbed to starvation.

With some 60 species the true thrushes constitute far the largest genus in the subfamily. They occupy a central place in that they appear to be unspecialized and to show the basic type from which the various more specialized groups have radiated. Moreover they are familiar to almost everyone, since in every continent except Australia there is at least one common garden species. No other genus of land birds is so widespread. Eurasia is especially rich in species, the Song thrush, Mistle thrush and blackbird being among the best known of European birds. Their place on garden lawns and playing fields is taken by, for example, the Olive thrush in southern Africa, the Rufous-bellied thrush in Brazil, the Clay-colored thrush in Central America and the American robin in North America.

Many of the true thrushes are noted for their songs, which characteristically are composed of a succession of short, richly warbled or fluty phrases; a few species are remarkable mimics. Their substantial cup nests are strengthened by a layer of mud, often mixed with decaying leaves, and are usually finished with an inner lining of grasses or similar material. Northern species are long-distance migrants, and tropical species nonmigratory, while some species from middle latitudes are partial migrants, some individuals moving south in winter and some remaining in their breeding area.

The ground thrushes are closely related to the true thrushes. They have the same general build but relatively longer, stouter bills, and are further distinguished by a striking, usually black and white, underwing pattern. They are shy birds, living near the ground in forests, and are mainly confined to Asia and Africa. The only exceptions are the widespread White's thrush whose

▲ **One of the most popular birds** in Britain, northern France and Germany, the robin has become the subject of a rich folklore. Of great interest are the origin and purpose of its conspicuous red breast. A Breton legend recounts how the robin's breast was covered with blood as it tried to pull a thorn from the crown of thorns as Christ hung on the cross. The breast in fact serves as a sign of imminent attack. When a male robin has to deal with an intruder to his territory he erects the feathers on his breast and throat, and the invader usually flees.

◄ **From Portugal to China** lives the Blue rock thrush (*Monticola solitarius*), a lively inhabitant of rocky areas.

breeding range extends, uniquely in the subfamily, to Australia, the Varied thrush of western North America and the Aztec thrush of Mexico.

The large group of robins, robin-chats and related species (including the nightingale) are small thrushes of woodland and tropical forest, mainly ground feeders and with proportionately longer legs than the true thrushes. A few, such as the alethes of tropical Africa, are habitual followers of army ants, feeding on insects flushed by the ants. Some have remarkably fine songs. Another group of small thrushes—chats,

wheatears, and their allies—inhabit more open country, nesting in holes or recesses in the ground; among these, the desert wheatears inhabit country as barren as any in which a bird can survive. These two groups of small thrushes have their headquarters in Asia and Africa. They are entirely unrepresented in the New World, where—apart from many species of true thrushes—the subfamily is represented by a much smaller variety of forms, most outstanding of which are the Hermit thrush and its relatives in North America, bluebirds, nightingale-thrushes and solitaires.

THE 11 SUBFAMILIES OF THRUSHES, FLYCATCHERS AND THEIR ALLIES

Thrushes

Subfamily: Turdinae
Three hundred and four species in 49 genera.

Worldwide (including many oceanic islands). From tropical forest to desert. Size: 4.3–13in (11–33cm) long, weight 0.28–7.7oz (8–220g). Plumage: varied; many species predominantly shades of gray, brown and white, but many (especially males) with bright patches of all colors except yellow; several species all-black; females generally similar to males in species lacking bright colors; in species with bright colors females are usually distinctly duller than males with contrasting patterning reduced or absent. Voice: many species very musical, producing some of the most beautiful of all bird songs; alarm calls usually sharp and staccato, churring or thin and high-pitched. Nests: open cups in various sites, eg trees, shrubs, on ground, in holes in the ground. Eggs: 2–6, rarely 7 (occasionally more in hole-nesters), whitish, blue, greenish or buff, unmarked or with brown or black spots or more diffuse markings; incubation: 12–15 days; nestling period: usually 11–18 days. Diet: invertebrates of many kinds, especially insects and earthworms; most species also take fruit.

Species and genera include: **alethes** (genus *Alethe*), **American robin** (*Turdus migratorius*), **Aztec thrush** (*Zoothera pinicola*), **blackbird** (*Turdus merula*), **bluebirds** (genus *Sialia*), **Clay-colored thrush** (*Turdus grayi*), **cochoas** (genus *Cochoa*), **Desert wheatear** (*Oenanthe deserti*), **fieldfare** (*Turdus pilaris*), **forktails** (genus *Enicurus*), **grandala** (*Grandala coelicolor*), **ground thrushes** (genus *Zoothera*), **Hermit thrush** (*Catharus guttatus*), **Island thrush** (*Turdus poliocephalus*), **Mistle thrush** (*Turdus viscivorus*), **nightingale** (*Luscinia megarhynchos*), **nightingale-thrushes** (genus *Catharus*), **Olive thrush** (*Turdus olivaceus*), **robin** or **Eurasian robin** (*Erithacus rubecula*), **robin-chats** (genus *Cossypha*), **Rufous-bellied thrush** (*Turdus rufiventris*), **solitaires** (genera *Entomodestes*, *Myadestes*), **Song thrush** (*Turdus*

philomelos), **true thrushes** (genus *Turdus*), **Varied thrush** (*Zoothera naevia*), **water-redstarts** (genus *Rhyacornis*), **wheatears** (genus *Oenanthe*), **whistling thrushes** (genus *Myiophoneus*), **White's thrush** or **Golden mountain thrush** (*Zoothera dauma*). Total threatened species: 5.

Babblers

Subfamily: Timaliinae
Two hundred and fifty-two species in 50 genera.

Asia, Africa, Australasia, one in western N America. All types of terrestrial vegetation, from desert scrub to swamp, tropical forest to alpine dwarf shrubs. Size: 4–14in (10–35cm) long, weight 0.2–5.3oz (5–150g). Plumage: highly variable, but many species are cryptic browns and grays; species living in dense forest often include bright yellows, reds and blues; no differences between sexes. Voice: great variety of calls, reminiscent of the entire range of songbird vocalizations; some species have group duets, in others there are antiphonal duets. Nests: usually above ground in bushes or trees, open or domed; rockfowl build mud nests. Eggs: 2–6; variety of colors, but often white or blue; unmarked; incubation period: 14–15 days; nestling period: 13–16 days. Diet: predominantly insects and other invertebrates.

Species and genera include: **Arabian** or **Arabian brown babbler** (*Turdoides squamiceps*), **babaxes** (genus *Babax*), **Black-capped** or **Black-headed sibia** (*Heterophasia capistrata*), **chatterers** (two species of the genus *Turdoides*), **Common babbler** (*Turdoides caudatus*), **Fulvous babbler** (*Turdoides fulvus*), **Iraq babbler** (*T. altirostris*), **Jungle babbler** (*T. striatus*), **laughing thrushes** (genus *Garrulax*), **minlas** (genus *Minla*), **scimitar babblers** (genus *Pomatorhinus*), **shrike-babblers** (genera *Pteruthius*, *Gampsorhynchus*), **tit-babblers** (genus *Alcippe*), **tree babblers** (genus *Stachyris*), **White-crested laughing thrush** (*Garrulax leucolophus*), **wren babblers** (genera *Kenopia*, *Napothera*, *Pnoepyga*, 1 species in *Ptilocichla*, *Rimator*, *Spelaeornis*, *Sphenocichla*), **yuhinas** (genus *Yuhina*).

Old World warblers

Subfamily: Sylviinae
Three hundred and thirty-nine species in 56 genera.

Chiefly Europe, Asia, Africa; small numbers in the New World. All types of vegetation, from grassland to forest. Size: most species 3.5–6.3in (9–16cm) long, weight 0.17–0.7oz (5–20g); several large exceptions, eg the grassbird with maximum length 9in (23cm), weight about 1oz (30g). Plumage: chiefly brown, dull green or yellow, often streaked darker; some tropical species (eg White-winged apalis) are brightly colored; in most species sexes are similar, exceptions include: blackcap, kinglets, some tailorbirds. Voice: calls varied, often harsh in the larger species; songs of some species are simple and stereotyped, but in others complex, varied and melodious. Nests: elaborate, carefully woven cup-shaped or spherical structures placed low in dense vegetation; tailorbirds and some other species stitch leaves together with cobwebs to form a cone in which the nest is sited. Eggs: usually 2–7, pale ground colors with dark spots or blotches; incubation period: 12–14 days; nestling period: 11–15 days, though young may fledge earlier (from 8 days), unable to fly, and are then attended by their parents for some days afterwards. Diet: predominantly insects; some species also eat fruit; many take nectar occasionally; kinglets regularly eat small seeds.

Species and genera include: **Aldabra warbler** (*Bebrornis aldabranus*), **Arctic warbler** (*Phylloscopus borealis*), **blackcap** (*Sylvia atricapilla*), **chiffchaff** (*Phylloscopus collybita*), **cloud-scraper cisticola** (*Cisticola dambo*), **Dartford warbler** (*Sylvia undata*), **fernbird** (*Bowdleria punctata*), **Garden warbler** (*Sylvia borin*), **gnatcatchers** (genus *Polioptila*), **gnatwrens** (genera *Microbates*, *Ramphocaenus*), **goldcrest** (*Regulus regulus*), **grassbird** (*Sphenoeacus afer*), **grass warblers** (*Cisticola*), **Great reed warbler** (*Acrocephalus arundinaceus*), **Icterine warbler** (*Hippolais icterina*), **kinglets** (four species in the genus *Regulus*),

Long-billed crombec (*Sylvietta rufescens*), **Marsh warbler** (*Acrocephalus palustris*), **Oriole babbler** (*Hypergerus atriceps*), **Red-faced crombec** (*Sylvietta whytii*), **Reed warbler** (*Acrocephalus scirpaceus*), **scrub warblers** (18 species belonging to the genera *Bradypterus*, *Sylvia*), **Sedge warbler** (*Acrocephalus schoenobaenus*), **spinifex-bird** (*Eremiornis carteri*), **tit-flycatchers** (five species belonging to the genus *Parisoma*), **tit-weaver** (*Pholidornis rushiae*), **whitethroat** (*Sylvia communis*), **White-winged apalis** (*Apalis chariessa*), **willow warblers** (genus *Phylloscopus*). Total threatened species: 4.

Old World flycatchers

Subfamily: Muscicapinae
One hundred and fifty-six species in 28 genera.

Europe, Asia, Africa, Australia, Pacific Islands. Chiefly woodlands, forests, shrubs. Size: 4–8in (10–21cm) long. Plumage: varies considerably, some species plain gray or brown, other black and white or bright blue, yellow or red; little difference between sexes in dull species, marked differences in brightly colored species. Voice: produce a wide range of notes; songs vary from the simple and monotonous to the complex. Nests: a few species are hole nesters, though they do not excavate their own holes; most species build cup nests on tree branches. Eggs: usually 2–6, range 1–8, whitish, greenish or buff, most often with spots; in hole-nesting species eggs are bluish without spots; incubation period: 12–14 days; nestling period: 11–16 days. Diet: mainly insects.

Species include: **Ashy flycatcher** (*Muscicapa caerulescens*), **Blue and white flycatcher** (*Ficedula cyanomelana*), **Collared flycatcher** (*F. albicollis*), **Dusky flycatcher** (*Muscicapa adusta*), **Flame robin** (*Petroica phoenicea*), **Mariqua flycatcher** (*Bradornis mariquensis*), **Pied flycatcher** (*Ficedula hypoleuca*), **Spotted flycatcher** (*Muscicapa striata*), **White-eyed slaty flycatcher** (*Dioptrornis fischeri*). Total threatened species: 2.

Fairy-wrens

Subfamily: Malurinae
Twenty-six species in 5 genera.

New Guinea and Australia. From margins of rain forest to desert steppes, salt pans, coastal swamp, heathland, spinifex tussocks, desert sandplains. Size: 5.5–9in (14–23cm) long, weight 0.25–1.3oz (7–37g). Plumage: varies from bright blue in some males to plain brown. Voice: brief contact calls, churrs and sustained reels of song. Eggs: 2–4, whitish with red-brown speckling; incubation period: 12–15 days; nestling period: 10–12 days. Diet: insects and seeds.

Species and genera include: **Black grass-wren** (*Amytornis housei*), **Carpentarian grass-wren** (*A. dorotheae*), **emu-wrens** (genus *Stipiturus*), **Eyrean grass-wren** (*Amytornis goyderi*), **grass-wrens** (genus *Amytornis*), **Gray grass-wren** (*A. barbatus*), **Purple-crowned fairy-wren** (*Malurus coronatus*), **Red-winged fairy-wren** (*M. elegans*), **Superb blue fairy-wren** (*M. cyaneus*), **true fairy-wrens** (genus *Malurus*), **White-throated grass-wren** (*Amytornis woodwardi*). Total threatened species: 3.

Parrotbills

Subfamily: Paradoxornithinae
Nineteen species in 3 genera.

E Asia with the Bearded tit occurring in W Asia and Europe. Reeds, grass, dense thickets, bamboo. Size: 3.5–11.5in (9–29cm) long, weight 0.2–1.3oz (5–37g) except for the largest species, the Great parrotbill (no data available). Plumage: varying shades of cinnamon-buff or gray; some species have whitish underparts, others have small areas of black on the head or throat. Voice: sounds range from twittering and pinging

notes to clear musical or mellow whistles, churring or curious wheezy notes, like the twanging of a guitar. Nests: grass and bamboo leaves bound together with cobwebs in a deep, compact cup shape; situated in reeds or low vegetation. Eggs: 2–7, blue or clay in color with irregular reddish brown, lavender or green marks. Diet: mainly insects; also grass seeds and, in the case of larger species, berries.

Species and genera include: **Bearded tit** or **Bearded reedling** (*Panurus biarmicus*), **Black-browed parrotbill** (*Paradoxornis atrosuperciliaris*), **Brown parrotbill** (*P. unicolor*), **Great parrotbill** (*Conostoma oemodium*), **Red-headed parrotbill** (*Paradoxornis ruficeps*), **Three-toed parrotbill** (*P. paradoxus*), **typical parrotbills** (genus *Paradoxornis*), **Yangtse parrotbill** (*P. heudei*).

Monarch flycatchers

Subfamily: Monarchinae
One hundred and thirty-three species in 25 genera.

Africa, tropical and eastern Asia, Australasia. Forest and woodland. Size: 5–12in (12–30cm) long (including tail), weight 0.5–1.4oz (15–40g). Plumage: often metallic black or gray, or chestnut with white underparts; sexes differ in appearance in some species. Voice: harsh or whistling calls. Nests: cup-shaped, often decorated with lichen, moss, bark or spiders' webs. Eggs: 2–4, white with brown spots or blotches. Diet: most species eat insects; a few also take fruit.

Species and genera include: **Frilled monarch** (*Arses telescophthalmus*), **paradise flycatchers** (genus *Terpsiphone*), **peltops flycatchers** (genus *Peltops*), **puff-backs** (genus *Batis*), **Restless flycatcher** or **scissors-grinder** (*Myiagra inquieta*), **Satin flycatcher** (*M. cyanoleuca*), **shrikebills** (genus *Clytorhynchus*). Total threatened species: 3.

Logrunners

Subfamily: Orthonychinae
Twenty species in 9 genera.

SE Asia, New Guinea, Australia. Desert scrub, woodland, rain forest, usually in dense shrub. Size: 4–12in (10–30cm) long, weight 0.7–2.8oz (20–80g). Plumage: most species are brown, black or white; differences between sexes in appearance vary from slight to marked. Voice: calls range from buzzing to whistling and bell-like sounds. Nests: cup-shaped or domed, usually placed in dense shrubs. Eggs: 1–3; white or pale blue. Incubation period: 17–21 days. Nestling period: 12–14 days. Diet: predominantly insects; also invertebrates and seeds.

Species and genera include: **Blue jewel-babbler** (*Ptilorrhoa caerulescens*), **Chiming wedgebill** (*Psophodes occidentalis*), **Chirruping wedgebill** (*P. cristatus*), **quail-thrushes** (genus *Cinclosoma*), **Western whipbird** (*Psophodes nigrogularis*).

Australasian warblers

Subfamily: Acanthizinae
Fifty-nine species in 19 genera.

SE Asia, New Guinea, Australia, New Zealand, Pacific Islands. Arid shrubland, woodland, forest. Size 3–8in (8–20cm) long, weight 0.25–1.4oz (7–40g). Plumage: usually brown, olive or yellow. Voice: twittering and warbling songs and calls. Nests: neat and domed, often with a hood. Eggs: 2 or 3, occasionally 4, white, sometimes with spots, or dark brown; incubation period: 15–20 days; nestling period: 15–20 days. Diet: insects and seeds.

Species and genera include: **Buff-tailed thornbill** (*Acanthiza reguloides*), **Rock warbler** (*Origma rubricata*), **scrub-wrens** (genus *Sericornis*), **whitefaces** (genus *Aphelocephala*).

Fantail flycatchers

Subfamily: Rhipidurinae
Thirty-eight species in the genus *Rhipidura*.

India, S China, SE Asia, New Guinea, Australia, New Zealand, Pacific Islands. Woodland and forest. Size: 5–8in (13–20cm) long, weight 0.25–0.9oz (7–25g). Plumage: black, gray, white, yellow or rufous; sexes similar. Voice: chattering or squeaky calls and songs. Nests: cup or goblet-shaped. Eggs: 2–5, white or cream with brown blotches; incubation period: 13–16 days; nestling period: 12–16 days. Diet: insects.

Species include: **Friendly fantail** (*Rhipidura albolimbata*), **Gray fantail** (*R. fuliginosa*), **Willie wagtail** (*R. leucophrys*).

Thickheads

Subfamily: Pachycephalinae
Forty-eight species in 10 genera.

Australasian and Oriental regions. From rain forest to arid scrub. Size: 5–10in (12–25cm) long, weight 0.5–3.5oz (15–100g). Plumage: mostly gray or brown, but males of some species have brighter colors. Voice: melodious whistling or bell-like songs. Nests: made of sticks, bark, grasses and spiders' webs and placed in a low fork in a tree. Eggs: 2–4, white to olive, sometimes with brown blotches; incubation period: about 17 days; nestling period: 13–16 days. Diet: insects and fruit.

Species and genera include: **Golden whistler** (*Pachycephala pectoralis*), **piopio** (*Turnagra capensis*), **pitohuis** (genus *Pitohui*), **Red-lored** or **Red-throated whistler** (*Pachycephala rufogularis*), **Rusty pitohui** (*Pitohui ferrugineus*), **shrike-thrushes** (genus *Colluricincla*), **shrike-tit** (*Falcunculus frontatus*), **whistlers** (genera *Hylocitrea, Pachycephala, Rhagologus*).

Some of these, including the Hermit thrush and solitaires, are among the world's finest songsters, noted for their pure and exquisitely modulated notes.

It seems certain that the main evolutionary radiation of the thrushes took place in East Asia, and it is there that the subfamily is present in greatest variety. The whistling thrushes, which include the largest of all thrushes, live along fast-flowing streams in the Himalayas and other mountains of eastern Asia. They have strongly hooked bills and forage for animal food among rocks at the water's edge. The forktails, slender birds with long tails, and the water-redstarts are also specialists in foraging along the banks of mountain torrents. The grandala, a long-winged and short-legged bird with blue plumage, is so unlike a typical thrush that its inclusion in the subfamily is at first sight surprising. Grandalas are highly aerial, social birds that live above the timberline in the Himalayas and associated mountains, where they feed in flocks on bare mountain slopes. Almost equally unthrushlike are the three species of cochoas. They are wide-billed birds of tropical forest in southeast Asia, with plumage patterned with green, blue and violet. Though little known, they are probably ecological equivalents of the cotingas of tropical America.   DWS

Babblers form a varied assemblage of small to medium-sized songbirds which are an important constituent of the bird populations of tropical Asia. In the middle altitudes of the Himalayas 5,000–10,000ft, (1,500–3,000m) they are the dominant passerines, with 71 species breeding in Nepal alone, out of a resident passerine community of about 350 species. Behavior and feeding ecology within the family are very diverse, with some species of active leaf-gleaners flitting in the forest canopy like warblers and other, robust, heavy-bodied genera rooting like thrushes among leaf litter on the forest floor. The "average" babbler falls between a sparrow and a thrush in size, with short, rounded wings and a longish, rather floppy, tail. They forage in bushes, low vegetation and on the ground.

In Africa the family is represented mainly by the chatterers, which are birds of scrub and savanna. In North Africa, the Middle East and Iran the Fulvous and Arabian babblers and their allies live in sparsely vegetated wadis in open desert. In the Negev Desert of Israel the Arabian babbler is the commonest resident bird, occurring wherever there are a few acacia bushes to provide cover and nest-sites. In contrast, the Iraq babbler inhabits the extensive swamps of the Tigris-Euphrates delta.

At the other extreme of the habitat scale a great diversity of different babblers inhabits the cloud forests of the eastern Himalayas, from tiny wren babblers skulking among rotting logs on the forest floor to the large scimitar babblers, probing with their hoopoe-like bills, and Black-capped sibia, drinking the sap oozing from holes in the trunks of oak trees, after the fashion of North American sapsuckers. Geographically close, but far off in terms of ecology,

◄ ▲ ► **Representative species** of four subfamilies of thrushes. (**1**) A Reed warbler (*Acrocephalus scirpaceus*). (**2**) A Chestnut-headed tit-babbler (*Alcippe castaneceps*). (**3**) A Pied flycatcher (*Ficedula hypoleuca*). (**4**) A Flame robin (*Petroica phoenicea*) holding an insect. (**5**) A White-crested laughing thrush (*Garrulax leucolophus*), (**6**) An Eastern bluebird (*Sialia sialis*). (**7**) A Red-faced crombec (*Sylvietta whytii*). (**8**) A Pied babbler (*Turdoides bicolor*). (**9**) A White-browed robin-chat (*Cossypha heuglini*). (**10**) A Song thrush (*Turdus philomelos*).

the babaxes inhabit the buckthorn scrub on the southern edge of the Tibetan plateau, in arid high-altitude desert.

In India the Common and Jungle babblers are among the most familiar birds of garden and roadside, moving in noisy bands from tree to tree and sometimes, especially in the early morning, hopping about on tarmac roads. Parties of 5–15 birds are the rule and these normally consist of extended families, with the whole group collaborating to incubate the eggs laid by the dominant female (and presumably fertilized by the dominant male). All members assist in feeding the nestlings, but despite this assistance the young birds grow no faster than other passerines, fledging in about 14 days.

Groups of Jungle babblers defend collective territories; encounters between neighboring groups are very noisy, with most of the birds on each side calling excitedly. Fighting sometimes breaks out in these skirmishes and antagonists can be seen rolling on the ground with their claws locked together, oblivious of the human observer.

The behavior of the more brightly colored laughing thrushes is similar to that of the Jungle babbler, but they often occur in larger groups of up to 100 birds. In the evening these break up into small parties of 2–10 birds which roost separately but within a fairly small area, recombining the next morning. The spectacular White-crested laughing thrush performs a remarkable communal display in which several members take part, prancing together on the forest floor, their white crests raised like helmets, uttering a series of laughing calls that gradually mount to a crescendo. At dawn and dusk these calls are normally answered by neighboring groups, producing a chorus of choruses which echo among the densely forested hills which they inhabit.

In the evergreen rain forests of Southeast Asia and the temperate forests of the Himalayas babblers are important members of the associations of several species of small insect-eating birds that join together for foraging expeditions: a striking feature of the area's bird life. Those involved include minlas, yuhinas, tree babblers, tit-babblers and shrike-babblers, which mix freely with warblers, tits, minivets, treecreepers and woodpeckers to form loosely organized parties, sometimes numbering several hundred, moving steadily through the forest throughout the day and only breaking up in the evening to roost in separate single-species groups.   AJG

Cooperative Breeding in Babblers

Considering the large number of species involved, the babblers are remarkable in being wholly nonmigratory. A few of the high-altitude laughing thrushes move small distances between their summer and winter altitude zones, but this probably entails movements of no more than a few miles. Because they are not called upon to do any very sustained flying, and because most species do not take insects on the wing, they tend to be poor at flying, and this is reflected in their short, rounded wings and heavy legs and feet. The fact that they are sedentary has probably contributed to the well-developed social behavior found among many species.

Being poor fliers, babblers tend to remain close to where they were born, giving a good opportunity for young birds to assist their parents in the rearing of their younger siblings. Because groups defend territories year-round there is no annual competition for space and it is more difficult for new territories to become established. In this situation a young bird that remains with its parents until its abilities are fully developed, perhaps after

several years, will stand a better chance of reproducing eventually than one that disperses immediately.

In order to form a new territory in the face of strong competition it may be necessary for several birds to collaborate. This is best achieved by groups of siblings, for as all share the same genes derived from their parents any help given to kin thereby benefits the survival of their own genes. In the Jungle babbler groups of sibling males or females sometimes split off from their parental group and roam about in marginal areas. If they encounter a similar coalition of the opposite sex, originating from another group, then they may combine to try to establish a new territory. However, sibling mating has not been recorded and breeding between unrelated individuals seems to be the rule.

The importance of kin associations in setting up new territories provides another incentive for birds to remain in their parental group until they can form a coalition of sufficient strength to attempt to defend their own ground.   AJG

▲ **One of Europe's smallest birds,** the Goldcrest.

◄ **Low-flying forager.** Where several genera of babblers are present each is equipped to exploit a particular section of habitat. The scimitar-babblers of Southeast Asia are active just above ground level. They fly around creepers and bushes with the ease of acrobats, using their long tails for balance. With their long bills they probe for insects. By contrast the terrestrial wren-babblers have long legs, short tails and short bills. This is the Rusty-cheeked scimitar-babbler (*Pomatorhinus erythrogenys*).

▼ **Spectacled warbler** (*Sylvia conspicillata*). The European populations of this species migrate to North Africa for the winter.

For many people the word "warbler" suggests a dull brownish bird singing a gentle, trilling song (ie warbling) from a concealed perch in dense vegetation. Such unobtrusiveness and drabness of plumage are indeed characteristics of many **Old World warblers**, but in fact this large subfamily contains numerous distinctive species to which the above description hardly applies. No fewer than 25 of the 56 genera contain only one species, although clearly many of these and other members of the subfamily are of doubtful affinity and some may not be true warblers at all. The taxonomic confusion surrounding warblers is highlighted by some of the vernacular names; the Oriole babbler, tit-flycatchers and tit-weavers are all currently regarded as warblers.

The great majority of species are Eurasian or African. The New World warblers have nine primary feathers and are not close relatives of the mainly Old World warblers which have ten primary feathers. However, some species of Old World warblers occur in the New World! There are 13 species of gnatwrens and gnatcatchers and 2 kinglets. In addition the Arctic warbler has extended its breeding range from Siberia into western Alaska, although even these birds return to the Old World to winter in southern Asia. Mainland Australia has only 8 resident species, including the distinctive Spinifex bird, and New Zealand only one, the fernbird. The archipelagoes of the Pacific and Indian Oceans contain a variety of unique warblers. The tiny populations of some of these island endemics make them highly vulnerable to extinction. The Aldabra warbler, whose population was fewer than 11 birds in 1983, is a good example of this.

Typical warblers are small birds with fine,

narrowly pointed bills. Their feet are strong and well suited for perching. Some (eg Dartford warbler) have long tails which counterbalance the body as the birds thread their way through dense foliage, carrying out inspections over and under leaves and twigs in their tireless search for insects.

Warblers' dependence on insect prey is the main reason why most warblers of high latitudes are strongly migratory. Most north Eurasian warblers winter in Africa or tropical Asia, some performing prodigious journeys. For example, Willow warblers nesting in Siberia travel up to 7,500mi (12,000km) twice a year, to and from sub-Saharan Africa. These long-distance migrants accumulate substantial reserves of fuel, in the form of fat deposits, before their journeys. It is not unusual for them to double their body weight in preparation for their migration. Those few warblers that remain in cold climates in winter are sometimes badly affected by food shortages in harsh weather. Dartford warblers in Britain, for example, often suffer large population decreases during severe winters.

Warblers are typically monogamous although instances of polygamy are known for a number of species (eg Sedge warbler). Voice has recently been shown to be important in some species for mate-attraction and mate-selection, in addition to being a primary means of advertising the positions of territory boundaries. Male Sedge warblers may cease to sing after pairing and individual Reed warblers with elaborate song repertoires tend to succeed in attracting females sooner than less accomplished singers. Some species (eg Icterine warbler) extend their repertoires by mimicking other bird species, for reasons that are not really understood. The Marsh warbler has gone further: its song consists entirely of imitations of other species. Each Marsh warbler mimics on average 80 species, over half of them African birds heard in the warbler's winter quarters. Voice also plays an important part in distinguishing species. For example, chiffchaffs and Willow warblers look almost identical, but have unmistakably distinct songs. Songs are generally delivered from perches, but warblers of low vegetation often use song flights as a means of broadcasting their songs for long distances. Examples of these include scrub warblers, such as the whitethroat, and many of the *Cisticola* grass warblers, such as the Cloud-scraper.

All warblers seem to be competing for the same basic food: insects. In practice there is often a high degree of spatial separation which minimizes competition for food between species and between individuals. Species that occur at high densities, notably the temperate-zone ones, are characteristically territorial. Typically the males defend territories against members of their own species and sometimes also against members of closely related species. For example, blackcaps and Garden warblers defend territories against each other as well as against other members of their own species. In the first case the territories of both species are large and supply most of the food of the nesting pairs and their broods. In the latter, however, breeding territories are small and perhaps serve mainly to space out nests to make it less profitable for predators to specialize in searching for them. Territorial behavior is not confined to the breeding season nor is it necessarily always directed at other warblers. For example, blackcaps using bird-tables or taking nectar from a particular bush will drive off species of similar or smaller size which try to feed there too.

Some warblers achieve ecological segregation by other means. Vertical separation sometimes occurs; for example, the Long-billed crombec forages lower down in the vegetation, where its range overlaps with that of a close relative, the Red-faced crombec, than it does elsewhere. Sometimes where species cooccur there is dietary specialization. For example, the nestling diets of Reed and Great reed warblers tend to differ where the two species are nesting in the same reedbed, but not where they occur apart from each other. Large warbler species are often found to coexist peacefully with smaller ones. Ecological segregation here may be due to specialization on prey of different sizes and to differences in foraging behavior. For example, blackcap and chiffchaff breeding territories often overlap in Europe since the two species share the same habitat, ie deciduous woodland. Blackcaps take fewer tiny insects than do the smaller chiffchaffs and, in addition, blackcaps feed to a large extent on settled insects whereas chiffchaffs often flycatch, or hover to take insects from the extremities of leaves and twigs where they may be inaccessible to blackcaps.   EFJG

Old World flycatchers are small woodland or forest birds; many can be recognized from their manner of capturing flying insects. They sit on a prominent perch and suddenly dash out, catch the prey in the air and then return to the perch.

Some species of flycatchers live in gardens and parks and are thus well known and provide much of interest to man, but they occur over most of Europe, Africa, Asia, Australia and the Pacific Islands from coastal shrubs to high altitude forests, up to 13,100ft (4,000m). The majority of species, however, are found in Southeast Asia and on New Guinea. In Southeast Asia, the Fiji Islands and Australia some flycatcher species (those of the three genera, *Petroica*, *Tregellasia* and *Eopsaltria*) are called robins by the Australians although these species look

▲ **The long wings and long tail** of the whitethroat (an Old World warbler) can be clearly seen when the bird is in flight. It breeds in much of Eurasia and migrates to North and tropical Africa for the winter. It is restless and perky.

◄ **Feeding time.** In Old World warblers of the genus *Sylvia* both parents normally care for the young. The range of the Subalpine warbler (*S. cantillans*), seen here, differs substantially from that of the whitethroat. Breeding takes place in southern Europe or northwest Africa, winter is spent in the eastern Mediterranean or North Africa.

like and behave like flycatchers. The name robin is said to have become popular thanks to nostalgia for the red-breasted robin of Europe (a thrush). In Europe flycatchers are popular garden birds, and some species can easily be attracted to nest boxes. Otherwise most flycatchers build small cup nests in forks of branches; among a few southern exceptions are some African species (genus *Muscicapa*) and the Japanese Blue and white flycatcher; these occasionally also use nest boxes.

Flycatchers vary greatly in appearance, from the very colorful to almost uniformly brown or gray. In many species the sexes differ considerably in plumage, but not in size, while in others, most often the duller-colored species, the sexes are very similar. Typical flycatchers have relatively broad,

flat bills with bristles around the nostrils, probably to help in catching flying insects. Their legs and feet are often weak, possibly because their feeding technique demands no more of them than sitting still and waiting. Spotted flycatchers are very fascinating to observe when catching insects on warm days. Then they use a sit-and-wait feeding strategy on low perches from which they sally out to capture prey in mid-air. In this way they may capture, on average, a prey every 18 seconds. In colder weather, with few flying insects, they have to hover among the foliage in the tree canopy, which is much more demanding of energy. Australian species in general have finer bills than most flycatchers and take most of their food on the ground. Not all flycatchers feed solely on insects; many also take berries and

fruits, for example, the Blue and White flycatcher in Borneo and the Dusky flycatcher and some of its relatives in Africa. One African species, the White-eyed slaty flycatcher, even takes nestlings of smaller birds.

Most flycatchers are thought to be monogamous. The Pied and Collared flycatchers in Eurasia, however, are polygamous and have a remarkable mating system in which males defend two or more distant territories in succession, to each of which they try to attract a female (see box). The Pied and Collared flycatchers are close relatives, males being black and white. They can easily be distinguished in the field from the white collar and rump of the Collared flycatcher, while the females of both species are gray-brown and almost indistinguishable from each other. In Eastern Europe, where both species occur together, they regularly hybridize and hybrids may locally make up as much as 5–10 percent of all birds present. Male hybrids do not seem to have any disadvantages in attracting a mate but they suffer from reduced fertility. The songs of pure species are very different, but Pied flycatcher males can switch to Collared flycatcher song in areas and situations where the two species are neighbors. In tropical areas some flycatcher species may form

The Deceptive Mating Behavior of Male Pied Flycatchers

The Pied flycatcher is an inhabitant of woodlands. It breeds in holes in trees and can easily be attracted to nest boxes. The male, after arriving in the breeding grounds in spring, sets up a territory around a nest-hole and tries to acquire a female (the "primary" female). If successful he then occupies a second more or less distant territory and attempts to attract another ("secondary") female. He rarely manages to obtain a third. The distance between a male's first territory and his second is on average 650ft (about 200m), but distances up to 2.2mi (3.5km) have been known, and several territories of other males lie in between. By having two distant territories males can hide from arriving females the fact that they are already mated. When trying to attract the secondary female, the male behaves exactly as when he was unmated and tried to attract the primary one. Males desert their secondary females after egg-laying and mainly help their primary female to feed the young. Since secondary females have to raise their young almost single-handed, some of the young may die from undernourishment. Thus males deceive females about their marital status and can increase their number of offspring at cost to the females. Approximately 15 percent of the males succeed in attracting more than one

female. Many more try but fail, while some males stay with their first female all the time.

Most male birds guard their females before egg-laying to prevent other males from copulating with them. Since Pied flycatcher males start visiting the second territory soon after having attracted the primary female, they cannot guard her uninterruptedly, and as a result run the risk of other males inseminating the female and siring some of her young. This has also been seen to happen; while the male is away the nearest neighboring males sneak into his territory and copulate with the female, which leads to shared fatherhood within broods. However, females of monogamous males are also the subjects of extra-pair copulations (there is a considerable risk if the male is more than 33ft, 10m, from the female), since their mates often have to chase intruding males from the territory. This leads to reduced paternity also for monogamous males. Thus, on average, in all broods the attendant male is the true father of only 75 percent of the young. Even though polygynous males may lose relatively more young per nest, due to shared fatherhood, than monogamous males, they in all father more young by having a secondary female than by being monogamous. Bigamy thus is an adaptive feature in the Pied flycatcher.

ALU

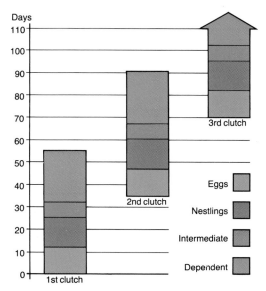

Days

▲ **Breeding with rapidity.** This diagram demonstrates how a female fairy-wren can, with the aid of helpers, reduce the period between successive clutches of eggs. For about 30 days after leaving the nest, young remain dependent on the parents, but after this they become independent and are available to help parents with later broods. For example young of the first clutch take over the care of the young of a second clutch leaving the female free to lay a third clutch.

◄ **The unforgettable bird.** According to Professor David Lack "There is hardly a corner in the world in which the English have not managed to find some red-breasted bird which they could call a robin." In Australia this common Old World flycatcher is known as the Red-capped robin (*Petroica goodenovii*).

▷ **Iridescent miniature** OVERLEAF the Red-winged fairy-wren of southwest Australia.

▼ **The rodent run.** Fairy-wrens are normally found (1) standing or hopping. If one is threatened by a predator it runs along the ground, tail down, squeaking (2–4). As a distraction the display is surprisingly effective.

small flocks in the nonbreeding season, like the Mariqua flycatcher, or may join parties of mixed birds, like the Ashy flycatcher. The Australian Flame robin which also forms flocks in autumn and winter even has communal roosts at night.

Most tropical species are resident, but some perform seasonal movements, and high-altitude species migrate towards lower altitudes in the nonbreeding season. Species in Europe and Asia migrate long distances and spend the winter in Africa, India or Southeast Asia.　　ALu

A species of **fairy-wren** can be found in nearly every kind of habitat throughout the 40 degrees of latitude covered by Australia and New Guinea, ranging from dense tall forest in the well-watered southwest Australia (Red-winged fairy-wren) to the spinifex-covered sand dunes of the interior desert (Eyrean grass-wren). Characteristically fairy-wrens have tails longer than their bodies and these are carried cocked, jauntily, most of the time.

The true fairy-wrens are endemic to Australia and New Guinea and wherever they occur the ground cover is generally thick and they hop rapidly through it on their long legs. Their wings are short and rounded and these diminutive birds rarely make prolonged flights. The males in this genus are brightly colored in enameled reds, blues, blacks and white while the females and immatures are usually brown. In the emu-wrens there are clear differences between the sexes, but in the other three genera the sexes are harder to tell apart in the field.

Most of the fairy-wrens depend largely on insects for food but the grass-wrens with their sturdier bills eat large quantities of seeds as well. Foraging is largely done on the ground as they bound along, though some species search through shrubs and even the canopies of tall trees. Because their wings are small and rather inefficient, fairy-wrens only rarely fly sorties after air-borne insects.

Throughout a wide variety of environments most species spend their lifetime within a prescribed area which they defend from trespass by members of their species outside the immediate family and within which they find all their requirements for

feeding, breeding and shelter. Such "territories" cover from 2.5–7.4 acres (1 to 3ha) and tend to persist from year to year with little change.

Despite their small size these birds may live for a surprisingly long time (more than 10 years), compared with their counterparts in the northern hemisphere. A long life and residential status seem to have encouraged them to maintain their family bonds beyond the usual period when offspring depend on their parents for food and protection; most fairy-wrens tend to live in groups with more than two adults capable of breeding yet only one female lays the eggs. Thus although fairy-wrens of both sexes are capable of breeding in the season after they are hatched, relatively few do so, opting to stay in the relative security of the family territory rather than disperse into the unknown and set up on their own. This "delayed" reproduction is encouraged by there being more males than females in many populations and by suitable breeding habitat often being in short supply: where young birds do disperse it is generally the females that leave.

In most species of fairy-wren the female builds the nest, lays and incubates the eggs and broods the young when they first hatch. Her mate may call her off the nest and escort her while she forages hurriedly before returning to brood. The young fledge after ten days or so in the nest and at first are unable to fly, though they will scuttle fast over the ground and hide. If a predator approaches a nest the parents (and other group members) perform a frenzied "rodent run" display: instead of hopping, which is their usual mode of progression, they run, keeping close to the ground, trailing their tails and squeaking, hence the name of the performance. This performance is surprisingly effective in distracting a variety of predators, from snakes to man.

The young are fed for several weeks after they have left the nest. Fairy-wrens nest several times during a season and the non-breeding members of the group may take over the raising of an early brood and so allow the breeding female to start a second (or third) nest. Later in the season young hatched earlier will attend their nestling-siblings and help to raise them, so that the

habit of "helping" is formed early in life.

Emu-wrens live deep in dense heathland: it is hard to catch more than a fleeting glimpse of them. Grass-wrens are birds of the deserts, arid shrublands and rocky plateaus and they, too, are rarely seen. In the last 35 years one new species has been discovered (the Gray grass-wren) and four others have been rediscovered after being unseen for 50 years or more (the Eyrean, Carpentarian, White-throated and the Black grass-wrens).

Most of the fairy-wrens have survived the environmental impact of European settlement and the accompanying exotic pests, the feral cat and the fox. However, the Purple-crowned fairy-wren does seem to be particularly vulnerable and to have decreased in numbers recently. This species lives in the gallery forest that lines a dozen tropical river-systems. Often only a few feet in width, this fringe vegetation is easily damaged by overgrazing and by stock trampling it down as they seek access to water. Hopefully this situation has been recognized in time, and adequate reserves will be maintained.

One of the great attractions of this family of small birds is that some species have thrived alongside the mushrooming of suburbia. In particular the Superb blue fairy-wren is common in the parks and gardens of six capital cities and brightens the lives of those who live there.   IR

Parrotbills are thought to have originated in China, as most species occur in that country. Though they have spread, their distribution remains basically Asiatic; there is just one exception: the Bearded tit. This species occurs in Europe, reaching as far west as Britain. It should be regarded as a somewhat aberrant representative of the subfamily as it differs from the typical parrotbills in having a more conventionally shaped bill. In this species, moreover, the sexes differ in appearance and the young resemble the female. The male has conspicuous erectile black moustaches and beautiful plumage in cinnamon-buff, gray and vinaceous rose. The Bearded tit produces "pinging" notes, which are frequently encountered in the extensive reed beds where the species breeds.

The typical parrotbills comprise the largest genus with 15 species, which range in size from 4.5–8.5in (11 to 22cm). Their distinguishing feature is the peculiarly shaped yellowish bill, which is shorter than the head—broad, highly compressed with an extremely convex outline to both

mandibles. They also have longish tails, which give them a superficial tit-like appearance.

Parrotbills are mostly found in hilly or mountainous regions, in mixed secondary forest and bamboo and in the dwarf rhododendrons of the Himalayas. Some species are found up to 12,000ft (3,700m), while other species extend to lowland areas. However, bamboo appears to be necessary for most species.

All species of parrotbills are gregarious, occurring in small restless flocks, which forage through the lower trees of forests, tall grasses and bamboos. There are also seasonal vertical movements by those species that breed at high altitudes. The Great parrotbill, which breeds between 10,000 and 12,000ft (3,000–3,700m), moves down to 6,000ft (1,850m) in the winter. This, the largest of parrotbills, is uniform mousy-brown with a heavy but normally shaped bill. The Yangtse parrotbill, which is superficially marked in such a way that it looks like a large version of the Bearded tit, has a massive yellow beak. It also has the most restricted range of any parrotbill, being recorded only along a 50mi (80km) stretch of reedbeds bordering the lower Yangtse. It is now considered an endangered species, particularly in view of cutting and reclamation and increase in navigation by powered vessels along the river during the last 50 years.

The uniformly brownish Three-toed parrotbill ranging from the Himalayas to Southwest China is unique in having its outer toe reduced to a clawless stump, adhering to the middle toe. Surprisingly enough the Brown parrotbill is barely distinguishable from the Three-toed parrotbill, and their ranges overlap slightly. Another pair of species are the Black-browed and Red-headed parrotbills, both of which have ginger-colored heads, pale brown backs and white underparts. However, the Red-headed parrotbill has a massive yellow bill twice the size of that of its sibling partner and presumably tackles much heavier seeds or insects.

PRC

Monarch flycatchers attract attention by their activity, quivering tail, harsh calls and metallic plumage. The paradise flycatchers are the most spectacular species with their 6in (15cm) long tail feathers. A range of closely related species is found from southern Africa across tropical Asia to Japan.

Africa, south of the Sahara, has many genera, as do Indonesia and New Guinea.

The subfamily extends as far as the Himalayas, Korea and Japan and has successfully colonized many of the islands of the Indian and Pacific Oceans, though not New Zealand.

Supposed species hybridize frequently and many species show several colors, the male having varying amounts of white, black and chestnut. New Guinea is the center of diversity of the monarchs with five or six species known to occupy one small area of forest. The peltops flycatchers sally from trees that extend above the forest canopy while other species occupy the canopy itself, subcanopy and understory. The sexes of the Frilled monarch differ strikingly in behavior. The rufous female, which has a long tail and wide beak, often sallies after insects in the subcanopy. The black and white male, on the other hand, gleans from trunks, branches and vines. As one would expect he has longer, more curved claws than the female.

Although most species have a long tail and plumage of chestnut, black or gray (glossed with blue or green), some species

differ from this pattern. The African puffback flycatchers are small, short-tailed, dumpy birds with a conspicuous breast band. Typically, monarch flycatchers have flat, broad beaks and small feet and often steep foreheads with a slight crest. Several species have brightly colored flaps or patches of bare skin around their eyes.

Although most monarch flycatchers sally after flying insects, several species are gleaners and the shrikebills occasionally take fruit. The Restless flycatcher hovers above the ground making a strange grinding noise, which has given rise to its other name, the scissors-grinder. The New Guinean and Australian species nest in

▲ ► **Representative species** of seven subfamilies of thrushes. (1) A Gray-headed parrotbill (*Paradoxornis gularis*). (2) A Yellow-rumped thornbill (*Acanthiza chrysorrhoa*). (3) A Gray fantail (*Rhipidura fuliginosa*) sitting on its nest. (4) An African paradise flycatcher (*Terpsiphone viridis*) holding an insect. (5) A Black-backed fairy-wren (*Malurus melanotus*). (6) A Golden whistler (*Pachycephala pectoralis*). (7) A Northern logrunner (*Orthonyx spaldingi*).

spring (September to December) and build neat nests on horizontal branches, often beautifully camouflaged with lichen. The Satin flycatcher often nests close to Noisy friarbirds—bold, aggressive honeyeaters.

HAF

The **logrunners** are a group of secretive birds, more often heard than seen. Most species are consequently rather poorly known—indeed the wedgebill was recently split into two species based on calls: the Chirruping wedgebill calls "tootsie-cheer" and the Chiming wedgebill "did-you-get-drunk." The wedgebills and whipbirds perform duets, the male eastern whipbird giving a characteristic whipcrack to which the female replies "cher, cher."

The name quail-thrush describes the genus *Cinclosoma* well, as they are thrush-like in proportions and plumage yet are ground-dwelling and eat seeds and insects. They mostly live in desert or eucalypt or acacia woodlands in Australia whereas most of the other logrunners occupy the understory of rainforest in eastern Australia and New Guinea, where they are chiefly insectivorous. Although most species are cryptically colored the Blue jewel-babbler male is blue and white. Most are dumpy birds with rather long tails; they have strong feet, which are used for digging. Logrunners often dig in areas from which Brush turkeys have removed the leaf litter for their mounds.

Logrunners may engage in noisy territorial battles in the breeding season, and perhaps most species are monogamous and territorial. Nests of dry sticks, bark, roots and grass are placed in thick foliage or on the ground, in winter and spring, but occasionally in the fall. Though quail-thrushes mostly nest between August and November, the desert species have been recorded breeding in all months of the year.

The Western whipbird was at one time considered rare or even endangered, but once its haunting, ventriloquistic call was learnt it was discovered in several places in southern Australia. Several species of logrunners have been affected by the clearing of forest or the overgrazing of shrubland in Australia, though none is currently threatened.

HAF

To many people the **Australasian warblers** are just dull little brown birds. However they are of great scientific interest because they display a variety of complex breeding biologies.

The *Gerygone* warblers are the most widespread members of the group occurring in

Australia, New Guinea, Indonesia, Malaysia, Burma, New Zealand and many Pacific Islands. They are delicate attractive birds with tinkling songs that flitter through the foliage after tiny insects. Scrub-wrens inhabit the understory of forests in Australia and New Guinea and thornbills are principally Australian, where they forage in a range of sites from the ground to the treetops.

Most Australasian warblers are small, even tiny, with short tails and wings and fine bills. Although many are dull brown or olive, many thornbills have contrasting rumps and the *Gerygone* warblers often have bright yellow underparts. The Rock warbler, which nests in caves in sandstone around Sydney, NSW, is dark gray above and reddish brown beneath. In appearance the sexes and ages are similar, often identical.

Insects are the primary food, but the whitefaces, which live in dry habitats, eat a lot of seeds. Where several species of thornbill occur in the same place each usually forages at a different level in the vegetation.

Evidence is slowly emerging that thornbills, despite their tiny size 0.25–0.28oz (7–10g), are long-lived, with 10-year-old birds being quite frequent in populations studied. Perhaps due to this they often do not breed in their first year. Breeding takes place from late winter to summer, and although some species breed as pairs cooperative breeding is more typical of the group.

The Buff-tailed thornbill lives in clans of about ten birds for most of the year. At the beginning of the breeding season these break up into pairs, trios and quartets which attempt to breed. Those that fail in their own breeding attempt help a neighboring pair or group, until the clan comes together again in the fall. A change in foraging coincides with the breakup of the clan. Larger groups feed more on the ground, pairs more on bark or among foliage.

Australasian warblers frequently join and may lead feeding flocks of mixed species in the nonbreeding season, a habit that does not help the bird-watcher confronted with a host of species of little brown birds.

HAF

Fantails frequently fly straight at human observers and hover a foot or two from them. Consequently they are regarded with great affection, to the extent that one species is called the Friendly fantail. In truth they are probably more interested in our flies than in us.

▲ **The deep nest** of the shrike-tit (a thickhead) is made of strips of bark woven together, felted with cobweb and decorated with moss and lichen.

◄ **The Black-throated wattle-eye** (*Platysteira peltata*), a monarch flycatcher, lives in southern Africa, from eastern Kenya south to Angola and Natal. It is almost always found near water.

► **One of the most extraordinary songs** in New Guinea is that of the Crested pitohui (*Pitohui cristatus*), a species of thickhead. It starts as a series of repeated identical notes but gradually the notes become shorter and the pitch falls. In one recorded example the song lasted almost 3 minutes. At the start there were 5 notes per second, at the end 13. During the song the pitch fell by half an octave.

New Guinea has the most species of fantail and here three or four species coexist in small patches of rain forest, foraging at different levels. Four species occur on the Asian mainland from India through Southeast Asia to southern China. Australia has three species, with the Willie wagtail occupying much drier and more open habitats than the other fantails. They have successfully invaded the Indonesian and Pacific Islands and spread as far east as Fiji and Samoa.

The most striking character of the group is the very long tail, which can be spread into an impressive fan and waved from side to side. The body is surprisingly small, legs are delicate, and the bill is short but broad, typical of a flycatcher. The Willie wagtail is black and white, other species are all black, gray and white or rufous and white.

Flies, beetles and other insects are snapped up in acrobatic sallies from perches in the understory or canopy. The Willie wagtail often uses a sheep's back as a perch, and frequently takes insects from the ground. The fanned tail and hyperactivity of these birds probably help to flush insects into the air.

The breeding biology of the Willie wagtail and of the Gray fantail in New Zealand have been well studied. Fantails suspend delicate nests of bark and moss from a low, thin branch. They breed from August to February and may have several successive clutches, with nests sometimes reused and later nests being built faster than early ones. The nestlings are often preyed upon by introduced weasels and mice. Willie wagtails place a nest of hair, wool, thistledown, bark and dead leaves on a horizontal branch or often a man-made structure. Nests are sometimes parasitized by Pallid cuckoos; despite this, young are reared from about 65 percent of nests.

All fantails seem common and popular and most adapt well to human disturbance, though some of the Pacific species have small distributions.   HAF

The popular name **thickheads** is hardly a complimentary one; preferable, for the largest genus, is whistlers as these include some of the finest songsters in a region not noted for its richness of birdsong.

Whistlers are found from Indonesia and Malaysia, through New Guinea and Australia to Fiji and Tonga. Most other genera occur in New Guinea or Australia. Only the piopio comes from New Zealand, and the taxonomic position of this species is confusing; it is often placed in its own family. The Golden whistler superspecies spans the range of the subfamily: some 70 forms are found, differing in plumage and in the extent of different appearances of the sexes. Shrike-thrushes and female whistlers are predominantly gray or brown, whereas male whistlers often have black and white heads and yellow or reddish breasts. Both sexes of shrike-tit have black and white striped heads, yellow breasts and green backs. Shrike-tits have massive beaks, hooked on each mandible. Other species have strong, slightly hooked beaks and strong feet.

Whistlers capture insects among foliage, whereas shrike-tits forage on bark and most of the other genera fossick among debris on or near the ground. Several species occasionally eat fruit, the pitohuis do so frequently.

The breeding season is from July to January and most species (including migratory species) are very faithful to their breeding territories from year to year. Nests are made of sticks, bark, grasses and spiders' webs, usually placed in a low fork. So far only the shrike-tit is known to be a cooperative breeder though the pitohuis live in groups. The Rusty pitohui associates with babblers, honeyeaters, cuckoo-shrikes and drongos in New Guinean lowland rainforests. Such mixed flocks are remarkable in that all members are a similar rufous color.

The piopio of New Zealand is possibly extinct, not having been seen since 1955. The Red-lored or Red-throated whistler from mallee-scrub on the borders of Victoria, New South Wales and South Australia is very rare and possibly endangered. Its habitat is rapidly being cleared.   HAF

TITS

Families: Paridae, Aegithalidae, Remizidae
Order: Passeriformes (suborder Oscines, part).
Sixty-two species in 10 genera.
Distribution: see map and table.

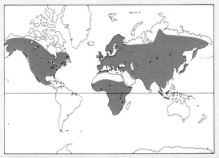

▶ **Representative species of the three families of tits.** (**1**) A Rufous-bellied tit (*Parus rufiventris*). (**2**) A Black-eared bushtit (*Psaltriparus melanotis*), one of the long-tailed tits. (**3**) Seven Long-tailed tits (*Aegithalos caudatus*) roosting. (**4**) A Yellow-cheeked or Chinese yellow tit (*Parus spilonotus*). (**5**) A Blue tit (*Parus caruleus*). (**6**) A verdin (*Auriparus flavifrons*), one of the penduline tits. (**7**) Head of a Bridled titmouse (*Parus wollweberi*) holding a worm. (**8**) An Azure tit (*Parus cyanus*).

TITS are small, active woodland and scrub dwellers: many are well-known visitors to bird feeders in gardens. Most are gregarious and vocal. The word "tits" derives from "titmice", the name for "true" tits (family Paridae) or, in North America, one group of *Parus* species (another group is called the chickadees). Other, unrelated, bird species are called tits, but here we include only members of three families currently thought to be closely related; they form a group probably closely allied to the nuthatches and creepers.

The **true tits** are by far the largest and most widespread of the three families, occurring from sea level to high mountains wherever there are trees: apart from treeless areas and offshore islands, only South America, Madagascar, Australia and the Antarctic are without true tits. Ten species are confined to North America, 10 to Africa south of the Sahara and the remainder are primarily Eurasian, though some of these spread into North Africa and one into Alaska. The North American and European species include some of the most "popular" of all birds, nesting in boxes in summer and common at bird-feeders in winter. They rarely cause any damage but provide hours of interest and enjoyment to home-bound observers.

In form and general appearance most of the true tits are fairly uniform and easily recognized as "tits" all over the world—a generalization borne out by the fact that all but two species are in the single genus *Parus*. Many have pale or white cheeks contrasting with black or dark caps; a number are

The 3 Families of Tits

True tits
Family: Paridae
Forty-six species in 3 genera.
Europe, Asia, Africa, N America (just into Mexico; also introduced to Hawaii). Chiefly woodland and forests. Size: 4.5–5.5in (11.5–14cm) long, weight 0.2–0.7oz (5–20g), except Sultan tit which reaches 8.7in (22cm), weight more than 1oz (30g). Plumage: chiefly brown, white, gray and black; some with yellow; three species have bright blue; only slight differences between sexes—females duller than males in some species. Voice: wide range of single notes, chattering calls and very varied complex songs, many whistled. Nests: all in holes, excavated in soft wood by some species. Eggs: usually 4–12, whitish with reddish-brown spots; incubation period: 13–14 days;

nestling period: 17–20 days. Diet: chiefly insects but also seeds, berries; some species store food for later retrieval.

Species include: **Black-capped chickadee** (*Parus atricapillus*), **Black tit** (*P. leucomelas*), **Blue tit** (*P. caeruleus*), **Bridled titmouse** (*P. wollweberi*), **Coal tit** (*P. ater*), **Crested tit** (*P. cristatus*), **Great tit** (*P. major*), **Marsh tit** (*P. palustris*), **Plain titmouse** (*P. inornatus*), **Siberian tit** (*P. cinctus*), **Sultan tit** (*Melanochlora sultanea*), **Tufted titmouse** (*P. bicolor*), **Willow tit** (*P. montanus*), **Yellow-browed tit** (*Sylviparus modestus*).

Long-tailed tits
Family: Aegithalidae
Seven species in 3 genera.
Europe to Asia, N America (just into C America). Mainly forest and woodland. Size: 3.5–5.5in (9–14cm) long, weight 0.25oz (7g). Plumage: chiefly black, gray, white, brown with pink in the Long-tailed tit. Voice: churring contact calls and subdued songs. Nests: purse-like structure of moss, feathers and lichens. Eggs: usually 6–10, white speckled with red spots in many species; incubation period: 13–14 days; nestling period 16–17 days. Diet: mainly insects.

Species include: **bushtit** (*Psaltriparus minimus*), **Long-tailed tit** (*Aegithalos caudatus*), **Pygmy tit** (*Psaltria exilis*).

Penduline tits
Family: Remizidae
Nine species in 4 genera.
N and C America, Africa, Eurasia. Open country in trees and bushes; reedbeds. Size: 4in (10–11cm) long. Plumage: mostly pale grays, white and yellows, but striking black mask and rich chestnut "saddle" in adult Penduline tit; a few species with bright yellow or red. Voice: fairly quiet, *ti-ti-ti*, thin whistles. Nests: purse-like with prickly twigs in verdin. Eggs: white except verdin (bluish-green) with red spots; incubation period: 13–14 days; nestling period: about 18 days. Diet: chiefly insects; some species also take small seeds.

Species include: **Fire-capped tit** (*Cephalopyrus flammiceps*), **Penduline tit** (*Remiz pendulinus*), **verdin** (*Auriparus flaviceps*).

crested. They have short sturdy bills and short legs. All spend most of their time in trees and bushes, though they will forage on the ground. They are extremely nimble and readily hang upside down on small twigs. Although they can fly long distances, they commonly only flit from one tree to the next.

True tits are monogamous in temperate areas, the male defending a territory against all comers. These territories are usually established in winter and early spring and break down when the young become independent, though in some species there is a brief resurgence of territorial behavior in the fall after the molt. Some species maintain their territories throughout the year. In Scandinavia the Willow tit may winter in groups of up to four in one territory; mortality in winter can be high and some territories do not have a pair by spring. In other species the birds may join up in flocks for much of the year, roving over large areas of woodland. Parties of mixed species of tits, often together with other small woodland birds, are a common feature of woodlands in Europe, Asia and North America. The behavior of tropical and African species is less well known. However, in the African

Black tit, territories are occupied by 3 or 4 birds during the breeding season and all help to raise the brood. The "extra" birds are usually males which have been raised in the same territory the previous year.

Of the two Southeast Asian species in separate genera, the Sultan tit is an enormous bird for a tit, about 8.7in (22cm) long, and weighing perhaps well over 1oz (30g). It is predominantly a glossy blue-black (the female is a little duller) with a bright yellow crown, an erectile crest and a yellow belly. It lives in rich forests and is not well known. Even less is known about the rather drab, greenish Yellow-browed tit, which lacks the distinctive patterning of most tits. It lives in high-altitude forests above about 6,000–7,000ft (2,000m). It was not until its nest was found in a hole in a rhododendron tree in 1969 that its breeding habits were known to be like those of other tits.

Many species have extensive ranges, the Great tit, Coal tit and Willow tit breeding from the British Isles across to Japan. The Marsh tit also breeds at both ends of this range, but has a gap of some 1,250mi (2,000km) in its range in Central Asia. The Siberian tit ranges from Scandinavia across Asia into Alaska and Canada. The Willow tit of Europe and Asia is very similar to the North American Black-capped chickadee; probably in prehistoric times a single species encircled the Northern Hemisphere; only later did they diverge into two species.

Most tropical and many temperate species are resident. Some, such as the Siberian tit, remain on their breeding grounds throughout the year despite very low winter temperatures (as low as −49°F, −45°C overnight); they roost in cavities in trees or even in mouse-holes in the snow, and go slightly torpid during the night, regaining their normal temperature at dawn. Some temperate species may migrate over long distances, especially when there are failures of the seed crops on which they are dependent in winter. Great tits from northern Russia have been known to winter as far afield as Portugal.

Most tits are primarily insect-eaters. Many also take seeds and berries, particularly species in colder climates where seeds are the main item of the winter diet. An abundance of an alternative food source is the reason why tits are so common in gardens and at bird feeders in winter. Some tits store food, primarily seeds, but sometimes also insects; such items are usually put behind cracks in the bark, but may also be buried under moss. The cache may not be used for some time, or the bird may store

▲ **An insatiable brood** of Coal tits begs for food from a returning parent. The white patches on the nape and crown of the adult distinguish this species from other similarly colored tits, such as the Marsh tit. The Coal tit prefers conifer wood habitats and nests in holes in banks and tree stumps.

◀ **The Southern black tit** (*Parus niger*) from Africa is one of the largest of true tits.

▶ **Frozen in flight,** a Marsh tit rises from a waterside feeding site. Its common name is a misnomer: this species has no particular preference for marshes. It is often seen in deciduous woods, hedges and sometimes in gardens. Its range is somewhat unusual. It is found in most of Europe, between the Black Sea and Lake Baikal, and in northern and eastern China and Hokkaido, Japan. There are no Marsh tits in the area between 52°E and 85°E.

food and collect it within hours. In the warm breeding season all species feed insects to their young. A pair of Blue tits may feed caterpillars to their nestlings at the rate of one a minute while the young are growing most rapidly, and bring well over 10,000 such items while the young are in the nest. Tits have been thought—although the evidence is not convincing—to be important in the control of forest pests, and large numbers of nesting-boxes have been put up for this reason. Tits are very versatile and quick to learn from one another. In 1929 some tits in Southampton were observed to remove the tops from milk bottles and drink the cream. This habit spread very rapidly throughout England by tits copying the skills from each other.

As far as is known, all *Parus* species are hole-nesters. A few nest in nesting-boxes in gardens; these species are well known and have been studied extensively (see pp92–9). The majority probably search for a hole which is suitable, because they do not seem to enlarge it in any way. However some, including the Crested tit, Willow tit and Black-capped chickadee, excavate their own nest-chamber in a soft piece of dead timber. This habit seems so fixed that they will excavate a new chamber even if the previous year's chamber is standing unused in the same tree. These species will normally not use nesting boxes, although if the boxes are filled with wood chippings they may then "excavate" them and find them acceptable! When suitable tree sites are in short supply, holes in the ground may be used.

Most species line their nests with moss, some adding hair or feathers; the female does the work, though the male may accompany her on trips to collect material. The eggs are laid at daily intervals. Clutches tend to be large, 4–5 in tropical species and more in temperate areas; as with other hole-nesting species, large clutches are thought to be related to the safety from predators of nests in holes, enabling large numbers of young to be raised. The average clutch of Blue tits in oak woodlands is about 11 eggs

Tufted Titmouse

Some of the 10 New World species of true tits are well known to the casual birdwatcher. The Black-capped chickadee and the Tufted titmouse (here illustrated) are a common sight at bird feeders, and the latter is particularly familiar since, unlike the chickadee, it will readily use a nesting box.

Although never reaching population densities as high as those of the Blue and Great tit in the Old World, the Tufted titmouse is very common throughout much of the eastern USA. It is rather scarcer in the

northern States, perhaps largely because, for this resident species, the winters are too severe.

However, in recent years it has gradually become more common in these States, especially in urban areas. Since its first appearance in Ontario in 1914, the Tufted titmouse had gradually established itself along the southern edge of this Canadian province. It seems almost certain that the widespread provision of food at bird-feeders is the key to this species being able to survive in such cold areas.

The Tufted titmouse is the only crested member of the family found in the eastern half of the United States. However, it has a crested counterpart to the west, the Plain titmouse, which lacks the rich orange-brown flank and the black above the beak. There is also a Bridled titmouse in the States bordering northwest Mexico, which people consider a separate species. All these North American crested birds are called "titmice" as opposed to the chickadees that make up the other members of the family. At one time the crested titmice of North America were put in a genus of their own, *Baeolophus*.

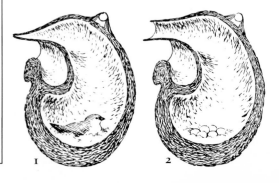

▲ **Putting the final touches,** a male Penduline tit hangs from its miraculous purse-like nest.

◄ **The Long-tailed tit's nest** ABOVE is constructed of feathers, mosses and spiders' webs.

◄ **An entrance leading nowhere** is built into the nest of the Cape penduline tit (**1**). The blind chamber to which it leads is thought to mislead predators. The true entrance lies above (**2**). It closes after the bird has entered or left the nest.

(exceptionally birds may lay as many as 18 or 19); these are probably the largest clutches of any song bird and only a few non-passerines such as gamebirds and ducks (which do not bring food to nestlings) lay larger clutches. In some species clutch size has been shown to vary with a number of factors: first-year birds lay smaller clutches than older, more experienced ones; clutches are smaller in the poorer habitats of gardens than in woodland; they are smaller later in the season when caterpillars are scarcer; and smaller when breeding density is high. Most species have a single brood, but some raise two broods in favorable seasons. Incubation is by the female alone. After leaving the nest the large brood is cared for by both parents for a week or so in temperate

species and probably for much longer in some tropical species.

Long-tailed tits are very small birds, their tail being perhaps half of their length. All seven species are highly social and live in flocks of 6–12 birds for much of the year. The Long-tailed tit and the bushtit roost in little groups, huddling together for warmth on cold nights. In Europe many Long-tailed tits die in very cold weather.

They build elaborate purse-like nests of feathers and moss—more than 2,000 feathers have been counted in a single nest. The beautifully constructed nest is bound together with spider's web and camouflaged with a covering of lichen; it may be 7in (18cm) or so deep in Long-tailed tits and up to 12in (30cm) or more in the bushtit, and it takes many days to complete. Although both members of a pair may roost in the nest at night, probably only the female incubates, acquiring a bent tail from sitting in the tiny nest. The Pygmy tit in Java also lives in flocks and builds similar nests, but little else is known of the behavior of this species.

In both the European Long-tailed tit and the bushtit, one or more "helpers" may assist the parents to feed the young at the nest. The helpers usually arrive after the nest has been built and the eggs laid: they may be birds that have lost their own nest to predators.

Penduline tits are named for their hanging nests. All are very small and have finer, more needle-pointed bills than the other tits. All the species are primarily resident. The Penduline tit has by far the greatest range, stretching from southern Europe across to eastern China. In Europe its range is extending slowly west and north. Penduline tits live in small parties for most of the year, many species in rather open, scrubby woodland, but the Penduline tit lives in small trees such as willows and tamarisks in marshes and spends much of its time hunting for its food amongst the reeds.

The Penduline tit and all *Anthoscopus* species build purse-like nests, of a strong felt-like construction. Indeed some nests are occasionally used as purses by certain tribes in Africa. *Anthoscopus* nests have a dummy entrance which is blind. The parents close the real one when they leave, thus making it hard for would-be predators to find their way in. The verdin builds a more normal domed nest with many thorns woven into it, and the Fire-capped tit nests in holes in trees like the true tits (it is arguable that it should be placed in the family Paridae).

CMP

The Great Tit

The World's Most Studied Bird?

The Great tit is perhaps the most studied wild bird in the world. The first person to realize the usefulness of the Great tit for purposes of study was H. Wolda in the Netherlands, who kept careful records for many years. Many of his results were published, together with new data, by H. N. Kluijver in 1951. This classic work in bird biology has inspired many other studies.

The Great tit is a common species over much of western Europe and Asia: except in the very coldest areas the birds are usually resident. In the wild it nests in holes in trees, but it readily accepts nest-boxes and often seems to prefer them to natural sites; all the birds within an area may nest in boxes. It is these characteristics that have made the Great tit (and to a lesser extent the Blue tit) such a convenient bird to study.

Great tits eat a wide variety of food. Although primarily insect-eaters they readily turn to seeds and nuts in winter when insects become scarce. The Great tit has a powerful beak with which it can hammer open seeds as large as hazel nuts, something that most of the smaller tits cannot do. Outside the breeding season, the birds often go about in small parties of perhaps 4–6 birds among other species of tits, each bird keeping an eye on where the others are feeding and what they are taking. As soon as one bird finds a new source of food the others will change their foraging technique to include the new item in their searches.

Great tits tend to settle in broadleaved deciduous woodland at densities of around one pair per 2.5 acres (1ha) and in coniferous woodland at about one pair per 5–12.5 acres (2–5ha). Long-term studies show that although the numbers of breeding pairs are relatively stable, there is a tendency to "see-saw" up and down from year to year. The most important factor in this is the presence or absence of beech mast. The beech tree tends to produce a rich crop of seeds at intervals of two years (or more) and tit numbers increase after a winter when the crop has been available, and decrease when there is no crop then. In northern populations the presence of beech crops also influences whether or not the birds will winter in the same area.

Birds emigrate ("irrupt") southward in years without a crop, but are more likely to remain on the breeding grounds in years when there is a good crop. Birds also come to bird feeders in gardens less often when beech mast is abundant, which leads some people to conclude that tits are very scarce in years when the reverse is in fact true.

Great tits stake out their territories in late winter and early spring, taking up the best areas first so that latecomers may have to settle in marginal areas. Some birds are even excluded from obtaining a territory at all; this can be demonstrated by removing established territory holders; the empty territories are usually filled by newcomers within 24 hours. The replacement pairs take up much the same areas as the original occupants, except that some occupants of adjacent territories expand their domain into the territory temporarily left vacant. If a tape-recording of Great tit song is played in the vacant territory it apparently "fools" would-be immigrants, as reoccupation by new owners is delayed. Territorial behavior breaks down when the birds have young, when they are too busy collecting food to be able to defend their territory.

In Central Europe Great tits start to build nests in early to mid April. Each egg weighs about 10 percent of the female's body weight and she may lay 10 eggs. She needs a plentiful supply of food in addition to her

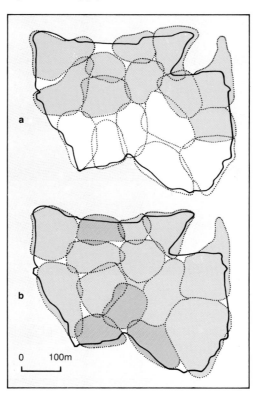

▲ **Rapid territorial expansion** in the Great tit. These maps show the distribution of Great tit territories in a small wood (45 acres 18ha). (**a**) Six pairs of birds were removed from their territories. (**b**) Within three days four new pairs had taken up residence (amber), while other residents of the wood had expanded their territories where their neighbors had been removed.

▶ **Head down, wings open,** a male Great tit threatens an intruder.

normal requirements, to form her own body weight in eggs over a period of just 10–14 days. The male brings food to the laying female. She also needs to lay as early as possible, since young born early in the season stand a better chance of surviving than those of later nests. However, the female's requirement for food is such that she cannot always lay at the time which would be best from the chicks' point of view; she has to wait until food is sufficiently abundant for her. Evidence for this is the fact that where food is put out for them just prior to laying the Great tits lay earlier than in adjacent areas where the birds are not fed. Great tits breeding in gardens also tend to lay earlier than those in woodland, probably again because the food put out for them by people enables them to do so.

After 13–14 days the eggs have hatched. Now the parents have to work exceedingly hard to feed their large and hungry brood. In the first days, the female may need to brood the young to keep them warm, but once they are 4–5 days old both parents spend almost all the daylight hours bringing food to the nest. Caterpillars collected from the trees are the main item. If caterpillars are sufficiently plentiful, between them the parents may bring them at a rate of one every minute; at the height of the nestling period 1,000 feeding visits may be made in one 16-hour day. In spite of this, the young beg for more. In a large brood the young leave the nest lighter in weight than those of smaller broods, showing that they have not received sufficient to bring them to full weight. This has important consequences, as the heavier young have a better chance of surviving to the next breeding season. The higher survival rate comes about not merely because of better nutrition in the nest, but because the heaviest chicks (and the earliest fledged) become dominant in the feeding flocks and so have the best opportunities for displacing their weaker comrades in disputes over food. In many species of tit only one brood is raised each year, but the Great tit may raise two if feeding conditions are good when the first brood leaves the nest.

Few of the very large number of young produced survive. About 1 in 10 of the eggs laid or about 1 in 6 of the newly fledged young end up as breeding adults. Roughly 50 percent of adult birds survive the winter to breed the following summer. Thus, on average, about one bird per pair survives to breed and one egg per brood does also. Of a thousand adult Great tits entering their first winter in Central Europe, perhaps one will live to reach the age of ten.   CMP

NUTHATCHES

Family: Sittidae
Order: Passeriformes (suborder Oscines, part).
Twenty-one species in 4 genera.
Distribution: N America, Europe, N Africa, Asia, New Guinea, Australia.

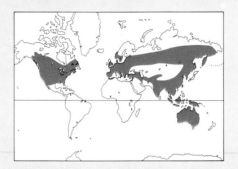

Habitat: woodlands, parks, rocks.

Size: length 4–7.5in (9.5–20cm), weight 0.35–1.75oz (10–60g).

Plumage: upperparts blue-gray; two species have a bright blue back (Azure and Velvet-fronted nuthatches); some species have a black stripe through each eye; underparts grayish white to brown. Little difference between sexes except in the Chestnut-breasted nuthatch: males chestnut underparts, females cinnamon.

Voice: repeated piping phrases, chattering calls.

Nests: the two sittellas build open nests in trees; all other species use holes in trees or rocks.

Eggs: 4–10; white with reddish spots; weight 0.04–0.09oz (1–2.5g).

Incubation period: 15–18 days (19 days in Wall creeper).

Nestling period: 23–25 days (28–29 days in Wall creeper).

Diet: insects and spiders, also seeds in autumn and winter (except in Wall creeper).

Species and genera include: **Azure nuthatch** (*Sitta azurea*), **Chestnut-breasted nuthatch** (*S. castanea*), **Corsican nuthatch** (*S. whiteheadi*), **Eastern rock nuthatch** (*S. tephronota*), **Eurasian nuthatch** (*S. europaea*), **Kabylian nuthatch** [R] (*S. ledanti*), **Red-breasted nuthatch** (*S. canadensis*), **Rock nuthatch** (*S. neumayer*), **sittellas** (genus *Neositta*), **Velvet-fronted nuthatch** (*S. frontalis*), **Wall creeper** (*Tichodroma muraria*), **White-breasted nuthatch** (*S. carolinensis*), **White-tailed nuthatch** (*S. himalayensis*).

[R] Rare

NUTHATCHES are the only birds able to climb not only up trees but also down them, headfirst. No other bird can move on trees with such versatility. The method employed differs from that of woodpeckers and treecreepers in that the tail is not used for support. When climbing the nuthatch's feet are not parallel but one is placed high, from which to hang, and the other low, for support. The word "nuthatch" is derived from the fondness of the Eurasian species for hazel nuts.

The species belonging to the main genus, *Sitta*, are so similar in form and habits that they are easily recognized as nuthatches. They are mostly gray-blue above (blue in some tropical species) with long bills and short necks. All except the Rock nuthatch and the Eastern rock nuthatch forage on trees, climbing around on trunks and thick branches. The two sittellas, which are confined to Australia and New Guinea, are similar to the true nuthatches except that they build open nests in trees, never using holes. The Wall creeper is similar to the true nuthatches in color but has a bill shaped more like that of the treecreepers. It also lives in the high mountains of Europe and Asia whereas nuthatches generally prefer woods from high altitudes down to sea level.

The Eurasian nuthatch has the most extensive range of all nuthatches, being distributed from North Africa and Spain across to Japan. The White-breasted nuthatch breeds in North America and the Chestnut-breasted nuthatch, whose behavior is similar to that of the Eurasian species, throughout the Indian subcontinent. Other species have smaller, often isolated ranges. The Wall creeper, however, has a restricted habitat but is found in high mountains from Spain across Eurasia to the eastern Himalayas.

Only a few species are known to undertake migrations. The Red-breasted nuthatch migrates from the woods of Canada as far as the southern montane woodlands of North America. In some winters the east Siberian subspecies of the Eurasian nuthatch moves west as far as Finland.

Most nuthatches eat insects and spiders; the Rock nuthatch also takes small snails. Nuthatches from more northern areas and

▶ **Descending nuthatch.** The Pygmy nuthatch (*Sitta pygmaea*) is the smallest species of nuthatch. It lives in the western USA, from the Rockies to the Pacific. Its plumage and habits are matched in the eastern USA by the Brown-headed nuthatch (*S. pusilla*).

▼ **Nuthatch postures.** (1) A solitary Corsican nuthatch feeding. The foot takes the weight of the bird, the right provides support. (2) Courtship feeding in Corsican nuthatches. (3) A Eurasian nuthatch in a threatening posture. (4) A Eurasian nuthatch making a defensive posture.

also some of the small species, for example the Corsican nuthatch, take tree seeds from the fall onwards and store them in bark crevices or under moss for later consumption. One pair of Eurasian nuthatches made a daily average of 921 collecting flights over three days, each time taking one or two sunflower seeds. The seed is hidden by covering it with bark or moss. When young hatch they are fed, in all species, by both parents on insects and spiders.

The true nuthatches are monogamous, each pair living in a territory which it will often defend throughout the year. The formation of new pairs takes place in the fall and through the winter, often in February. (In winter nuthatch pairs often associate in feeding flocks with parties of tits.) All nuthatches of the genus *Sitta* are hole-nesters, some excavating their nest-chambers in rotten wood. Rock nuthatches make a nest-chamber by closing up a rock niche with a hemispherical mud wall and entering through a specially constructed tube. Some nuthatches (eg the Eurasian nuthatch but also the Chestnut-breasted and White-tailed nuthatches) use mud to reduce the size of an entrance: the hole is covered until there is just enough space left to accommodate the width of the bird's body. Using a similar technique all cracks and small openings in the cavity are sealed. In dry periods Rock nuthatches (and also other species in Asia) use animal dung as building material, and also caterpillars, other larvae and insects which are squashed with the bill. Berries have also been found in walls made by Rock nuthatches. The White-breasted nuthatch rubs insects round the entrance hole while the Red-breasted uses smeared resin as a protection.

Inside their holes nuthatches construct nests. Various materials are used. The Eurasian nuthatch and its Asiatic relatives (such as the Chestnut-breasted and White-tailed nuthatches) make a nest of thin flakes of bark (mainly pine). Some species use fine grasses and feathers. The rock nuthatches use exclusively mammal hair and filaments, often fragmented owl pellets. North American nuthatches also use bark and animal hair.

Most pairs produce just a single brood during the breeding season, which is incubated by the female alone. During the incubation period the male brings food for the female. Both adults feed the young. The young can fly and climb well by the time they fledge. At this point they require just one week to become independent.

HL

TREECREEPERS

Families: Certhiidae, Climacteridae, Rhabdornithidae
Order: Passeriformes (suborder Oscines, part).
Fourteen species in 4 genera.
Distribution: See map and table.

► **At the nest-hole,** a female White-throated treecreeper (an Australasian treecreeper). Treecreepers' life is centered on trees, with different species sometimes concentrating on trunks or branches.

▼ **Fan-like wings spread,** a Common treecreeper (an holarctic treecreeper) returns to its nest.

TREECREEPERS are small, mostly brown birds which are usually seen climbing steadily up the trunk of a tree and along its branches, then planing down to the base of another tree to repeat the process. They have long toes with deeply curved claws for climbing, and a slightly downcurved bill for probing into crevices and under flakes of bark in search of insects. Apart from these adaptations to their niche, however, the members of the three families of treecreepers have little in common. Even their climbing techniques differ. In the Holarctic treecreepers the feet are held parallel and are moved simultaneously, whereas in the Australasian treecreepers one foot is always held in front of the other and the lower foot is brought up to the level of the upper before the latter is moved higher. Moreover most species of Australasian treecreepers spend much time on the ground.

The five species of Holarctic treecreepers belonging to the genus *Certhia* are unique among treecreepers in possessing pointed tail feathers with stiffened shafts, which are used as a prop when climbing. This adaptation is also seen in the unrelated woodpeckers and woodcreepers. The five *Certhia* species are very similar in appearance and habits, being mainly solitary. The circumpolar Common treecreeper, known as the Brown creeper in America, overlaps the range of all four of the other species to some extent. In Britain, where it is the only treecreeper, this species inhabits open deciduous woodlands, but in Europe this habitat is occupied by the Short-toed treecreeper and the Common is confined to coniferous forests. Four species occur in the Himalayas up to the timberline (about 11,500ft; 3,500m), all moving down to the foothills and adjacent plains during winter. The Himalayan treecreeper apparently favors conifers and avoids pure oak forest, where it is replaced by the Brown-throated treecreeper. The Stoliczka's treecreeper has the most restricted distribution of all, but it is not known how this bird differs from the others in its habitat or niche requirements.

Although the Spotted creeper is included in the Holarctic treecreepers it lacks the modified tail of the main genus *Certhia* and differs markedly from all other treecreepers in its nest, which is built on a horizontal branch usually in a fork. It is beautifully camouflaged, being decorated externally with spiders' eggs bags, lichen and caterpillar frass (excrement). This peculiarity suggests that it may have closer relatives in other nonclimbing families. Similarly, though once considered allied to the Australasian treecreepers, the Philippine creepers lack the sexual differences and modifications of the foot of the latter and may instead represent a branch of the diverse Asian babblers (Timaliinae). Little is known about these birds. They reputedly gather at times to visit flowering plants in open areas but their tongue is not particularly specialized for nectar-feeding. Of the two Philippine creepers the larger Plain-headed creeper prefers the higher montane forest regions, while the Stripe-headed creeper occupies lower areas.

The six species of Australasian treecreepers are all found on the Australian mainland, but one also occurs in New Guinea. They overlap little in their distribution except in southeastern Australia, where the White-throated often coexists with the Red-browed in eucalypt forests, and with the Brown in woodlands and partly cleared areas. The larger Brown is often found on the ground but the other two are similar in size and live almost entirely in trees. However, the White-throated uses rough-barked trees more than the Red-browed, preferring the fibrous bark of the trunk, while the latter concentrates on the smooth branches of such trees.

The White-throated treecreeper is the only species that occurs in rain forests and possibly had a different ancestor to the other

Australasian treecreepers. It differs in many respects, including patterns of sexual differences, juvenile plumage and egg coloration. In the White-throated, females have an orange spot on the cheek while females of the other species are characterized by rufous stripes on the chest. Juvenile White-throated treecreepers have whitish streaks on the scapular feathers (above the shoulders) and a bright chestnut patch on the rump (in females), features lacking in the other species. In contrast with the other species, the White-throated has relatively unmarked eggs, and only the female builds the nest. It has a much longer incubation period, a special territorial display, and calls specific to each sex. Moreover, it roosts externally whereas the other species generally sleep inside hollow spouts.

Social organization varies greatly among the Australasian treecreepers. The White-throated breeds in pairs but is normally solitary during the nonbreeding season. By contrast, the Red-browed and Brown treecreepers live in pairs or groups of up to six. These groups usually consist of the breeding pair and their male offspring, females tending to disperse in their first year. Both species breed communally, nonbreeding birds feeding the incubating female and young. In the Brown, however, birds sometimes attend two nests in different territories contemporaneously. This unique behavior results from, firstly, some birds continuing to attend nests in their natal territory even after they have become breeders with their own separate territory, and secondly some nonbreeders attending the young of their brothers or stepbrothers, as well as their father. The parents benefit from this "help" from these extra attendants but the latter may also benefit in the future from the help of the young they attend. RAN

The 3 Families of Treecreepers

Australasian treecreepers
Family: Climacteridae
Six species of the genus *Climacteris*.
Australia and New Guinea. Forest and woodland. Size: 5–7.5in (12–19cm) long, weight 0.7–1.4oz (20–40g). Plumage: upperparts brown to black, underparts striped or rufous; broad, pale wing-bar. Voice: loud piping notes, trills, chatters; harsh grates, rattles. Nest: cup in hole of tree or hollow branch. Eggs: 2–3, white with sparse brown dots (White-throated treecreeper) or pinkish, densely marked with red-brown and lilac-gray; incubation period: 16–23 days; nestling period: 25–26 days.

Diet: insects (especially ants).

Species include: **Brown treecreeper** (*Climacteris picumnus*), **Red-browed treecreeper** (*C. erythrops*), **White-throated treecreeper** (*C. leucophaea*).

Holarctic treecreepers
Family: Certhiidae
Six species in 2 genera.
Eurasia to Indo-China, Africa, N America. Forest, woodland. Size: 5–6in (12–15cm) long, weight 0.25–0.6oz (7–16g). Plumage: upperparts brown, underparts paler in *Certhia*; blackish spotted white in *Salpornis*. Voice: high-pitched, thin whistles and songs. Nest: cup on a loose platform of twigs, usually wedged against a tree trunk behind a flap of loose bark in *Certhia*; cup cemented to a horizontal branch with cobwebs, decorated on the outside in *Salpornis*. Eggs: in *Certhia* 3–9 (usually 5 or 6), white with red-brown dots; in *Salpornis* 2 or 3, pale turquoise with black and lilac markings; incubation period: 14–15 days; nestling period: 15–16 days. Diet: insects and spiders.

Species include: **Brown-throated treecreeper** (*Certhia discolor*), **Common treecreeper** or **Brown creeper** (*C. familiaris*), **Himalayan treecreeper** (*C. himalayana*), **Short-toed treecreeper** (*C. brachydactyla*), **Spotted creeper** (*Salpornis spilonotus*), **Stoliczka's treecreeper** (*C. nipalensis*).

Philippine creepers
Family: Rhabdornithidae
Two species of the genus *Rhabdornis*.
Philippine Islands. Forest, second growth. Size: 5–6in (13–15cm) long. Plumage: upperparts brown, underparts white with blackish streaks on flanks. Voice: unknown. Nest: holes in trees. Eggs: unknown. Diet: unknown.

Species: **Plain-headed creeper** (*Rhabdornis inornatus*), **Stripe-headed creeper** (*R. mystacalis*).

WHITE-EYES
AND THEIR ALLIES

**Families: Zosteropidae, Dicaeidae,
Pardalotidae, Nectariniidae**
Order: Passeriformes (suborder Oscines, part).
Two hundred and fifty-five species in 24
genera.
Distribution: see maps and table.

White-eyes   Flowerpeckers

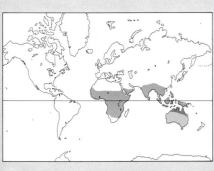

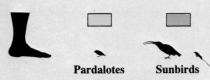

Pardalotes   Sunbirds

▶ **Extremely common and very well known**
ABOVE in eastern Africa (Abyssinia to South
Africa) is the Pale white-eye (*Zosterops
pallida*). Here one is seen taking pollen from a Bird of
paradise flower (*Strelitzia reginae*) in South
Africa. Otherwise this species eats mainly soft
fruit and berries.

▶ **Pardalotes are confined to Australia** BELOW
with the Spotted pardalote (*Pardalotus
punctatus*) being restricted to eastern Australia.
It is a fairly sedentary species which lives in
forests and woodlands, but its habits are both
arboreal and terrestrial. Here a male is seen
looking out of his nest-hole.

WHITE-EYES—small greenish birds with
white eye-rings—forage in gardens
and forest edges, and flock around bird
tables in parts of Africa, Asia, New Guinea,
Australia and South Pacific islands. They
have short, pointed bills and brush-tipped
tongues, with which to collect nectar. They
also hunt insects and spiders by gleaning
foliage, probing into small crevices and
hawking. They appear in orchards and eat
fruits as well as aphids. With versatile feeding habits they exploit a variety of resources
to survive, and breed even on small wooded
islands where most other passerines fail to
establish themselves.

Some white-eyes on continents migrate
regularly in winter to lower latitudes,
though part of the population remains
resident in the cold region. They also disperse in flocks to remote islands. In the
1850s white-eyes from Tasmania colonized
New Zealand across 1,200mi (2,000km) of
sea. Successive generations on oceanic
islands and isolated mountains differentiated into new forms by becoming large (eg
the Black-capped speirops) and/or losing
certain pigments from plumage (eg the Cinnamon white-eye) or even the white eye-
ring (eg Olive black-eye). As such differenti-
ations take place in a relatively short geo-
logical time, successive invasions of original
stock have led to the present coexistence of
two or three species on some islands. Yet the
similarities between some distant species,
resulting from convergence, are so remarkable that it is often difficult to establish true
affinities among them.

Most white-eyes pair for life and breed in
small territories. Members of a pair often
perch together and preen each other. On
Heron Island, Great Barrier Reef, where the
Gray-breasted white-eye maintains a very
high density with more than 400 adults in
40 acres (16ha), they attempt to nest two
or three (occasionally four) times between
September and March (southern summer).
From a clutch of three eggs, two young usually fledge after 11 days of incubation and
12 days of feeding in the nest by both
parents. Birds nesting in their first year produce fewer young than older birds (they have
fewer clutches); when an adult loses its
mate it tends to pair with another bird of
similar age rather than a first year bird. Very
few change partners. Juveniles suffer a
higher mortality than adults, but for those
that survive the first year the mortality rate
remains constant thereafter and the oldest
birds die in the 10th or 11th year. In cyclone
years the population is reduced considerably, but it recovers in the following year

after an extended breeding season.

The same ritualized form of aggression
used in territorial defense is used in winter
when fighting over food. Aggressive birds
flutter their wings at their opponent. Equally
matched birds may take to the air to fight,
after a period of mutual display. Sometimes
they supplant a feeding bird or attack and
chase an approaching bird with beak clatter
or challenge calls.

Some specialized species on islands are in
danger of extinction as their population size
is small and their available habitats are
being destroyed through local development.
The Norfolk white-throated white-eye of
Norfolk Island, the largest member of the
genus *Zosterops*, is one such species. White-
eyes are kept as cage-birds in some Asian
countries because of their attractive songs.
However, they do not breed in aviaries.

Although they are considered pests by orchard-keepers they also consume large quantities of pest insects wherever they occur.   JKi

Flowerpeckers are small dumpy birds, associated with mistletoes, berry-bearing shrubs, trees and vines. They also visit flowers for small insects and possibly nectar. Hence they are called flowerpeckers, berry-peckers and the Mistletoe bird. Thirty-five species belong to the main genus *Dicaeum*, distributed in southern Asia and the islands, east and south to New Guinea and Australia. Many of them are notable as seed dispersers. The Mistletoe bird in Australia excretes a mistletoe seed within half an hour of ingesting a berry. It occurs wherever mistletoes grow, be it the arid center of the continent or the rain forest of the tropical coast. It is only absent from Tasmania, where mistletoe is absent. The greatest variety of flowerpecker species is seen in New Guinea where there are eight species of berrypeckers belonging to four genera. In some berrypeckers the sexes have a different appearance with females duller and larger (an unusual character for passerine birds). The Crested berrypecker is the only crested member of the family and is much larger than the others. It was once placed in a separate family of its own (Paramythiidae).

Flowerpeckers and berrypeckers generally nest in pairs and outside the breeding season they form small flocks or sometimes congregate in large numbers on fruiting shrubs.   JKi

The **pardalotes** are often grouped with flowerpeckers because they have small bodies with stumpy bills and short tails, and plumage having some bright colors and 9 instead of 10 primary flight feathers. These features are now considered to be a result of convergence rather than revealing affinities with flowerpeckers. Biological analysis showed that they are not members of the flowerpeckers as was once thought. Unlike flowerpeckers they forage in outer foliage for small insects and nest in hollows or burrows. Strictly endemic to Australia, the pardalotes probably evolved in association with eucalypts and acacia from among the old passerine colonizers of Australia. Their distinct territorial calls and displays at nest-sites are features of the Australian bushlands (they are absent from rain forest in the breeding season, which starts in winter in the subtropical region and extends to spring and summer in southern parts of the range). The Striated paradalote has several distinct geographical subspecies which were once treated as separate species. However, where their ranges overlap they hybridize.

JKi

Sunbirds are small, brightly colored, nectar-feeding birds of the Old World tropics. As the ecological counterparts of hummingbirds of the New World, sunbirds are closely associated with flowers that depend on them for pollination and offer large quantities of nectar as the tempting reward.

Africa and its islands are the home of most sunbirds (76 of 116 species), but other species inhabit the Middle East, India, Ceylon, the Himalayas, Burma through Malaysia, the East Indies, New Guinea and Australia. The Palestine sunbird alone is found in Israel and Palestine. Many colorful, long-tailed species of the genus *Aethopyga* occur in India and the Himalayas, while spider-hunters are restricted to Malaysia.

The largest sunbird is the Giant sunbird, which is restricted to the island of Sao Tomé in the Gulf of Guinea. Other large, spectacular species, the Golden-winged sunbird, Scarlet-tufted malachite sunbird and Tacazze sunbird live in the mountains of East Africa. Three medium-sized species of West Africa, the Superb sunbird, Splendid sunbird and Johanna's sunbird, and several Himalayan species are renowned for their spectacular colors. Most highly colored species in Africa are found in open habitats while plain-colored species inhabit shady forests.

Spider-hunters lack the bright plumage colors of other sunbirds and their bills are larger, stronger and downcurved. They feed primarily on spiders as their name implies. Their nests are cup-shaped like those of many passerine birds, not hanging, bag-like structures. Both sexes incubate, unlike other sunbirds where this is the job of the female.

Sunbirds are small to very small birds with long, thin, curved bills. Fine serrations on the edges of the delicate bill help to capture and hold insects. The nostrils are covered by flaps (opercula) which keep out flower pollen. The tongue is mostly tubular except for its split tips. Sunbirds have strong feet with short toes and sharp claws that aid difficult perching while feeding at flowers.

▶ **Sunbird feeding territories** in central Kenya. Golden-winged sunbirds feed at flowers of the mint *Leonotis nepetifolia* during months when flowers and nectar are scarce in their mountain habitats. The number of flowers in a territory is predictably close to the number required to supply a sunbird's daily energy needs. As the number of new flowers on a site changes from day to day the boundaries of the territory expand or contract.

Territorial defense requires constant vigil and also investment of energy in frequent chases and eviction of intruders of several species of sunbirds, which try to feed at the same nectar-rich flowers. Golden-winged sunbirds invest energy in territorial defense when they expect to recover that investment plus some "profit." Return on the investment derives from being able to obtain more nectar from undefended flowers and being able to rest rather than feed as a result. When Golden-winged sunbirds can get adequate nectar from flowers that are common property they do not defend a territory but instead share flowers with others.

▶ **A Greater double-collared sunbird** (*Nectarinia afra*), an African species.

The 4 Families of White-eyes, Flowerpeckers and Sunbirds   Ⓡ Rare.

White-eyes and allies
Family: Zosteropidae
Eighty-five species in 11 genera. Africa, Asia, New Guinea, Australia, Oceania (introduced to Hawaii). Woodland, forest, gardens. Size: 4–5.5in (10–14cm), weight 0.3–1.1oz (8–13g); in some species females are smaller than males. Plumage: greenish with yellow, gray, white and brown parts; most species have a conspicuous white ring round the eye; in some species males are brighter than females. Voice: males produce a rich warbling song at dawn; a high-pitched plaintive note is produced for keeping contact across long distances; other distinct notes used in alarm, distress and for courtship; beak clatter also used in aggression. Nest: cup shape, slung in a tree fork under cover. Eggs: 2–4, whitish or pale blue without spots (2 species have spotted eggs); size: 0.5 × 0.4in to 0.8 × 0.6in (1.4 × 1cm to 2 × 1.5cm); incubation period: 10–12 days; nestling period: 11–13 days. Diet: insects, nectar, berries; fruits in winter.

Species include: **Black-capped speirops** (*Speirops lugubris*), **Gray-breasted white-eye** (*Zosterops lateralis*), **Cinnamon white-eye** (*Hypocryptadius cinnamomeus*), **Norfolk white-throated white-eye** (*Zosterops albogularis*), **Olive black-eye** (*Chlorocharis emiliae*). Total threatened species: 4.

Flowerpeckers and allies
Family: Dicaeidae
Forty-nine species in 6 genera. Southern Asia, New Guinea, Australia. Woodland, forest. Size: 3–6in (8–15cm), weight 0.2–0.7oz (5–20g); Crested berrypecker is 8.3in (21cm) long, weight 1.5oz (42g). Plumage: upperparts dark and glossy, underparts light; in species with dull plumage no difference between sexes, in others males have patches of bright colors. Voice: faint metallic notes and high-pitched twittering; some species produce series of rapid oscillating notes. Nests: open, cup-shaped or pendant with a side entrance. Eggs: 1–3, white with or without brownish blotches; 0.6 × 0.4in to 1.2 × 0.8in (1.5 × 1cm to 3 × 2.1cm); incubation period: 12 days; nestling period: about 15 days. Diet: berries (swallowed whole), insects, spiders.

Species include: **Crested berrypecker** (*Paramythia montium*), **Mistletoe bird** (*Dicaeum hirundinaceum*).

Pardalotes or diamond birds
Family: Pardalotidae
Five species of the genus *Pardalotus*. Australia. Woodland and forest. Size: 3–5in (8–12cm) long, weight 0.3–0.5oz (8–13g). Plumage: back is slate to olive, head and wings black with white spots or stripes, bright yellow or orange patches; females duller than males in some species. Voice: 2–5 distinct notes, repeated. Nests: cup-shaped or dome-shaped, placed in tree hollow or at the end of a tunnel 16–28in (40–70cm) long dug in a bank or down from the surface of sand. Eggs: 3–5, white; 0.6 × 0.5in to 0.7 × 0.6in (1.6 × 1.3cm to 1.9 × 1.5cm); incubation period: 14–16 days; nestling period: about 25 days. Diet: small insects and spiders.

Species include: **Striated pardalote** (*Pardalotus striatus*).

Sunbirds and spider-hunters
Family: Nectariniidae
One hundred and sixteen species in 6 genera. Old World tropics, from Africa to N Australia including Himalayas. Lowland forest, second growth, gardens, thornscrub, moorlands, rhododendron forest. Size: 3.5–12in (9–30cm) long including the tail, which accounts for about a third of length; weight 0.2–0.7oz (5–20g). Plumage: males are bright iridescent blue and green, often with bright red, yellow or orange underparts; females usually duller—olive green, gray or brown with tinges of yellow below and some streaks or spots; the colors of some males are highlighted by yellow or red display tufts at the bend of the wings and by long central tail feathers; male spider-hunters lack metallic colors as do some forest sunbirds of Africa. Voice: produce sharp and metallic songs—loud, high pitched, fast and tinkling. Nests: purse-shaped structure, embedded or suspended; side entrance is often covered with a porch-like projection; often decorated or held together by spider webs; nests of spider-hunters are cup-shaped. Eggs: 2, sometimes 3, whitish or bluish white with heavy dark spots, blotches or streaks; incubation period: 13–15 days; nestling period: 14–19 days. Diet: flower nectar and insects especially spiders; rarely fruit.

Species and genera include: **Amani sunbird** Ⓡ (*Anthreptes pallidigaster*), **Giant sunbird** (*Nectarinia thomensis*), **Golden-winged sunbird** (*N. reichenowi*), **Johanna's sunbird** (*N. johannae*), **Palestine sunbird** (*N. osea*), **Scarlet-tufted malachite sunbird** (*N. johnstoni*), **spider-hunters** (genus *Arachnothera*), **Splendid sunbird** (*N. coccinigastra*), **Superb sunbird** (*N. superba*), **Tacazze sunbird** (*N. tacazze*).

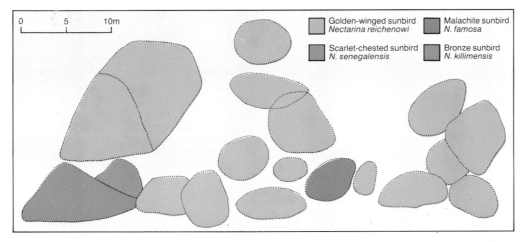

Golden-winged sunbird
Nectarina reichenowi

Malachite sunbird
N. famosa

Scarlet-chested sunbird
N. senegalensis

Bronze sunbird
N. killimensis

The variable tail shapes include long central feathers in males of some species.

Although many sunbirds aggregate in large numbers at suitable flowers, they rarely form cohesive flocks. Some species, especially insect-eating species of *Anthreptes*, participate in parties of mixed species. Many species are highly nomadic and are known to wander great distances in search of nectar.

Sunbirds feed on insects and nectar. Even subtle differences in sunbird bill sizes affect abilities to feed at different kinds of flowers. Small, short-billed sunbirds find insects in the foliage and extract minute volumes of nectar from small insect-pollinated flowers. Large, long-billed species depend more on nectar in large, conspicuous red or orange flowers with long corollas that should exclude short-billed species. Short-billed sunbirds, however, often pierce the bases of these flowers to obtain the nectar. Sunbirds normally perch while feeding at flowers; they rarely hover like hummingbirds. Typical sunbird flowers in Africa include species of the following: *Erythrina*, *Spathodia* and *Symphonia*.

Many mistletoe flowers depend on sunbirds for pollination. They literally explode when a sunbird visits them. A new mistletoe flower houses spring-like filaments and anthers bearing pollen. When a sunbird pokes its long bill into one of the slits on the side of the flower, the trap is sprung and the flower bursts open to spray a cloud of fresh pollen onto the forehead of the sunbird for transport to another flower.

Studies in Kenya of sunbirds feeding at one mistletoe (*Loranthus dshallensis*) revealed that whereas young sunbirds exploded flower after flower in their own faces and became covered with pollen, adults often ducked quickly after they tripped the trigger.

Nesting by sunbirds is related to rainfall and in turn to peaks in the availability of flowers and insects. Some species may breed at almost any time of the year, and pairs may renest up to five times in succession. In contrast to hummingbirds, which are promiscuous, sunbirds are monogamous. Male sunbirds feed their young, but do not help with nest-building or incubation. Instead they often defend flowers which are their mate's energy supply.

Breeding male sunbirds have a reputation for being extremely pugnacious. Subordinate species in East Africa may breed successfully only when large dominant species do not usurp their nectar supplies.

FBG

HONEYEATERS AND AUSTRALIAN CHATS

Families: Meliphagidae, Ephthianuridae
Order: Passeriformes (suborder Oscines, part).
One hundred and seventy-four species in 40
genera.
Distribution: see map and table.

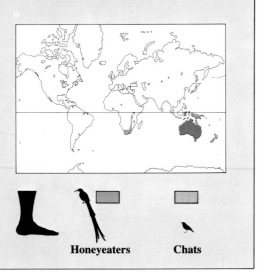

Honeyeaters   Chats

▶ **The Orange chat** ABOVE is a brilliant
inhabitant of a dull, arid habitat.

▶ **Sweet tastes** BELOW are evident in the diet of
Lewin's honeyeater (*Meliphaga lewini*). Here one
is eating a paw-paw fruit. The species eats
mostly fruit but also honey and insects. It
inhabits rain forest in eastern Australia.

▷ **Dining on waratah** OVERLEAF a Noisy
friarbird (*Philemon corniculatus*). Another
species of eastern Australia and southeast New
Guinea it is a raucous bird. Its bare head has
earned it the alternative common name of
leatherhead.

ONEYEATERS all have a long protrusible
tongue with a brush-like tip which they
use to extract nectar from flowers. They are
important pollinators of Australian flowers
and many have co-evolved with certain species of plants. Otherwise they are extremely
variable in size and habits. They are one of
the dominant passerine families in
Australasia and represent a very successful
adaptation to a wide variety of food-types.
Almost all feed on nectar and many on
insects and fruit, some predominantly so.

Honeyeaters are often the most numerous
species present in an area and there may be
more than 10 different honeyeater species
in 2.5 acres (1ha). None are truly terrestrial
or found in arid country, unlike their close
relatives the Australian chats, and only the
Singing honeyeater occurs in open country
and coastal dunes.

In general they are longish, streamlined
birds with long, pointed wings and undulating flight. Bold and vigorous, they have
strong legs and sharp claws which enable
them to clamber agilely around flowers and
foliage as they feed, sometimes upside-
down. Nearly all have rather long, downcurved and sharply-pointed bills, with many
variations on this shape associated with differences in diet. Most honeyeaters are drab
but a few are brightly colored, resembling
their counterparts, the sunbirds of Africa
and Asia and hummingbirds of America.

There were once at least five honeyeaters
in Hawaii but the kioea and one moho
became extinct about 1840 and two other

mohos were last seen earlier this century.
Only the ooaa still lives in the forests of
Hawaii, feeding on insects and some nectar.
Bellbirds and the starling-like tui are found
throughout New Zealand, especially in or
near forest, but the stitchbird disappeared
from mainland New Zealand around 1885
and is now confined to one offshore island.

The sugarbirds of South Africa resemble
large honeyeaters but opinion is divided as
to whether they are really members of the
family Meliphagidae or merely convergent
in appearance and habits. Recent evidence
suggests that they are not true honeyeaters.

Honeyeater diversification has been so
great that 14 of the 38 genera in this family
contain only a single species, and 10 genera
only two species each. The largest group,
the "typical" honeyeaters (*Meliphaga*), contains 36 of the 169 honeyeater species. Olive
in color and very similar in appearance,
their relationships are complex. Most are
smallish, foliage-gleaning insectivores with
relatively short, straight bills.

No honeyeater is truly solitary and some
are very gregarious. Cooperative breeding
occurs in the White-naped honeyeater and
is widespread in the miners. Species such as
the Noisy miner live in dense colonies—up
to 4 birds per acre (10 per hectare)—broken
into territorial, family groups which forage
together and unite to mob predators and
other birds. Only the female incubates and
meanwhile the males in a group may help
feed the nestlings of neighbouring groups.
Over 20 different males may help a female
with the nest and feed nestlings during a
season and the feeding rate may exceed 50
visits an hour. Even the fledglings from one
brood may feed their siblings in the next.
The groups have a clear-cut hierarchy and
sometimes indulge in elaborate communal
displays called "corroborees."

Only the two *Ramsayornis* honeyeaters
build nests with domes; all others have cup-
shaped nests. In most species the female

Honeyeaters as Pollinators

Many Australian flowers rely on honeyeaters
for pollination and reward them with copious
nectar. Some plants have only generalized
flowers (eg eucalypts), which are also visited
by insects, but others have flowers adapted to
birds, especially in the families Proteaceae and
Ericaceae. Long, narrow tubular corollas,
sometimes defended by hairs, deter insects but
not birds and are often yellow or red—a color
insects see badly. Bird-pollinated flowers are
often clumped and a banksia inflorescence
8–16in (20–40cm) long may contain over
5,000 flowers.

Bird pollination probably developed from
insect pollination, as honeyeaters evolved
from insectivorous birds. All honeyeaters still
eat insects to obtain essential nutrients
although some have become very reliant on
nectar for energy.

Pollen deposited on the forehead, face, chin
and beak of a honeyeater, often visible as a
yellow patch, is transferred to the stigmas of
the next flowers visited. Honeyeaters typically
carry thousands of pollen grains from several

different plant species at a time and their
relationships with Australian flowers are
much less specific than those between
hummingbirds and flowers in tropical
America. However, a process of co-evolution
has produced some elaborate mutual
adaptations such as the long, curved beak
which Western spinebills use to probe the
long tubular flowers of kangaroo-paws and
jug-flowers.

Some plants produce only a few flowers at
a time, albeit over prolonged periods, which
forces honeyeaters to move between plants
and promotes cross-fertilization, a genetic
advantage. Indeed, many bird-pollinated
plants are probably incapable of self-
pollination. The greater mobility of birds
makes them more effective at outcrossing
than insects and they are less affected by
adverse weather. The unpredictable climate
and flowering patterns in much of Australia
results in many honeyeaters being migratory
or nomadic as they follow the nectar flow
opportunistically.

The 2 Families of Honeyeaters and Australian Chats $\boxed{\text{E}}$ Endangered. $\boxed{\text{V}}$ Vulnerable.

Honeyeaters
Family: Meliphagidae
One hundred and sixty-nine species in 38 genera.

Australia, New Guinea, New Zealand, SW Pacific and Bonin Islands, Hawaii, Indonesia, S Africa. Mostly forest and woodlands containing nectar-producing plants such as eucalypts and banksias; some species in heathlands and open country but none fully terrestrial. Size: 3–18in (8–45cm) long (including tail of longest sugarbird), weight 0.2–5oz (6.5–150g). Plumage: most species dull green, gray or brown, some with black, white or yellow markings.

Sexes similar in most species but different in some. Voice: small species often musical, larger ones raucous. Nests: cup-shaped, built by the female. Eggs: 2 (1–4), white, pinkish or buff with reddish-brown spots; incubation period: 13–17 days; nestling period: 10–16 days (17–21 days for sugarbirds). Diet: nectar, insects and sometimes fruit.

Species and genera include: **Noisy miner** (*Manorina melanocephala*), **ooaa** $\boxed{\text{E}}$ (*Moho braccatus*), **Painted honeyeater** (*Grantiella picta*), **Singing honeyeater** (*Meliphaga virescens*), **stitchbird** $\boxed{\text{V}}$ (*Notiomystis cincta*), **tui** (*Prosthemadera novaeseelandiae*), **wattlebirds** (genus *Anthochaera*), **Western spinebill** (*Acanthorhynchus superciliosus*), **White-naped honeyeater** (*Melithreptus lunatus*), **Yellow-faced honeyeater** (*Meliphaga chrysops*), **yellow-winged honeyeaters** (genus *Phylidonyris*).

Australian chats
Family: Ephthianuridae
Five species in 2 genera.

Australia. Open scrubland, dry woodland, desert and margins of water. Size: 4–5in (10–13cm) long, weight 0.4oz (10–11g). Plumage: red, yellow or black and white; males more brightly marked than females. Voice: metallic twanging contact calls, aggressive chattering calls and high-pitched whistles. Nest: cup-shaped nest in a bush close to the ground or on ground. Eggs: usually 3–4, white or pinkish white with reddish brown spots; $\frac{1}{2}$–$\frac{3}{8}$in. Diet: insects taken on ground.

Species: **Crimson chat** (*Ephthianura tricolor*), **Gibber chat** (*Ashbyia lovensis*), **Orange chat** (*Ephthianura aurifrons*), **White-fronted chat** (*E. albifrons*), **Yellow chat** (*E. crocea*).

incubates alone but in some both sexes incubate; both parents feed the young. Most honeyeaters breed in the spring but some also breed in the fall or have protracted breeding seasons. They have a typical passerine molt after the spring breeding attempt.

Most honeyeaters are very generalized feeders, with few anatomical specializations for extracting nectar from particular types of flowers. They differ greatly in their dependence upon nectar and insects, although all take insects for the essential nutrients not present in nectar and some are almost entirely insectivorous. The widespread Singing honeyeater balances its diet between nectar, insects and fruit, while the Painted honeyeater is almost entirely fruit-eating—it is nomadic in its search for mistletoe berries.

Ecologists often divide honeyeaters into long-billed and short-billed forms. The small to medium-sized honeyeaters with rather short, straight bills (eg *Melithreptus*, *Meliphaga* and *Manorina* species) are more insectivorous in their habits and tend to segregate by habitat.

The long-billed honeyeaters eat more nectar than insects, and the small red honeyeaters and spinebills use their long, curved bills to feed from tubular flowers. This group also includes the medium-sized yellow-winged honeyeaters, which are generalized nectar-eaters visiting a wide range of flowers, and the wattlebirds which tend to prefer eucalyptus and banksia flowers.

How can several species of long-billed honeyeaters live in the same area when they are competing for a limited nectar supply? The answer seems to lie in a balance between small, efficient honeyeaters and large, aggressive ones. The larger species, such as wattlebirds, aggressively exclude other honeyeaters from dense clumps of

flowers where nectar levels are highest, but cannot defend all the flowers over a wider area. This allows the smaller honeyeaters, which can still feed profitably on the poorer nectar sources, to co-exist with larger species. Thus a hierarchy of aggression based on size maintains a diversity of birds even where nectar abundance varies greatly.

If nectar is really scarce some honeyeaters probably switch to a more insectivorous diet but most move to areas richer in nectar. In the tropical rain forests of New Guinea and northeastern Australia most honeyeaters are sedentary but in the more arid areas they are markedly nomadic. Even in the mediterranean and temperate coastal areas many honeyeaters show extensive movements. In southeastern Australia, the Yellow-faced honeyeater and the White-naped honeyeater regularly migrate northward each fall and return in spring, although some birds remain in the south during winter and elsewhere movements are purely local.

The **Australian chats** are colorful birds whose brush-tipped tongues and egg coloration suggest they may be related to honeyeaters. Males are red, yellow, or black and white, but females are duller in four of the five species. Chats live in open country, usually in groups, taking insects on the ground. They nest in low bushes, often in loose colonies. Most are well adapted to dry, even desert, conditions.

Crimson chats and Orange chats occur throughout the semi-arid saltbush, samphire and savanna of the inland plains. Highly gregarious, they sometimes form large flocks. Both species, but especially Crimson chats, are very nomadic and occasionally erupt coastwards in adverse seasons. Both sexes build the cup-shaped nest, incubate the eggs and feed the young. The rare Yellow chat is known only from swamps near the north and northeast coasts and from reeds around water in the interior.

White-fronted chats are fairly common throughout southern Australia in samphire, saltbush and the edges of swamps. Most birds breed in the south of their range. Tasmanian birds and some mainland populations are sedentary but others move northwards when not breeding.

In the more robust Gibber chat the sexes are similar in color. Their name comes from the stony Gibber plains around Lake Eyre in central Australia where they live. Some birds are sedentary but others make local movements. Breeding occurs whenever conditions are suitable, the nest being placed on the ground   RDW

BUNTINGS AND TANAGERS

Family: Emberizidae
Order: Passeriformes (suborder Oscines, part).
Five hundred and fifty-two species in 136
genera.
Distribution: Worldwide except extreme SE
Asia and Australasia.

▶ **Reed bunting** ABOVE, widespread from
Europe to East Asia. Female (here) has black
and whitish moustache streaks—males have
distinctive head markings in breeding season,
as do males of most Eurasian buntings of the
genus *Emberiza*.

▶ **Male Lapland longspur** or bunting BELOW
by nest. Females do all the incubating but males
share the feeding of young. The "long spurs"
are the elongated toes of this species.

▼ **Unique coloration** of male Painted bunting
(*Passerina ciris*), from the southern USA to
Central America: no other bird has a blue head
and red underparts. The female Painted
bunting is a brilliant yellow-green.

THE term **bunting** is derived evidently from
an old English word "buntyle," the original meaning of which is somewhat obscure.
Whatever its meaning, the name was given
to several grain-eating, ground-feeding
birds in western Europe. The name was later
carried by early settlers and pioneers from
Britain to other parts of the world and there
applied to some not particularly closely
related birds: in North America, for example, to some members of the subfamily Carduelinae, the cardinal grosbeaks. Ironically,
most true buntings of the New World are
called sparrows.

The true buntings almost certainly
evolved in the New World. More than three-quarters of the world's species are found in
the Americas, and there occupy a diverse
and broad range of habitats. Of the 60 or
so species in North America, for example, we
find species inhabiting arctic tundra, boreal
forest, prairies and meadows, deserts, alpine
meadows, salt and freshwater marshes, and
oak and pine woods. Probably, ancestral
open-country buntings crossed the Bering
Sea into Asia, the genus *Emberiza* evolving
in temperate Asia where it is best represented, and spreading westward into Europe
and Africa. Interestingly enough, there are
only a couple of buntings breeding in tropical Asia, the Crested bunting and the
Chinese blue bunting, and the group has
failed to penetrate or persist in the East
Indies–Australasia region, although the Cirl
bunting and the yellowhammer have been
introduced with some success into New
Zealand.

The true buntings are characterized by a
stout, conical bill adapted for crushing and
taking the husks off seeds. The upper and
lower parts of the bill can be moved sideways in some species; juncos for example
are particularly adept at manipulating,
cracking, and discarding the husks off seeds
with their bills. True buntings show considerable diversity in plumage and voice—
somberly plumaged species such as the Corn
bunting, dull grayish-brown with heavy
streaks, contrast with the more brightly-plumaged ones, such as the yellowhammer
with bright yellow underparts and streaked
yellow head, and the Lapland longspur with
black, chestnut and white head markings.

In temperate and arctic regions, buntings
are mostly monogamous, with a few males
attracting more than one female in some
species studied. The Lark bunting and Corn
bunting, however, are usually polygamous,
with some males reportedly attracting up to
seven females at a time, and other males
within a population attracting no female at
all. It is generally supposed that this mating
system occurs when there are large differences in quality of territory among males,
so that a female is better off pairing with an
already mated male in a good territory
rather than with a bachelor male in a poor
territory.

Most species are territorial. In migratory
species, the male arrives before the female
and defends the territory against other
males. Often the male reoccupies the same
territory he held the year before. Most breeding activities—courting, pairing, nesting,
and raising young—occur within the territory. Collecting food for young may or may
not occur within territory boundaries—
American tree sparrows defend large territories, usually more than 2.5 acres (1ha),
within which food is collected, whereas
Clay-colored sparrows defend small territories of usually less than 11,000sqft
(1,000sqm) and forage exclusively outside
the territory, often on communal feeding
grounds. Once the breeding season is over,
territorial boundaries break down and
adults and young gather together in loose
flocks.

Courtship in buntings usually involves a
male advertising his presence by singing.
When a female approaches, the male dives
and chases her through the vegetation.
These courtship chases frequently involve
the male buffeting the female, and end with
both birds tumbling to the ground in a mass
of feathers. Song flights occur in open-country species; males of Lapland longspurs,
Snow buntings in the Arctic and Chestnut-collared longspurs and Lark buntings on the

North American prairies, for example, typically rise a few yards above ground and then slowly circle back to earth, holding their wings at an angle above the body, and uttering their song.

Nests are usually placed on the ground or low in a bush, and tend to be neat compact cups built of dried vegetation (grass, weeds) and lined with hair, mosses, fine vegetation fibres, wool and/or feathers. Females are usually solely responsible for incubating eggs and brooding young, and males usually contribute substantially to feeding young, at both the nestling and the fledgling stages.

The **Plush-capped finch** is somewhat of an enigma. Little is known of its reproductive biology, vocalizations, foraging or social behavior; most of what we do know comes from collecting trips in South America and from museum specimens. Adults measure about 6in (15cm) in length, and have a striking plumage: dark gray upperparts, chestnut underparts, black nape, and yellow crown of stiff, erect, "plush-like" feathers— hence the name. In overall appearance, this bird resembles the tanagers, except that it has a short, thick, stubby bill more akin to the buntings—indeed, it appears to be a link between these two groups.

Plush-capped finches inhabit forest edges and clearings in the cloud forests of the Andes from Venezuela to northern Argentina. Reports from Colombia and Ecuador indicate that it forages close to the ground, eats insects, and occurs primarily on its own or in pairs, but will join mixed-species flocks.

RWK

THE 5 SUBFAMILIES OF BUNTINGS AND TANAGERS

Old World buntings and New World sparrows

Subfamily: Emberizinae
Two hundred and eighty-one species in 69 genera.

Practically worldwide; absent from extreme SE Asia and Australasia (introduced to New Zealand). Almost cosmopolitan in the New World: open woodlands, grasslands, arctic tundra and alpine meadows, and desert regions; primarily open country, hedgerows, parkland, "edge" habitats in Eurasia. Size: 4–8.5in (10–22cm) long; weight 0.4–1.4oz (11–40g). Plumage: ranges from dull brown and gray to bright blue-green, yellow and red; several groups have sharply patterned plumages. Voice: alarm calls usually loud and easily localized, anxiety calls frequently ventriloquial; songs short and simple to long and melodious, containing whistles, chatters and trills. Nests: woven, cup-shaped nests usually well concealed on ground or in low bush. Eggs: usually 4–6, base color off-white, light brown or light blue, usually with brownish, reddish or blackish marks; incubation period 10–14 days; nestling period 10–15 days. Diet: primarily grains; adults eat seeds and berries; nestlings are fed almost exclusively on arthropods.

Species and genera include: **American tree sparrow** (*Spizella arborea*), **Black-headed bunting** (*Emberiza melanocephala*), **Black-throated finch** (*Melanodera melanodera*), **Chestnut-collared longspur** (*Calcarius ornatus*), **Chinese blue bunting** (*Latoucheornis siemsseni*), **Cirl bunting** (*Emberiza cirlus*), **Clay-colored sparrow** (*Spizella pallida*), **Corn bunting** (*Emberiza calandra*), **Crested bunting** (*Melophus lathami*), **Galapagos finches** (*Geospiza, Camarhynchus, Certhidea, Pinaroloxias*), **Gough Island bunting** (*Rowettia goughensis*), **grassquits** (*Tiaris*), **Lapland longspur** (*Calcarius lapponicus*), **Lark bunting** (*Calamospiza melanocorys*), **Red-headed bunting** (*Emberiza bruniceps*), **Reed bunting** (*E. schoeniclus*), **Rock bunting** (*E. cia*), **Rustic bunting** (*E. rustica*), **Savanna sparrow** (*Passerculus sandwichensis*), **seedeaters** (*Sporophila*), **Snow bunting** (*Plectrophenax nivalis*), **Yellowhammer** (*Emberiza citrinella*), **Zapata sparrow** (*Torreornis inexpectata*). Total threatened species: 3.

Tanagers and honeycreepers

Subfamily: Thraupinae
Two hundred and thirty-three species in 56 genera.

Western hemisphere from Canada to northern Chile and central Argentina, including Antilles; nearly all tropical. Forests, scrub, thickets, plantations, parks, gardens; lowlands to high

Island Species

Island species are of special interest, for their rarity, or relationship to mainland species. Among buntings, the Zapata sparrow is confined to a few marshes in Cuba. The Ipswich (a subspecies of the Savanna) sparrow, occurs only on the shifting sands of windswept Sable Island, some 100mi (160km) east of Nova Scotia. The Gough Island bunting is a recent offshoot of the South American Black-throated finch, but the origins of the Tristan da Cunha species are obscure. On the Pacific Galapagos Islands, 6 of the 13 species are seed eaters, 6 insect eaters, and one insectivore occupies a woodpecker-type niche (a 14th species occupies Cocos Island, 600mi/965km northeast). In this classic adaptive radiation, mainland buntings found their way to the Galapagos Islands and in the absence of competitors evolved to fill various unoccupied niches.

RWK

mountains. Size: 3.5–11in (9–28cm) long; weight 0.3–1.4oz (8.5–40g). Plumage: exceedingly varied; many bright colors to gray, olive, black and white. Sexes alike or very different. Voice: on the whole, poorly developed, some species songless, a few persistent and pleasing songsters. Nests: usually well-made open cups in trees and shrubs, rarely in crannies. Euphonias build covered nests with side entrance. Eggs: usually 2, up to 4–5 in euphonias and the few species that breed in temperate zones; blue, blue-gray, gray or white, spotted, blotched and scrawled with lilac, brown or black; incubation period 12–18 days, nestling period 11–24 days. Diet: mainly fruits and arils, also nectar, insects.

Species include: **Blue-and-yellow tanager** (*Thraupis bonariensis*), **Blue-gray tanager** (*T. episcopus*), **chlorophonias** (*Chlorophonia* species), **Crimson-backed tanager** (*Ramphocelus dimidiatus*), **dacnises** (*Dacnis* species), **Diademed tanager** (*Stephanophorus diadematus*), **Dusky-faced tanager** (*Mitrospingus cassinii*), **flower-piercers** (*Diglossa* species), **Green honeycreeper** (*Chlorophanes spiza*), **orangequit** (*Euneornis campestris*), **Paradise tanager** (*Tangara chilensis*), **Red-legged honeycreeper** (*Cyanerpes cyaneus*), **Rose-breasted thrush tanager** (*Rhodinocichla rosea*), **Sayaca tanager** (*Thraupis sayaca*), **Scarlet tanager** (*Piranga olivacea*), **Scarlet-rumped tanager** (*Ramphocelus passerinii*), **Silver-throated tanager** (*Tangara icterocephala*), **Spot-crowned euphonia** (*Euphonia imitans*), **Summer tanager** (*Piranga rubra*), **Yellow-rumped tanager** (*Ramphocelus icteronotus*). Total threatened species: 3.

Cardinal grosbeaks

Subfamily: Cardinalinae
Thirty-seven species in 9 genera.

Central Canada to central Argentina. Temperate zone woodlands, tropical rain forests, thickets, arid scrub, plantations, gardens, fields. Size: 4.5–9.5in (11.5–24cm) long. Plumage: brilliant and varied, or olive, gray, blue-black. Males and females either alike or very different. Voice: Many are superb and persistent songsters. Nests: massive or loosely built open cups in trees and shrubs, rarely on ground. Eggs: 2–5, white, greenish, bluish, or blue, unmarked or speckled or scrawled; incubation period 11–14 days, nestling period 9–15 days. Diet: seeds and grains, fruits and insects.

Species include: **Black-headed grosbeak** (*Pheucticus melanocephalus*), **Blue-black grosbeak** (*Passerina cyanoides*), **Buff-throated saltator** (*Saltator maximus*), **cardinal** (*Cardinalis cardinalis*), **dickcissel** (*Spiza americana*), **Indigo bunting** (*Passerina cyanea*), **Painted bunting** (*P. ciris*), **pyrrhuloxia** (*Cardinalis sinuata*), **Rose-breasted grosbeak** (*Pheucticus ludovicianus*), **Yellow-green grosbeak** (*Caryothraustes canadensis*).

Swallow-tanager

Subfamily: Tersininae
Tersina viridis.

S America from eastern Panama to northern Argentina. Open woodland, clearings with scattered trees, and suburban gardens. Size: about 5in (13cm) long; weight 1–1.1oz (28–32g). Plumage: male largely iridescent turquoise blue with a black mask, black-barred sides and white abdomen; female bright green. Voice: a pebbly twitter of up to 7 syllables. Nests: a shallow cup of vegetable materials in long tunnels in masonry, cliffs or earthen banks. Eggs: 2 or 3, shiny, unmarked white, weight 0.1oz (2.8g); incubation period 13–17 days; nestling period 24 days. Diet: fruit, insects.

Plush-capped finch

Subfamily: Catamblyrhynchinae
Catamblyrhynchus diadema.

Western S America. Biology little known (see text).

► **Rainbow or Orange-breasted bunting** (*Passerina leclancherii*) of Mexico.

To contemplate the colorful, constantly changing throng of **tanagers**, peaceably eating in a tree laden with berries, is one of the delights of bird watching in the tropics. From warm lowlands to high, cold mountains, their amazingly varied plumage adds touches of warm color to the foliage of trees and shrubs. The small tanagers of the genus *Tangara* display every bright color in the most varied patterns: one of them, the Paradise tanager, is splendidly attired in scarlet, golden yellow, shining apple green, purplish blue, turquoise, and black.

Tanagers are compactly built, with short to medium-length and often rather thick bills, generally notched or hooked at the tip. Their tails are short to medium-length, and their wings have only nine primary feathers instead of the usual 10.

With one known exception (see box), even the most brilliant tropical tanagers wear the same colors throughout the year. Of the four species that nest north of Mexico, the Scarlet tanager, which performs the longest migration, shows the greatest seasonal color changes in the male—from scarlet to yellowish; male Western and Hepatic tanagers travel less far and change only slightly; male Summer tanagers winter in the tropics in their full coats of red. At the other extreme of the family's range, the three partly migratory species—Diademed, Blue-and-yellow, and Sayaca—that breed as far south as central Argentina change

▲▼► **Representative species of buntings and tanagers,** males in breeding plumage.
(1) Swallow tanager (*Tersina viridis*) catching insects. (2) Black-headed bunting (*Emberiza melanocephala*). (3) Corn bunting (*E. calandra*) in middle of "bunch-of-keys" rattling song (plumage of both sexes similar). (4) Rose-breasted thrush tanager (*Rhodinocichla rosea*) foraging in leaf litter. (5) Buff-throated saltator (*Saltator maximus*) eating a banana. (6) Rose-breasted grosbeak (*Pheucticus ludovicianus*) male in winter. (7) White-throated sparrow (*Zonotrichia albicollis*). (8) Plush-capped finch (*Catamblyrhynchus diadema*). (9) Red-legged honeycreeper (*Cyanerpes cyaneus*) feeding on nectar.

little. Wholly tropical tanagers are nonmigratory but may wander up and down the mountains with the changing seasons. In the small tanagers of genus *Tangara*, and many other tanagers that are paired throughout the year, the sexes are nearly or quite alike. Among tanagers that travel in small flocks in which pairs are not obvious, the female may be much duller than the male, as in the Scarlet-rumped tanager and the Yellow-rumped tanager.

Largely fruit-eating, the tanagers are probably by far the most important disseminators of tropical American trees and shrubs, as they do not digest the seeds that they swallow. Tanagers vary their diet with insects gleaned from foliage or caught in the air. Some work along horizontal limbs, bending over now on this side and now on that to pluck insects and spiders from the lower side. Species other than honeycreepers (see box) occasionally sip nectar. Summer tanagers, expert flycatchers, tear open wasps' nests to eat larvae and pupae. Gray-headed tanagers regularly accompany the mixed flocks of small birds that follow army ants to capture insects that the ants drive up from the ground litter. The Rose-breasted thrush-tanager is one of its few members that forage on the ground, flicking aside fallen leaves with its bill.

Although tanagers are nearly always monogamous, bigamy is occasional in the Blue-gray tanager and Scarlet-rumped tanager. Males of many species feed their mates. The open, cup-shaped nest, high in a tree or low in a shrub, rarely on the ground, is built by both sexes in many species, by the female only, attended by a songful partner, in others. The eggs, most often two in the tropical species, are laid early in the morning and incubated by the female alone, even when she is no less colorful than her mate. He frequently escorts her when she returns to her eggs. The incubation period varies with the form and situation of the nest. In low, open, thick-walled nests, such as those of the Scarlet-rumped and Crimson-backed tanagers, it is 12 days. In the smaller, usually higher, less conspicuous mossy nests of Silver-throated tanagers and other species of *Tangara*, it is usually 13 or 14 days. In the covered nests with a side entrance that euphonias hide in crannies, it is prolonged to 15 or 18 days.

The insides of the hatchlings' mouths are red. Nearly always, their father helps to feed them and to clean the nest, but only their mother broods. Sometimes a young Golden-masked tanager in immature plumage helps its parents to feed a later brood; and in this and other species of *Tangara*, as also in the Dusky-faced tanager, three or four adults may attend one or two nestlings. The nestling period varies in the same way as the incubation period; 11 or 12 days in species with low, open nests, 14 or 15 days in those whose nests are usually higher, 19 to 24 days in the covered nests of euphonias and chlorophonias.

The 25 species of euphonias differ in many ways from other tanagers. Among the smallest tanagers, they are mostly blue-black above and often also on the throat, with yellow on the forehead and sometimes also crown, and yellow underparts. Although not brilliant songsters, many utter bright, clear notes which make them attractive pets and, unhappily, sometimes lead them to be confined in miserably small cages. In addition to insects and many kinds of fruits, they eat so many mistletoe berries that they are among the chief disseminators of these abundant parasites on tropical trees. The tiny, nearly downless nestlings are fed by regurgitation rather than directly from the bill, as is usual among tanagers. When the parents arrive together with food, the male regularly feeds them first. Spot-crowned euphonias sleep singly in snug pockets in moss, instead of roosting amid

▶ **The cardinal.** Seen here beside Roosevelt Lake, Arizona, the cardinal may be found from the eastern and southern USA to Mexico, and is common in wood margins, hedgerows and suburbs. The more yellowish-brown female also has a crest and pink bill.

▼ **Electric breeding plumage** of the male Red-legged or Blue honeycreeper—the only tropical species of the subfamily whose males are known to shed their breeding plumage (for the green of the female). Long, downcurved bill points to its nectar staple diet, but honeycreepers take a wide range of other foods.

Honeycreepers

The 27 species of honeycreepers, dacnises, flower-piercers, and allies, here included with the tanagers, are often classified with the bananaquit (*Coereba flaveola*) in a separate family, the Coerebidae. With the exceptions of the Red-legged honeycreeper in Cuba and the orangequit of Jamaica, all are confined to the tropical American mainland and closely adjacent islands. Mostly under 5.5in (14cm) long, they wear varied plumage. Most colorful are the lowland honeycreepers, whose males are clad in blue, turquoise, purple, green, and yellow. Their bills are long and slightly downcurved in the four species of *Cyanerpes*, intermediate in the Green honeycreeper, short and sharp in the nine species of *Dacnis*. More frequently than tanagers with thicker bills, these birds probe flowers for nectar. They also eat much fruit, catch insects in the air, or pluck them from foliage; they come readily to feeders where fruit is displayed. They are almost or quite songless.

The 11 species of the less colorful but more tuneful flower-piercers of the genus *Diglossa*, attired largely in blue, cinnamon, olive, and black, prefer cooler regions where flowers abound, from the upper levels of the tropical zone to the chilly *páramos*. Their queer, uptilted bills are efficient instruments for extracting nectar from tubular flowers. The tip of the upper mandible hooks over the tube and holds it while the sharp lower mandible pierces the corolla, and the two tubes of the tongue suck out the sweet liquid. Thus, they take nectar from the flower without pollinating it. Small flying insects balance their diet. They lay two eggs in thick-walled open cups at the same time as their neighbors the hummingbirds do, at a season when few other birds are breeding. Also like hummingbirds, whose diet closely resembles theirs, they feed their nestlings by regurgitation instead of directly from the bill, like other honeycreepers.   AFS

foliage like other tanagers. The chlorophonias of wet mountain forests are essentially, as their name implies, green euphonias (adorned with blue and yellow), and have quite similar habits. AFS

Among the **cardinal grosbeaks** are familiar birds of suburban gardens in temperate North America and little-known species in tropical rain forests. A favorite is the high-crested, black-throated cardinal, who wears his warm red plumage amid winter's snow. His mate is much duller. Thanks largely to people who provide seeds in winter, during the last century the cardinal has extended its breeding range from the Ohio Valley to above the Great Lakes in southern Canada. Along the USA–Mexican border, it coexists

with the equally high-crested and thick-billed pyrrhuloxia, more gray than red.

The lovely little buntings of the genus *Passerina* live chiefly in the USA and Mexico. One of the most elegant, the Painted bunting, has a blue head, yellow-green mantle, red rump and underparts, and dark wings and tail. The almost solid-blue male Indigo bunting, which nests in bushy places through much of the eastern half of the USA, wears a brownish dress much like the female's in its winter home in southern Mexico and Central America. Also highly migratory is the Rose-breasted grosbeak, which after nesting in woodland edges and similar habitats in the northeastern USA and southern Canada travels as far as Venezuela and Peru. In winter plumage, males retain enough red on their breasts to distinguish them from the browner females. Equally migratory is the dickcissel, which sings its name in open fields chiefly in the Mississippi Valley and winters as far south as Venezuela and Trinidad, in vast numbers where rice is grown, sometimes causing heavy losses. Huge numbers roost on sugarcane leaves in neighboring fields.

Among the nonmigratory tropical members of this subfamily are the Blue-black grosbeak and his brown mate, both of whom sing beautifully in rain forests and bushy clearings. They eat maize, whether in the milk or dry, but, not being gregarious, they do only slight damage to the crop. More closely confined to mid and upper levels of

rain forests is the Slate-colored grosbeak, whose nearly uniformly dark bluish gray plumage contrasts with his heavy, bright red bill.

Most cardinal grosbeaks consume many insects and soft fruits as well as weed seeds and grains. More closely allied to the tanagers in their preference for fruits, although least like them in their largely grayish and olive-green plumage, often with a white eyebrow, are the dozen species of saltators, which inhabit semi-open and scrub country through much of tropical America. The widespread Buff-throated saltator is a frequent attendant at feeders where bananas are offered. Never having learned to hold food with a foot while they prepare it for eating, these birds and some of their relatives rest a fruit precariously on a horizontal branch while they bite off pieces.

The social habits of cardinal grosbeaks vary greatly. Solitary and pugnacious in the breeding season, lovely male Painted buntings may occasionally wound and even kill their adversaries. At the other extreme are Yellow-green grosbeaks, who at all seasons travel in loose flocks through rain forests and shady clearings, displaying no territorial exclusiveness. Parents feeding nestlings are joined by one or more helpers.

The cup-shaped nest is usually built by the female, but male cardinals and Blue-black grosbeaks share the task. Although in most species only the female incubates, male Rose-breasted and Black-headed grosbeaks take turns on the eggs, often singing while they sit. Male cardinals, Buff-throated saltators and Blue-black grosbeaks bring food to their incubating partners. Nearly always the father helps to feed the young, but male Painted buntings are unreliable attendants, and the polygamous male dickcissel neglects his offspring. AFS

In plumage the **swallow-tanager** resembles tanagers, but differs in its broad, flat bill and pointed, swallow-like wings. Like tanagers, they eat much fruit; like swallows, they catch many insects in flight. From warm lowlands where they live when not breeding, they ascend into the mountains of northern South America to nest at 2,600–5,900ft (800–1,800m). The female, with token assistance by an attentive mate, builds the nest. She alone incubates but both parents feed the nestlings. Highly social birds, Swallow-tanagers engage in mass displays, all simultaneously "curtseying" or bowing deeply down and up, while facing one another or perching close together.

AFS

WOOD WARBLERS

Family: Parulidae
Order: Passeriformes (suborder Oscines, part).
One hundred and twenty species in 26 genera.
Distribution: N and S America, the West Indies.

Habitat: forests and brushlands.

 Size: 4–7in (10–18cm) long, weight 0.2–0.9oz (7–25g), sexes similar.

Plumage: among the brightest of North American birds. Female plumage usually similar to male's but duller.

Voice: distinct musical songs, often more than one per species; a wide variety of call notes.

Nest: well built, in tree or on ground.

Eggs: 2–8 (usually 4–5); white to green, usually with brown spots or splashes.

Incubation period: 10–14 days; nestling period: 8–12 days.

Diet: invertebrates, especially insects; some fruit.

Species include: **American redstart** (*Setophaga ruticilla*), **Bachman's warbler** E (*Vermivora bachmanii*), **Black-and-white warbler** (*Mniotilta varia*), **Blackpoll warbler** (*Dendroica striata*), **Kirtland's warbler** E (*D. kirtlandii*) **Olive warbler** (*Peucedramus taeniatus*), **ovenbird** (*Seiurus aurocapillus*), **Semper's warbler** E (*Leucopeza semperi*) **Tennessee warbler** (*Vermivora peregrina*), **Yellow-rumped warbler** (*Dendroica coronata*).

E Endangered.

► **Bill-full of grubs** from mother Yellow warbler (*Dendroica petechia*) for her young, as father looks on. Females are responsible for incubation at the well-constructed nest, and for most feeding of the newly hatched young; males make greater feeding contributions as the young grow. After fledging, some of the young may disperse with their mother, the rest with the father. They may be fed for up to two weeks after leaving the nest. Warblers are typically single-brooded in the temperate zone, but will nest again if the nest is broken up—as quite frequently happens—by other birds, mammals or snakes.

Wood warblers are of great interest to birders and professionals alike, because of their bright plumage and large number of species. They are the most diverse and abundant family of forest-dwelling birds breeding in eastern North America: five to six nesting species of a single genus, *Dendroica*, may constitute as much as 70 percent of the birds occupying the region's spruce forests.

Western North America has a poorer wood warbler fauna, which declines as one proceeds into Mexico, Central America, and South America. High-latitude breeders migrate to warmer climes for the northern winter, the majority wintering within the tropics. Numbers of migrants also decline markedly as one moves from Mexico and northern Central America southward. Few winter south of the Equator.

With few exceptions, wood warblers are small foliage-gleaners. Their bill is generally narrow and pointed, although species that capture much of their food on the wing have a broad bill like that of the tyrant flycatchers. The ovenbird and waterthrushes are largely ground foragers, with a life-style similar to that of thrushes. The Black-and-white warbler has even adopted a nuthatch-like life-style, and moves about easily on trunks and large limbs.

As a group, the warblers have some of the brightest and most variable plumages of North American passerine families. Colors include yellow and blue in abundance, with red and orange as well. Males and females often have similar plumage, but in migratory species males are brighter than females. Many have conspicuous wing and tail markings of white, or, less frequently, yellow. Young usually resemble females until their first breeding season, when they molt into adult plumage. However, the American redstart and the Olive warbler have subadult male plumages and do not molt into the adult male plumage until their second breeding year. Ground-dwellers, such as the ovenbird and waterthrushes, have plumage of olive, brown and dull white, spotted below (hence "-thrush").

The life spans of warblers are poorly known. The oldest bird known in the wild is a Black-and-white warbler that lived at least 11 years and three months. However, most warblers that fledge are unlikely to breed more than once. All species probably breed the year following their birth, although first-year males of some species have lower opportunities of breeding than older individuals.

Warblers are first and foremost insect feeders, and this habit accounts for their strongly migratory habit at high latitudes. Some feed partially on fruit outside the breeding season, a few on nectar or pollen. The Yellow-rumped warbler subsists on fruits, largely bayberry or wax myrtle, during the winter. Elsewhere, a few will feed on nectar or pollen at this time. In fact, the faces and throats of many Tennessee warblers, otherwise white, olive, and gray, become yellow or red from pollen as a consequence of feeding at flowers during the tropical winter.

Some warblers have elaborate courtship maneuvers, consisting of intricate flight patterns. Prior to mating, the songs of some species differ from the songs usually sung after breeding, which suggests the importance of song in courtship. A well-constructed nest is built either in trees or on the ground. Females are largely or totally responsible for brooding, and the newly-hatched young are fed mainly by the females, but males make greater feeding contributions as the young grow. After fledging, some of the young may disperse with the female, the others with the male. They may be fed for as much as two weeks after leaving the nest. Warblers are typically single-brooded in the temperate zone, but will nest again if their nests are broken up. Predation on nests by birds, mammals or snakes appears to be heavy.

Warblers are intensely territorial during the breeding season, but later in the year may join flocks led by chickadees and titmice. Yellow-rumped warblers frequently form large, unstable, single species flocks, which move about rapidly. Many warblers join flocks of other species on their tropical wintering grounds, often one per flock, suggesting that they are aggressive towards their own species at this time.

Although some warblers are among the most abundant of North American birds, a few species are rare or endangered. The Kirtland's warbler has declined to a few hundred known birds, which breed in a few Michigan counties.

In fact, habitat destruction on the wintering grounds may provide a serious threat to many species of wood warblers. Neotropical forests are being destroyed at an alarming rate, to the point that few will remain by the year 2000, unless unforeseen changes occur. This area includes Mexico and northern Central America, where a high proportion of warblers winter. Some thrive in second-growth vegetation, but others appear dependent on the pristine forest, and are likely to disappear with those forests.

DHM

VIREOS

Family: Vireonidae
Forty-three species in 4 genera.
Order: Passeriformes (suborder Oscines, part).
Distribution: N, C and S America, West Indies (Vireoninae only).

Habitat: scrub, woodlands, forests.

Size: Vireoninae (true vireos and greenlets): 4–6in (10.2–15.3cm) long, weight 0.3–0.7oz (9–22g); Cyclarhinae (pepper-shrikes): 5–6.5in (12.7–16.5cm) long, 0.6–1.3oz (20–39g); Vireolaniinae (shrike-vireos): 5–6.5in (12.7–16.5cm) long, 0.7–1.2oz (22–36g); males and females similar in size.

Plumage: chiefly green above, but some species of *Vireo* are gray or brown on the back; yellow or white on belly. Males and females similar but male Black-capped vireo has a black crown (female gray), and male Chestnut-sided shrike-vireo much wider and brighter barring on throat, breast and "face" than females.

Voice: rarely musical, repetitive song of the same or different whistled or "burry" notes (a gravelly roll to certain syllables); up to 15 different calls in some species.

Nest: bag-like, suspended by rim from fork.

Eggs: 2 in tropical species to 4–5 in northern species; whitish with brown spots at the broad end; incubation period 11–13 days; nestling period 11–13 days.

Diet: arthropods and some fruit in summer and winter.

Species include: **Bell's vireo** (*Vireo bellii*), **Black-billed pepper-shrike** (*Cyclarhis nigrirostris*), **Black-capped vireo** (*Vireo atricapillus*), **Black-whiskered vireo** (*V. altiloquus*), **Blue mountain vireo** (*V. osburni*), **Chestnut-sided shrike-vireo** (*Vireolanius melitophrys*), **Cozumel vireo** (*Vireo bairdi*), **Gray-headed greenlet** (*Hylophilus decurtatus*), **Gray vireo** (*Vireo vicinior*), **Hutton's vireo** (*V. huttoni*), **Jamaica vireo** (*V. modestus*), **Philadelphia vireo** (*V. philadelphicus*), **Red-eyed vireo** (*V. olivaceus*), **Rufous-browed pepper-shrike** (*Cyclarhis gujanensis*), **Scrub greenlet** (*Hylophilus flavipes*), **Solitary vireo** (*Vireo solitarius*), **Warbling vireo** (*V. gilvus*), **White-eyed vireo** (*V. griseus*), **Yucatan vireo** (*V. magister*).

VIREOS are small scrub and forest songbirds restricted to the New World. Most have stout, fairly heavy to quite heavy beaks; those of pepper-shrikes, shrike-vireos, the Blue Mountain vireo, and some races of the Black-whiskered vireo are almost massive. The beak of most true vireos is characterized by a tiny hook on the cutting edge at the tip of the upper mandible—a feature found in pepper-shrikes and shrike-vireos as well, but lacking in greenlets.

Greenlets are more uniform in color—greenish on the back with varying amounts of yellow buff and white on the face and underparts—than are vireos, which have plumage of these colors as well, but also include species which are brown (Cozumel vireo) or gray (Gray vireo) above. True vireos differ further from greenlets by the presence of whitish or yellowish eye-stripes or eye-rings and all but the Red-eyed vireo and its closest relatives also have faint to strongly marked wing bars. Wing bars are lacking in greenlets, pepper-shrikes and shrike-vireos, but the pepper-shrikes have a distinctive, reddish stripe above the eyes and shrike-vireos have strongly patterned facial and crown markings of yellow, bluish-green, or chestnut.

To a varying degree all vireos appear to eat some fruit. Arthropods are taken mostly from leaves and twigs by Red-eyed and White-eyed vireos; Red-eyed, Solitary and Yellow-throated vireos forage mostly in treetops, whereas White-eyed vireos and other closely related scrub-dwelling species forage low in vegetation. Out of the whole family, only the Gray vireo takes prey from the ground and then only in about 5 percent of its foraging bouts. Greenlets generally either take arthropods in low scrub or forage high in the canopy. Vireos also flycatch, taking insects on the wing. Pepper-shrikes and shrike-vireos apparently only glean prey from leaves, twigs, branches, trunks and flower parts. Other than on migration, vireos are not noted for long-distance flights; the Gray vireo, however, may fly several hundred feet at a time within its territory—up to 20 acres (8ha)—in the desert scrub and canyon country it favors.

Tropical and subtropical vireos and their allies, as far as is known, are territorial all the year round, gathering in pairs or family groups. The temperate zone resident, Hutton's vireo, forms winter flocks with chickadees, nuthatches and kinglets. Red-eyed vireos and their close relatives form small flocks in winter moving from one fruiting tree to another. The remaining migrant species maintain winter territories which are defended against other individuals of the same species. Distance of migration varies from as little as 100mi (160km) in Gray vireos to more than 3,000mi (4,800km) in Red-eyed vireos.

Solitary and White-eyed vireos and their close relatives sing throughout the year. In summer, Red-eyed and Bell's vireos are among the most persistent singers of all New World songbirds. Although as a rule members of the vireos are not known for their beautiful voices, individual pepper-shrikes often have pleasant warbled, albeit repetitive, song types within their repertoires. Such song stands in sharp contrast to the police-whistle trill of the Blue Mountain vireo and the monotonous chatter song of several Caribbean and circum-Caribbean scrub-dwelling species. Female song has only been documented in the Gray vireo in which it is a regular feature of nest changeover by incubating or brooding adults. Males of most vireos sing when on the nest, probably as a reminder to the female of the nest location and as a stimulus for her to return to it once her hunger is satisfied.

In tropical and temperate regions in the Northern Hemisphere nesting begins between late April and mid-May and in all except the Red-eyed, Black-whiskered, the Yucatan and the Philadelphia vireos nests are built by both sexes. In the aforenamed species a singing male accompanies his female as she builds, but does not actually participate in construction. Nest building requires from 4–5 days in Bell's vireos and most other temperate zone species and up to 25 days in the Chestnut-sided shrike-vireo.

The nest has an outer layer of coarse strips of bark and leaves, or in some species moss, bound together by spider silk and decorated with whitish spider egg cases, and an inner layer of fine grass stems carefully coiled around the bowl of the nest. In species in which both sexes build, males are capable of building rough bag nests by themselves, but the lining is done by the female.

In temperate zone species eggs are laid within a day of nest completion. Males of all species except the Red-eyed vireo and closely related forms sit on eggs at intervals during the day when the female is not incubating. When hatching occurs the male Red-eyed vireo and his Black-whiskered and Yucatan vireo close counterparts finally participate in the care of young and share with the female feeding of arthropods to nestlings. Upon fledging individual young appear to be fed exclusively by one parent or the other for up to 20 days after leaving the nest.

Some vireos are highly susceptible to nest parasitism by the Brown-headed cowbird, and their breeding success is accordingly reduced. Bell's vireo, a heavily parasitized species, often buries cowbird eggs laid in its nest by adding additional nesting material to the interior of its nest thereby effectively walling in eggs of the social parasite. Solitary vireos have been observed tossing cowbird eggs from the nest, although cowbird young may also be raised by this species.

JCB

◄ **Typical vireo nest** is bag-like and hangs from the crotch of a thin branch. Two is a typical brood size in the tropics, but clutches in the temperate zone may be twice as large.

▼ **Most common bird of deciduous forests** in the eastern USA, the Red-eyed vireo (male illustrated) has a persistent robin-like song.

AMERICAN BLACKBIRDS

Family: Icteridae
Order: Passeriformes (suborder Oscines, part).
Ninety-four species in 24 genera.
Distribution: N and S America.

Habitat: grasslands, savannas, marshes, woodlands, and forests

Size: 6–21in (15–53cm) long, weight 0.7–16oz (20–454g).

Plumage: chiefly black with bold patches of yellow, orange or red; brown common among both sexes of grassland species and females of many others. Differences between males and females pronounced in temperate, migratory species and among polygynous species at all latitudes.

Voice: a wide range of single notes and chattering calls. Songs range from simple and harsh to long, complex and musical.

Nests: trees, shrubs, on ground, and in emergent aquatic vegetation; occasionally on cliffs.

Eggs: variable in background color and amount of spotting; weight 0.07–0.5oz (2.1–14.2g); incubation period 12–15 days; nestling period 9–35 days.

Diet: arthropods, seeds, fruit, nectar, and small vertebrates.

Species include: **Bay-winged cowbird** (*Molothrus badius*), **bobolink** (*Dolichonyx oryzivorus*), **Brown-headed cowbird** (*Molothrus ater*), **chopi** (*Gnorimopsar chopi*), **Common grackle** (*Quiscalus quiscula*), **Giant cowbird** (*Scaphidura oryzivora*), **Melodious blackbird** (*Dives dives*), **Jamaican blackbird** (*Nesopsar nigerrimus*), **Martinique oriole** (*Icterus bonana*), **Montserrat oriole** (*I. oberi*), **Montezuma oropendula** (*Psarocolius montezuma*), **Red-eyed** or **Bronzed cowbird** (*Molothrus aeneus*), **Red-winged blackbird** (*Agelaius phoeniceus*), **Scarlet-headed blackbird** (*Amblyramphus holosericeus*), **Scarlet-rumped cacique** (*Cacicus uropygialis*), **Screaming cowbird** (*Molothrus rufoaxillaris*), **Shiny** or **Common cowbird** (*M. bonariensis*), **St Lucia oriole** (*Icterus laudabilis*), **Tricolored blackbird** (*Agelaius tricolor*), **troupial** (*Icterus icterus*), **Yellow-headed blackbird** (*Xanthocephalus xanthocephalus*). Total threatened species: 1.

THE American blackbirds are common and conspicuous birds over much of North and South America, and their habit of forming large flocks outside the breeding season attracts the attention of even casual observers of birds. The family also includes the cowbirds, most of which are brood parasites, laying their eggs in the nests of other species. Sometimes very closely related blackbirds have strikingly different social systems.

The majority of species are tropical. There are centers of species richness in southern Mexico (24 species) and in Colombia (27 species), both regions with diverse habitats. Many species are found in temperate areas with an abundance of marshes, such as northern Argentina and adjacent Uruguay (19 species), and the Midwest of the USA (10 species). Blackbirds breed in all habitat types but especially in open environments such as grasslands, savannas, marshes. Forest species favor edges and disturbed sites rather than mature forest, but a few tropical species breed in primary forest. Blackbirds are generalized foragers, eating a wide variety of invertebrates and plant materials. Many species are insectivorous during the breeding season but seed-eaters during the remainder of the year.

Blackbirds are medium-sized birds, ranging in size from that of a large sparrow (females of some orioles and tropical marsh-nesting species) to that of a crow (tropical oropendolas). Bills and eyes are brightly colored in many species but legs are dull. In many tropical species, males and females are alike in plumage; striking sexual differences are found among high-altitude migratory species and among species in which males hold harems (polygynous) at all latitudes. Females of all species achieve adult plumage within one year, but males of many polygynous species retain a subadult plumage until they are two years old. Juvenile plumages are always female-like and subadult plumages of males are intermediate between those of females and adult males.

During the nonbreeding season blackbird flocks may be extremely large. Social groups during the breeding season are much smaller, but the Tricolored blackbird of California breeds in dense colonies that may contain over 100,000 birds. Territorial blackbirds breed in all habitat types occupied by the family. Colonial breeders are found principally among marsh-nesters, species that breed in isolated trees in open savannas where nesting sites are limited but feeding areas are widely dispersed, and among the partly fruit-eating tropical oropendolas and caciques that form conspicuous colonies in isolated trees in forest clearings.

Among the blackbirds can be found most of the social systems of the avian world. Most species breed as mated pairs on large territories, but there are also colonial species, species with highly clumped territories, and monogamous, polygynous and promiscuous species. A few species live in year-round flocks and up to eight individuals may attend a single nest.

Among the brood-parasitic cowbirds are two species (Brown-headed cowbird of North America and Shiny cowbird of South America) that lay their eggs in the nests of hundreds of other species of birds. Two others (Red-eyed cowbird and Giant cowbird) parasitize primarily other members of the blackbird family, especially orioles, caciques and oropendolas. The Bay-winged cowbird takes over active or inactive nests of other species of birds but incubates its own eggs and feeds its own nestlings. Finally, the Screaming cowbird is known to parasitize but a single host, the Bay-winged cowbird. Adaptations of cowbirds for brood parasitism include short incubation times, the habit of throwing out an egg of the host

▲ **Yellow-headed blackbirds** of western North America. During the nonbreeding season, most blackbirds gather into flocks. In the southern USA winter roosts of Red-winged blackbirds, Common grackles and Brown-headed cowbirds have been estimated to contain up to 50 million individuals!

▶ **Gaping for food.** American blackbirds obtain much of their food by inserting the closed bill into some potential food source, and then forcibly opening it. Blackbirds "gape" into rotting wood, flowers, curled leaves, clumps of grass, soil, and objects lying on the surface of the soil. In all cases, gaping exposes food, usually arthropods, not available to a bird gleaning prey from the surface.

◀ **Common grackle** may be a pest in ricefields and cornfields. The species flocks with Red-winged blackbirds, cowbirds and starlings. Open-country blackbird species have become more, tropical forest species less, numerous since the arrival of European settlers.

for every egg they deposit and a tendency towards mimicry of the eggs and nestlings of their hosts.

Regardless of the form of breeding social organization, male and female blackbirds assume very different roles. Nests are built exclusively by females in every species that has been studied except two. Incubation of eggs by males has never been reported, even

among species with identical males and females. Males do not bring food to their incubating spouses but many stand guard near the nest. Males of most monogamous species feed nestlings and fledglings, but males of only about one-third of the polygynous species do so. Polygynous males feed preferentially at the nest containing the oldest nestlings. Among monogamous species, males and females have about the same number of vocalizations, but males of polygynous species utter a greater variety of sounds than do females.

Among West Indian species, several of which are restricted to single islands where their populations were never very large, those considered threatened (but not yet listed by the ICBP) include the St. Lucia oriole, the Martinique oriole, the Montserrat oriole and the Jamaican blackbird. In South America the troupial, the chopi, and the Shiny cowbird are often kept as caged birds because of their beautiful songs.   GHO

FINCHES

Family: Fringillidae
Order: Passeriformes (suborder Oscines, part).
About 153 species in 33 genera.
Distribution: N and S America, Eurasia, Africa
(except Madagascar); introduced to New
Zealand, Hawaiian finches confined to
Hawaiian Islands

▼ **Commonest finch in Europe,** the chaffinch
breeds in all kinds of woodland, making its nest
usually quite low down in a tree or bush. Male
(here) and female feed the young with
caterpillars, which they bring one at a time.
Most other finches bring their young seeds,
which they carry in large quantities in the crop,
prior to regurgitating the meal at the nest.

FINCHES of one kind or another are
familiar to everyone. Not only do they
breed commonly in our parks and gardens,
they are also frequent visitors to feeding
trays in winter. However, few people are
familiar with more than a handful of species.

Finches have stout bills, strong skulls,
large jaw muscles and powerful gizzards, all
for coping with hard seeds. Other seed-
eating birds share these features, but the
Fringillidae are distinguished by the
presence of 9 instead of 10 large primary
feathers in each wing, 12 large tail feathers,
and the fact that the female is responsible
for building the cup-shaped nest and for
incubating the eggs.

The three species of fringilline finches
have fairly long tails, peaked heads and
prominent shoulder patches and wing
markings. Chaffinches breed in all kinds of
woodland, and over much of Europe are one
of the commonest birds, usually comprising
between one-fifth and two-fifths of the total
woodland bird population. The brambling
replaces the chaffinch as a breeding bird in
the subarctic birch woods of northern
Europe, and also extends across Asia to
Kamchatka, migrating south for the winter,
and concentrating in areas with beechmast.
The rare Blue chaffinch occurs only in high-
altitude pine forests of the Canary Islands.

The fringilline and cardueline finches differ in the way they feed their young, and
the dispersion system that results from this.
Although the main food of all species is
seeds, fringilline finches feed their young
entirely on insects (especially caterpillars),
while cardueline finches feed their young
either on a mixture of seeds and insects or
on seeds alone. The raising of young entirely
on a seed diet is comparatively rare among
birds, but has been recorded for crossbills,
siskins, redpolls and linnets. Also, while
fringilline finches carry insects to their
young one or a few at a time in the bill, cardueline finches carry large quantities of

▲ **Greenfinch on dried flowerhead** of willowherb (*Epilobium* species). Greenfinches breed through most of spring and summer, changing their diet as different plants come into seed.

seeds in their gullets and regurgitate them to the young. Some species, including the bullfinch, have special throat pouches for this purpose.

The fringilline finches defend large territories while breeding, and pairs spread themselves fairly evenly through the habitat. The food is obtained from the territory itself, and the young are fed at frequent intervals (about every 5–10 minutes). The carduelines nest solitarily or in loose colonies, within which each pair defends only a small area around its nest; they forage away from the colonies in flocks, wherever seeds happen to be abundant at

the time. They pack large amounts of seeds into their crop, and feed their young at infrequent intervals (about 20–60 minutes). The pair forage and visit the nest together.

The fringilline finches sing only on their territories, and the song serves to advertise the occupation of the territory and to attract a mate. The cardueline finches sing anywhere they happen to be, and the song serves as a form of self advertisement. Many cardueline finches have special song flights over their breeding areas.

Like other birds, all these finches breed when their food is most plentiful, but the timing varies between species, according to what they eat. The chaffinch, which eats caterpillars, has a short breeding season in late spring, while the cardueline finches, which need seeds, have long and varied seasons, in which individual pairs often raise more than one brood. The greenfinch, linnet and bullfinch, which eat a variety of seeds, breed for almost the whole growing season, continually changing their diet as different plants come into seed. The European goldfinch, which likes the seeds of thistles and related plants, breeds later in summer, while the American goldfinch, which depends even more on thistles, breeds later still. The regular start of its breeding season is the latest in North America. The crossbills nest in any month, whenever conifer seeds are sufficiently available; in larch forests this is mainly in late summer or early fall, in spruce forests in fall to winter, and in pine forests in spring. If spruce and pine are available in the same area, breeding can occur continuously for 10

▼ ► **Representative species of finches.**
(1) Kauai akialoa (*Hemignathus procerus*) of Hawaii. (2) Common or Red crossbill (*Loxia curvirostra*). (3) Pine grosbeak (*Pinicola enucleator*). (4) Hawfinch (*Coccothraustes coccothraustes*). (5) Maui parrotbill (*Pseudonestor xanthophrys*). (6) European goldfinch (*Carduelis carduelis*). (7) Siskin (*C. spinus*). (8) Two-barred crossbill (*Loxia leucoptera*). (9) Ou (*Psittirostra psittacea*). (10) Apapane (*Himatione sanguinea*). (11) Parrot crossbill (*Loxia pytopsittacus*).

The Finch's Bill

The beak of a finch is modified internally for shelling seeds. Each seed is wedged in a groove on the side of the palate and crushed by raising the lower jaw onto it. The husk is peeled off with the aid of the tongue and discarded, while the kernel is swallowed.

The cardueline finches can extract seeds from the seed-heads of plants. Species differ in the size of seeds they prefer, and in the types of seed-head they can best exploit, corresponding with differences in the size and shape of their bills. Hawfinches have big powerful bills for crushing large hard tree fruits, such as cherry stones. Goldfinches have long tweezer-like bills for probing into thistles, and other composite plants; they are the only species able to eat the seeds of teasel, which lie at the bottom of long, spiked tubes. The male European goldfinch has a slightly longer beak and can reach teasel seeds more easily than the female, which in consequence rarely feeds from this plant. Siskins also have tweezer-like bills, and feed largely from seeds in small cones, such as alder.

Bullfinches and Pine grosbeaks have rounded bills adapted for eating buds and berries, the bullfinch in general taking smaller items than the grosbeaks. The crossbills use their crossed mandibles to help them extract seeds from hard closed cones. The three species in Europe have different-sized bills and feed primarily from different conifers: the slender-billed Two-barred crossbill eats seeds mainly from the small soft cones of larch, the medium-billed Common crossbill feeds mainly from the medium cones of spruce, and the large heavy-billed Parrot crossbill mainly from large hard cones of pine.

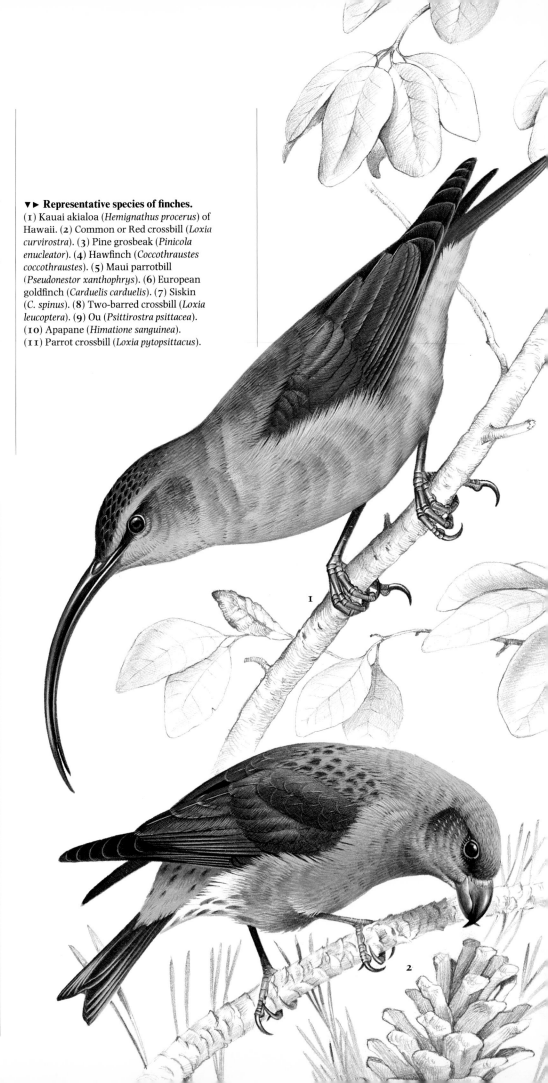

months. Thus crossbills are often forced to nest when days are short and cold, and the ground is snow covered. In the Moscow region, some nests were found in February, when air temperatures were −2°F (−19°C); inside the nest the temperature was as high as 100°F (38°C) while the female brooded.

Another major event in the annual cycle of finches is migration, and here again food plays an overriding role. The main distinction is between species which feed from low herbaceous plants and those which feed high in trees. Herbaceous plants produce an abundance of seeds every year, but at times of snow these seeds may be unavailable. Most finches that depend on such seeds migrate south for the winter, and in Europe many thousands winter in the Mediterranean region. Such species have fairly fixed migration routes and show strong homing tendencies, returning to the same areas for breeding and wintering in successive years. Examples include the European goldfinch and linnet.

The tree feeders have a different problem because, although their food is generally available above the snow (enabling them to winter much further north), in any one locality the seed crops vary enormously from one year to the next. In some years the trees and bushes are laden with fruits but in other years they are barren. In different parts of a continent, however, the crops are not necessarily in phase with one another, so in a year when the crops may fail in one region, they may be good in another. With such a fluctuating food supply, there would be little point in individuals migrating to the same places every year. In consequence, the migrations are highly variable both in direction and distance travelled. When seed crops are good in the north most of the birds stay there. However, when the northern crops fail, most of the birds move further south. As band (ring) recoveries testify, individuals of such species may breed or winter in widely separated regions in different years. Enormous year-to-year fluctuations of populations may be seen at any one locality, but the continental population as a whole probably does not fluctuate to such a large extent. This system applies particularly to siskins and redpolls, but also to bullfinches, Pine and Evening grosbeaks.

The most famous of all eruptive finches are the crossbills. Every few years these birds move out of their breeding areas and occur in enormous numbers outside the normal range. Sometimes, the movements are so spectacular as to attract general attention; as long ago as 1251, the English chronicler, Matthew Paris, wrote about these strange birds which invaded his homeland in great numbers, and caused devastation to the apple crop (for the birds are often forced on to unusual foods when away from their favorite conifers). Eruptions of crossbills have since been recorded from all their main centers, including parts of North America, Japan and the Himalayas, but have been best documented in Europe. On this continent between 1800 and 1965, crossbills erupted at least 67 times at intervals of up to 17 years. Only recently have band recoveries confirmed that some birds return to their regular range in later years. From a batch of birds banded in Switzerland on migration, some were recorded the following fall and winter in southwest Europe, having continued their journey; others were recorded in later years 2,500mi (4,000km) northeast, in the northern USSR.

Because of their song, bright colors, engaging habits and simple seed diet, finches have for centuries been kept in cages as pets. Some species breed readily in captivity, and from the wild serin of the Canary Islands all the various strains of domestic canary were derived. Certain finches are also important as pests, notably the bullfinch which eats buds of fruit trees, sometimes devastating orchards.

In the past, man must have had an enormous influence on the distribution and numbers of the different finches. Deforestation must have greatly reduced the habitat available to certain species, but the spread of cultivated and urban environments provided new habitats for others. One adverse trend in recent decades has been the increasing use of herbicides in agriculture. These chemicals kill the weeds on which several species depend, and in the long term deplete the "seed bank" in the soil. Plowing and other soil disturbance turns buried seeds to the surface, where they are available to certain finches, but farmland offers much less food for finches than in times past.

IN

Hawaiian finches (also known as Hawaiian honeycreepers) are thought to be derived from a single finch-like species that crossed more than 1,860mi (3,000km) of ocean to colonize the Hawaiian Archipelago. In the near absence of competition, these immigrants, resembling the Nihoa finch, evolved specialized feeding behavior and remarkable bills to exploit highly diverse island ecosystems—from shrubby coral atolls and rocky islets to mountain rain forests receiving more than 400in (1,000cm) of rain per year.

Many seed-eaters retained finch-shaped bills; an extinct, unnamed Oahu species had one of the most massive known. In contrast, the insectivorous creepers have thin warbler-like bills. The Kauai akialoa's decurved bill, 2.6in (6.6cm) long (one-third the bird's length), is used for seeking insects in thick mosses or deep cracks. The Maui parrotbill chisels into branches for insects with its broad lower mandible. Most remarkable is the akiapolaau, which chips into soft wood with its stout lower mandible while holding its curved upper mandible, with which it later probes for insects, out of the way.

Nectar-sipping species such as the Black mamo and iiwi have bills that closely match the flower corollas that provide their food, and possess tubular tongues to aid in sucking nectar.

Other members of the group eat berries, fruit, snails and seabird eggs. The colorful red apapane and dazzling orange iiwi fly many miles each day in their search for nectar-bearing flowers, and their evening flights in the thousands can be very spectacular.

The Hawaiian finches have extended breeding seasons beginning in January and continuing through July or August. Because many species are rare and frequent rugged, wet terrain, nests of only half of them are known. Their nests are open, constructed of twigs and lined with fine fibers, and are well concealed in terminal leaf clusters. The Nihoa finch nests in rock cavities, while the Laysan finch, which belongs to the same genus, prefers to nest in grass tussocks on its sandy island.

These amazing birds have been decimated by changes in their island homes. At least 15 species, known from undescribed fossils, survived until Polynesians, beginning about AD400, converted their dry lowland forest habitats to agriculture. Of the 28 species known from records made in more recent times, 8 are extinct and 12 are endangered. Habitat destruction by man and ungulates (primarily cattle, goats and pigs) and introduced predators and diseases have greatly reduced the numbers of all surviving species. It is hoped that ambitious conservation programs currently under way will protect most of those species that still survive.

CBK

▲ **Heavy-billed Parrot crossbill** male regurgitating a meal of seeds for its young.

◄ **The Common or Red crossbill** of Europe, North Africa, Asia and North to Central America reveals its whereabouts by the presence on the ground of open fir cones, from which it has taken the seeds. Male crossbills are brick red in color, the females and young are greenish.

The 3 Subfamilies of Finches

E Endangered. V Vulnerable. R Rare. Ex Extinct. Ex? Probably Extinct.

Fringilline finches
Subfamily: Fringillinae
Three species of the genus *Fringilla*.
Eurasia, Canary Islands. Woodland and forest. Size: about 6in (15cm) long, weight 0.9–1.0oz (26–30g). Plumage: males very colorful: in chaffinch, blue head, greenish back, and pink breast; in brambling, black and buffish back and orange underside; in Canary Islands chaffinch, mainly bluish; females generally duller, and in chaffinch mainly pale green. All species have conspicuous shoulder patches, wing and tail markings.
Voice: chaffinch has "spink, spink" call, and loud musical song, lasting 2–3 seconds and consisting of a succession of "chip" notes, followed by a flourish. Brambling has a harsh "tswark" note, and a softer "tchuck," mostly used on the wing and a long drawn-out "dwee" note, which constitutes the song.
Nests: mainly of grass, moss and other vegetation, usually in a tree or bush. Eggs: 3–5, dark greenish-blue with purple-brown streaks and spots that have a paler rim; incubation period 12–14 days; nestling period: 11–17 days. Diet: seeds; young fed on insects, especially caterpillars.

Species: **brambling** (*Fringilla montifringilla*), **Canary Islands chaffinch** (*F. teydea*), **chaffinch** (*F. coelebs*).

Cardueline finches
Subfamily: Carduelinae
About 122 species in 17 genera.
N and S America, Eurasia, Africa (except Madagascar). Woodland and forest. Size: 4–7.5in (11–19cm); weight up to 3.5oz (100g). Plumage: varied in color but generally with prominent wing and tail markings, many species streaked, especially in juvenile plumage. Voice: very varied, but most have pleasant, musical songs of pure notes; a few, such as the bullfinch, have rather coarse, creaky songs. Nests: built mainly of grass, moss and other vegetation, usually in a tree or a bush. Eggs: 3–5, whitish with brown spots; incubation period 12–14 days; nestling period 11–17 days. Diet: seeds; young fed on seeds and insects or seeds alone.

Species include: **American goldfinch** (*Carduelis tristis*), **bullfinch** (*Pyrrhula pyrrhula*), **Common** or **Red crossbill** (*Loxia curvirostra*), **European goldfinch** (*Carduelis carduelis*), **Evening grosbeak** (*Hesperiphona vespertina*), **greenfinch** (*Carduelis chloris*), **hawfinch** (*Coccothraustes coccothraustes*), **linnet** (*Acanthis cannabina*), **Parrot crossbill** (*Loxia pytopsittacus*), **Pine grosbeak** (*Pinicola enucleator*), **redpoll** (*Acanthis flammea*), **Two-barred** or **White-winged crossbill** (*Loxia leucoptera*). Total threatened species: 3.

Hawaiian finches
Subfamily: Drepanidinae
Twenty-eight species in 15 genera.
Hawaiian Islands. Native forests and shrublands. Size: 4–8in (10–20cm) long, weight 0.4–1.6oz (12–45g). Plumage: green, yellow, brown, black, red, and orange. Males and females usually similar; males brighter than females in some. Voice: variable, from musical trills to fragmented squeaky phrases and whistled notes. Nests: open cups, occasionally in tree cavities. Eggs: normally 2–3, whitish with gray to reddish-brown scrawls; incubation period 13–14 days; nestling period 15–22 days. Diet: mainly insects and nectar, but also snails, fruit, seed-pods, and seabird eggs.

Species include: **akiapolaau** E (*Hemignathus munroi*), **apapane** (*Himatione sanguinea*), **Black mamo** Ex (*Drepanis funerea*), **iiwi** (*Vestiaria coccinea*), **Kauai akialoa** Ex? (*Hemignathus procerus*), **Kauai creeper** R (*Oreomystis bairdi*), **Laysan finch** (*Telespyza cantans*), **Maui parrotbill** V (*Pseudonestor xanthophrys*), **Molokai creeper** E (*Paroreomyza flammea*), **Nihoa finch** (*Telespyza ultima*), **ou** E (*Psittirostra psittacea*), **poo-uli** R (*Melamprosops phaeosoma*). Total threatened species: 12.

WAXBILLS AND WEAVERS

Families: Estrildidae, Ploceidae
Order: Passeriformes (suborder Oscines, part).
Two hundred and sixty-seven species in 45
genera.
Distribution: see map and table.

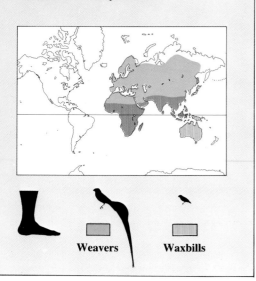

Weavers   Waxbills

► **Plague-like flock** of Red-billed queleas
ABOVE threatens serious damage to grain crops
in the vicinity. Attempts at pest control south
of the Sahara have so far failed. Flocks may
number over a million birds.

► **Spectacular Gouldian finch** BELOW (male
illustrated) is a popular cage bird in its various
color forms; it is now protected by the
Australian Government's ban on import and
export of fauna.

▼ **Blue-capped cordon bleu** (*Uraeginthus
cyanocephala*) of East Africa is another cagebird
favorite. The colorful waxbills are probably the
single most important family for aviculturists.

THE **waxbills** are notable for their extraordinary diversity of plumage. Some species are relatively somberly clad in grays,
browns and white but many of them make
up for their lack of bright coloration with
attractive markings. The Double-bar finch,
Pictorella finch and Zebra finch all illustrate
this tendency. Other species are richly colored, including the blue of cordon bleus,
reds of firefinches and green and yellow of
the Green avadavat. The most colorful of
them all is, however, the Gouldian finch,
whose combination of green, yellow, cobalt-
blue, turquoise, purple and white give it a
bizarre, and perhaps (depending on taste),
beautiful appearance. This species also
shows an interesting variation in head
coloration: the heads of roughly 75 percent
of Gouldian finches in the wild are black but
most of the remaining 25 percent are red.
There is another so-called yellow-headed
form (in reality it is orange in color), which
occurs in about one in every thousand or
so wild birds.

Most waxbills are social and occur in
flocks in the nonbreeding season, sometimes
aggregating in large mixed species groups.
The behavior of individuals within flocks
tends to be synchronized; they feed
together, take-off simultaneously, show
coordinated flight movements and perform
acts, such as preening and bathing, at the
same times. Experimental work on captive
birds, and recordings made from flocks living under natural conditions, have shown
that both calls and visual stimuli are important in synchronizing behavior. Flight move-

ments, for instance, are coordinated, at least
in part, by so-called "flight calls" which are
given by birds taking-off and in flight. The
acts of preening and flying down from
perching places to the ground in order to
forage are, on the other hand, synchronized
by the sight of other birds performing these
acts. There is greater emphasis on coordina-
tion by calls in forest-inhabiting species, in
which members of flocks may have difficulty
in maintaining visual contact with one
another, than in species which inhabit open
country.

The Mouse of the Avian World

The relative ease with which the Zebra finch
can be kept and bred in captivity recommends
it as a laboratory animal. Indeed, it is widely
used in experimental work in many parts of
the world, particularly in laboratories in
Europe and the USA. Some research workers
have even predicted that it will become as
familiar in laboratories as the mouse.

One significant line of research in which the
Zebra finch has been involved illustrates the
ways in which early experiences of an animal
can affect the development of patterns of
behavior which are not performed until it
reaches maturity. It is possible to alter the
normal nestling environment of the Zebra
finch and therefore its experiences during
development, by allowing it to be foster-reared
by Bengalese finches. Adult pairs of the latter
species will incubate Zebra finch eggs and rear
the nestlings, as if they were their own. Young
Zebra finches which have been reared in this
way, however, become sexually imprinted on
their foster-parents, and as a consequence,
show abnormal mate choice when they

become adult. If they are given access to both
Bengalese and Zebra finch females, they prefer
to court, and pair with, members of the foster
species, rather than their conspecifics. The
effects of imprinting are remarkably stable.
Foster-reared male Zebra finches can be
persuaded to pair, and nest, with females of
their own kind, if they are caged with them
alone, in the absence of Bengalese finch
females. But even this experience does not
affect subsequent mate choice. When such
males are separated from their Zebra finch
mates and given the choice between
unfamiliar Zebra finch and Bengalese finch
females, they still prefer the latter species.
Similar experiments have shown that the
male Zebra finch also learns features of its
courtship song during its early development.
It does so by listening to the songs of its father.
Birds reared by their natural fathers imitate
their songs and consequently have typical
song repertoires of the Zebra finch; males
foster-reared by Bengalese finches, sing like
members of this species.   SME

Pair-bonds are strong in most species and members of pairs keep together during the nonbreeding season. They indulge in gestures, such as clumping (perching in contact) and preening one another, which probably serve to maintain and strengthen bonds between them. Breeding occurs in the wet season, when the food on which the nestlings are reared, mostly seeding grasses and insects, is abundant. Predators, including hawks, snakes and small mammals, take a heavy toll of eggs and nestlings and breeding success is often poor. Records of several African species show that only 18–30 percent of the eggs laid survive to produce fledglings; most of the rest are destroyed by predators. Nestlings possess conspicuous marks on the palate and tongue which are revealed whenever they gape for food. There are additional luminous spots at the base of the bill in some species. These markings probably stimulate parents to feed their young and also help them to locate the nestlings' mouths in the semi-darkness of the nest.

Waxbills adapt well to life in captivity and have become popular cage birds. Two species in particular, the Bengalese finch and the Zebra finch, are now thoroughly domesticated and are available in a number of different color varieties. Together with other species, they are kept by aviculturists throughout the world. Unfortunately, the demand for most African and Asian finches is met by trapping them in the wild. Dealers in these two continents export enormous numbers of finches worldwide. It has been

estimated, for example, that Europe alone imports $7\frac{1}{2}$ million birds a year, a very large proportion of which are wild-caught waxbills. The extent to which the trade is depleting natural populations is unknown, but other aspects of it, such as severe mortality of birds in transit, caused by overcrowding or insufficient food, are undesirable. In fact, it is questionable whether the trade is necessary at all. Aviculturists faced with the non-availability of certain species from the wild have been highly successful in breeding and maintaining captive strains. The Australian Government's ban on the import and export of fauna in the 1960s, for example, meant that new stocks of African and Asian species were no longer available to Australian aviculturists, and of Australian finches to aviculturists in other parts of the world. Serious bird breeders in Australia have nevertheless established strains of many non-native species, including cordon bleus, firefinches and waxbills, while European aviculturists still keep and breed viable stocks of at least thirteen of the Australian species. SME

The Waxbills and 4 Subfamilies of Weavers ® Rare.

Waxbills
Family: Estrildidae
One hundred and twenty-four species in 27 genera.
Africa, Asia and Australia. Dry savanna, thorn scrub, open grassland, reedbeds, tropical forests, semideserts. Size: 3.5–5.5in (9–14cm) long. Plumage: a great variety of color patterns and markings. Males and females distinctly different in some species, similar in others. Voice: a range of calls in social situations, eg flock synchronization, contact; a quiet song during courtship and in a solitary context by males. Nests: mostly built of grasses, domed with a side entrance; some species nest in holes. Eggs: usually 4–8, white, length 0.5–0.7in (13–17mm). Diet: mostly grass seeds. Some species take insects, particularly when rearing young.

Species include: **Beautiful firetail** (*Emblema bella*), **Bengalese finch** (domesticated) or **White-backed munia** (*Lonchura striata*), **Double bar finch** (*Poephila bichenovii*), **Golden-breasted waxbill** (*Amandava subflava*), **Gouldian finch** (*Chloebia gouldiae*), **Green avadavat** (*Amandava formosa*), **Pictorella finch** (*Lonchura pectoralis*), **Pink-billed parrotfinch** ® (*Erythrura kleinschmidti*), **Red-billed firefinch** (*Lagonosticta senegala*), **Red-cheeked cordon bleu** (*Uraeginthus bengalus*), **Zebra finch** (*Poephila guttata*).

Weavers
Family: Ploceidae
One hundred and forty-three species in 18 genera.

Buffalo weavers
Subfamily: Bubalornithinae
Three species in 2 genera.
Africa south of the Sahara. Semi-arid areas, thorn-bush scrub, savanna and acacia country. Size: 8–9.5in (22–24cm) long. Plumage: two species black, one white and brown with scarlet rump. Voice: noisy when breeding (colonial), harsh chattering and guttural calls. Nests: large, untidy domed nests of thorny twigs. Eggs: 3–4, length 1.1in (25–28mm), pale blue or grayish, marked with olive. Diet: seeds, fruits and insects.

Species: **Black-billed buffalo weaver** (*Bubalornis albirostris*), **Red-billed buffalo weaver** (*B. niger*), **White-headed buffalo weaver** (*Dinemellia dinemelli*).

Parasitic viduine weavers and whydahs
Subfamily: Viduinae
Nine species of the genus *Vidua*.
Distribution: Africa south of the Sahara. Savanna and open plains; also villages and gardens. Size: 4.5–16in (11.5–41cm) long. Plumage: mainly black or steely-blue, some with some white or yellow; many females with sparrow-like plumage.

Voice: chirping and soft warbling songs. Males mimic the song of host species. Nests: parasitic in their nesting habits. Eggs: white, length 0.6–0.7in (15–19mm). Diet: seeds and insects.

True weavers
Subfamily: Ploceinae
Ninety-four species in 7 genera.
Distribution: mainly Africa, some extending to Arabia, India, China and Indonesia. Habitat: savanna and forest. Size: 4.5–25.5in (11.5–65cm) long (longest is Long-tailed widow bird *Euplectes progne*). Plumage: many bright yellow, red or glossy black. Females of most *Ploceus* species have sparrow-like plumages, males brighter. Voice: loud chattering, various chirpings and twittering. Nests: often nesting colonially; domed nests suspended from branches. Eggs: 2–4, length 0.7–1in (18–25mm), vary greatly in color and markings: white, greenish, bluish or pink. Diet: seeds, vegetable matter and insects.

Species include: **bishops** (9 species in the genus *Euplectes*), Cuckoo weaver (*Anomalospiza imberbis*), **fodies** (genus *Foudia*), **Grosbeak weaver** (*Amblyospiza albifrons*), **Red-billed quelea** (*Quelea quelea*), **Village weaver** (*Ploceus cucullatus*), **Yellow bishop** (*Euplectes capensis*). Total threatened species: 4.

Sparrow weavers, sparrows and snow finches
Subfamily: Passerinae
Thirty-seven species in 8 genera.
Distribution: Africa, Europe, Asia, introduced to the Americas, Australasia and many islands. Dry bush to full desert, savanna, forest, rocky mountain sides. Also villages and towns. Size: 4–7in (10–18cm) long. Plumage: mainly brown and gray, but sometimes with black or bright yellow. Snow finches show varying amounts of white. Voice: loud chirpings, twitterings and some simple trilled songs. Nests: many species gregarious, breeding in colonies in trees or bushes, making grassy domed nests. Also in holes in trees, rocks or buildings. Eggs: 3–7, length 0.8in (18–22mm), whitish, creamy or pinkish suffused with mauve-brown, grayish or lilac markings. Diet: mainly seeds, vegetable matter and some insects. True sparrows (*Passer*) largely seed-eaters with marked preference for cereals; House sparrows can exist mainly on bread and household scraps.

Species incude: **House sparrow** (*Passer domesticus*), **Pale rock sparrow** (*Petronia brachydactyla*), **Rock sparrow** (*P. petronia*), **snow finches** (*Montifringilla*), **Tree sparrow** (*Passer montanus*), **Yellow-throated sparrow** (*Petronia xanthocollis*).

The weaver family can be divided into four subfamilies. Most **true weavers** are thick-set seed-eating birds with strong short bills and many have the ability to construct elaborately woven nests. Some forest species have less robust bills and are mainly insectivorous.

The majority of the true weavers are confined to Africa and its neighboring islands and can be separated into two groups. The first group are exclusively tree dwellers, nearly all with bright yellow or red plumage, and build elaborately suspended nests which are tough, with the entrance on the underside, or protected by a tunnel. The tunnel may be as much as 2ft (60cm) long and the nests are often built at the tips of twigs or palm fronds, often sited near water. In a nesting colony, the tree-top is often filled with their nests, slung on branches very close together. The Village weaver may build several nests, advertising each to any interested female. He hangs upside down at the entrance, located in the bottom of the nest, with much wing flapping and chattering.

The second group comprises the fodies and bishops, which build globular nests and, except for the fodies, often place them in grass or herbage instead of suspending them in trees. Territorialism is highly developed in these birds and in a grassy area of a flood plain several species may have their territories. The Yellow bishop can have several females nesting in his territory, so that he spends a great deal of his time patrolling his boundaries giving aggressive calls.

Among the three species of diochs, the Red-billed quelea has been known from its earliest recorded history as a menace to

▲ **Representative species of waxbills and weavers.** (1) Golden palm weaver (*Ploceus bojeri*), male displaying at nest.
(2) White-backed munia (*Lonchura striata*), wild form of the domesticated Bengalese finch.
(3) House sparrow (*Passer domesticus*), in flight.
(4) Golden bishop (*Euplectes afer*) male courtship flight. (5) Pin-tailed whydah (*Vidua macroura*). (6) White-headed buffalo weaver (*Dinemellia dinemelli*). (7) Social weaver (*Philetairus socius*) with nests in background.

▶ **Trapeze-like foundation** OVERLEAF of nest laid by male Red-headed weaver (*Anaplectes rubriceps*).

crops of small grain. This species is completely colonial in its habits and is often found in concentrations of over a million birds. Large-scale efforts at control, coupled with research, began in the Sudan in 1946, and by 1953 had become necessary in other territories, but in spite of immense slaughter the plague continues.

There are also two species in separate genera outside the two main groups, the Grosbeak weaver, which has a very heavy bill and weaves a superior globular nest of extremely fine fibers, and the Cuckoo weaver which is a small yellow bird that parasitizes grass-warblers.

The **viduine weavers** and **whydahs** parasitize species of waxbills. The young of each host species carry distinctive colors and markings on their palates, which serve to release the feeding behavior of the parents. Chicks of the parasitic whydahs mimic these markings with extraordinary accuracy.

The **buffalo weavers** inhabit the drier areas of Africa, feeding on the ground in the manner of starlings. They have a mixed diet, and build large untidy nests of thorny twigs, which are highly protective.

The **sparrows** have a tendency to associate with man, and at least eight of the species regularly nest in the eaves of inhabited buildings. The House sparrow is the most persistent of all and is only rarely found breeding away from man. The Tree sparrow fills the same niche in the eastern parts of its range, where the House sparrow is absent. Despite the close association with man, House sparrows are extremely wary birds and not easily kept in captivity. Many of the sparrows are gregarious and breed in colonies, although the nests do not form communal structures as do those of some other species of weavers.

The Rock sparrows are mainly gray and brown birds with a yellow patch on the throat. However, the African species, including the Yellow-throated sparrow, which extends to India, are birds more of trees than rocks. The remaining two species, the Rock sparrow and the Pale rock sparrow, are more typical "rock" sparrows, as they typically nest in holes in rocks or walls.

The snow finches spend their lives almost entirely on the ground and are among the highest-nesting of living birds, since they occur at from 5,900 to 15,000ft (1,800–4,600m). They are gregarious in winter, forming flocks, which may descend to lower altitudes in severe weather, although they do not leave the mountains altogether.

PRC

STARLINGS, ORIOLES AND DRONGOS

Families: Sturnidae, Oriolidae, Dicruridae
Order: Passeriformes (suborder Oscines, part).
One hundred and fifty-four species in 26 genera.
Distribution: see maps and table.

Starlings

Orioles   **Drongos**

▶ **Returning to the nest,** a male European starling pauses on his perch before flying the last few feet to feed his young in their tree-hole nest. Jaunty, loquacious and gregarious, the European starling is at once one of the most successful and most damaging of birds. It is a fearsome competitor and will oust other birds, such as woodpeckers and hoopoes, from their holes.

The male European starling sometimes mates with a second female while his first mate is still incubating her clutch of 4–6 eggs. In such cases, the male goes on to help feed the chicks of his first mate, rarely those of the second. Some females lay their eggs in nests of other starlings rather than in one of their own, in cuckoo-like fashion.

Throughout history, one of the greatest scourges of man's crops has been the locust and the delectation for this pest of several species of **starling**, such as the Rose-coloured starling, the Common mynah and the Wattled starling brought them to man's attention many centuries ago. Other species are better known as pests.

Most species of starling are resident but some migrate. The Violet-backed starling and the Blue-eared Glossy starling undertake local migrations in Africa and the Brahminy starling makes similar movements in India. The Gray starling migrates from its breeding areas in eastern USSR, northern China and Japan to winter in southern China and the Philippines. Northern populations of the European starling migrate to milder climates for the winter, those from Siberia heading south towards the northern shores of the Indian Ocean while Scandinavian birds migrate southwest towards the Atlantic seaboard. Some starlings are nomadic. This applies particularly to the Wattled starling, which settles to breed where locusts abound but moves on when the insects disappear, and the breeding sites of the Rose-coloured starling, which winters in India, are determined by the abundance of insects—an area that has a large colony of birds one year may be deserted the next.

Starlings are small- to medium-sized birds that make their presence felt near human habitations by their ceaseless activity, loud calling and squabbling. In general appearance, they are rather variable since forest-dwelling forms, like the African glossy starlings, tend to have broad, rounded wings whereas those species that live in drier, more open habitats, such as the European starling, have longer and more pointed wings. The legs and feet are fairly large and strong and the birds tend to walk, rather than hop. In the oxpeckers, the toes are also long and sharp to enable them to cling to the pelts of large mammals. The bill is rather stout and usually straight and reasonably long. Such a bill allows starlings to be catholic in their choice of food, and most eat invertebrates and fruit. Some are more omnivorous and include nectar and seeds in their diets. The tongue of the Brahminy starling bears a brush-like tip which is used for collecting pollen and nectar and the brush-like crests of some of the mynahs are believed to be important in pollination.

Some of the south-east Asian starlings have areas of bare skin on the head, especially around the eye; these areas are yellow in the Andaman starling, blue in Rothschild's mynah and red in the Sulawesi starling. The amount of naked skin reaches its maximum in the Bald starling, where feathering is restricted to a narrow strip of bristles running down the crown. The Hill mynah and the Wattled starling develop fleshy wattles on the head; in the latter species the wattles appear, and head feathering is lost, mainly by birds coming into breeding condition but the wattles are subsequently resorbed and feathers grow anew. The Rose-coloured and Brahminy starlings have long feathers on the head that can be raised into a crest, and the Sula starling has a stiff crest that is permanently erect.

Most starlings breed in holes in which they build a bulky nest. Holes in trees and cliffs are commonly used, while close to human habitation nests may be made inside buildings. The Thin-billed chestnut-winged starling nests in holes behind waterfalls, and several species use holes made by other birds. Some starlings bore their own holes, such as the Bank mynah in river banks and the Woodpecker starling in dead trees. A few species do not nest in holes, however: the Superb starling builds a domed nest in bushes and the Shining starling builds hanging nests, weaver fashion.

In many of the species that have been studied, both sexes incubate the eggs but the male usually plays the lesser role. In the Spotless starling the male does not incubate at all and yet in no species are males known to feed the female on the nest. Nestlings are fed by both parents but the role of the male can be variable. Cooperative breeding, where three or more fully grown birds may feed a brood of chicks in one nest, has now been demonstrated in some African starlings.

Most starlings are gregarious, breeding in colonies, feeding in flocks and roosting communally at night. Several species of starling may roost together and they may also roost among other birds. Roosts are usually in trees but the European starling has recently adopted a habit of roosting in cities in flocks that can contain over a million birds.

During the last 400 years four species are known or thought to have become extinct, two from Indian Ocean islands and two from islands in the Pacific. Rothschild's mynah survives in a small population in a forest nature reserve on Bali, Indonesia. The European starling, on the other hand, is one of the most successful birds, with a world population running into hundreds of millions. The most dramatic example of the species' success, however, comes from its introduction to North America: about 100

individuals were released in New York in 1890—only 90 years later it is now one of the most numerous birds in North America.

The European starling causes extensive damage in Eurasia and North America by eating grapes, olives, cherries, germinating wheat and cattle food, while in northern Europe and central Asia and in New Zealand it is held to be useful on account of its destruction of insects. Many species are kept as cage birds, especially those, like the Hill mynah, with a capacity to mimic speech. The feathers of some African glossy starlings are used for human adornment and several species are killed for food, including the European starling in southern Europe. The Wattled starling's ability to resorb its wattles has been studied in cancer research, while its ability to re-grow feathers has been investigated by optimistic seekers of cures for human baldness! CJF

The name **oriole** appears to have been derived from the Latin *aureolus*, meaning golden or yellow. Most of the orioles are yellow and black, although some are crimson and black. They are not closely related to the

---

The 3 Families of Starlings, Orioles and Drongos

E Endangered. V Vulnerable. R Rare.

Starlings
Family: Sturnidae
One hundred and six species in 22 genera.
Africa, Europe, Asia, Southeast Asia, Oceania (just into Australasia), introduced to North America, New Zealand, southern Australia and many tropical islands. Forest, savanna, steppes and temperate grassland. Size: 6–18in (16–45cm) long, weight 1.5–6oz (45–170g). Plumage: chiefly dark but usually with iridescent sheens of green, purple and blue; some with brilliant orange and yellow, some with dull gray, some with bare skin or fleshy wattles. Males and females usually similar but with males brighter than females in some. Voice: vociferous, with wide range of whistles, squawks and rattles. Some mimic other animal sounds, including human speech. Nests: most in holes in which a bulky nest of dried grass is built; usually natural holes in trees, cliffs, or buildings or holes made by other species, but some excavate own; some build domed or pendulous nests; many colonial or loosely so. Eggs: usually 1–6, pale blue with brownish spots, but some genera without spots; incubation period 11–18 days; nestling period 18–30 days. Diet: most eat fruit and insects, some also

seeds, nectar and pollen; oxpeckers specialize on insects parasitic on large mammals.

Species include: **Andaman starling** (*Sturnus erythropygius*), **Bald starling** (*Sarcops calvus*), **Bank mynah** (*Acridotheres ginginianus*), **Blue-eared glossy starling** (*Lamprotornis chalybaeus*), **Brahminy starling** (*Sturnus pagodarum*), **Chestnut-bellied starling** (*Spreo pulcher*), **European starling** (*Sturnus vulgaris*), **Glossy starling** (*Aplonis panayensis*), **Golden-breasted starling** (*Spreo regius*), **Gray starling** (*Sturnus cineraceus*), **Hill mynah** (*Gracula religiosa*), **Ponape mountain starling** V (*Aplonis pelzelni*), **Red-winged starling** (*Onychognathus morio*), **Rose-colored starling** (*Sturnus roseus*), **Rothschild's mynah** E (*Leucopsar rothschildi*), **Santo mountain starling** R (*Aplonis santovestris*), **Shining starling** (*A. metallica*), **Spotless starling** (*Sturnus unicolor*), **Sula starling** (*Basilornis galeatus*), **Sulawesi starling** (*B. celebensis*), **Superb starling** (*Spreo superbus*), **Thin-billed chestnut-winged starling** (*Onychognathus tenuirostris*), **Violet-backed starling** (*Cinnyricinclus leucogaster*), **Wattled starling** (*Creatophora cinerea*), **Woodpecker starling** (*Scissirostrum dubium*), **Yellow-billed oxpecker** (*Buphagus africanus*).

Orioles and figbirds
Family: Oriolidae
Twenty-eight species in 2 genera.
Africa, Asia, the Philippines, Malaysia, New Guinea and Australia. One species present in Europe. Most species present in the eastern quarter of the family's range. Woodlands and forest. Size: 8–12in (20–30cm) long, weight about 2.5oz (70g). Plumage: predominantly yellow, and yellow and black, occasionally crimson and black in orioles; female orioles, with few exceptions, are less brightly colored than males and in a number of species are also streaked. The figbirds are duller olive green, gray and yellow, with bare red skin around the eyes in the male. Voice: orioles have clear liquid calls and a growling or bleating call; some orioles are capable mimics. Figbirds have peculiar chattering calls. Nests: open cup-shaped nests high in trees. Eggs: 2–4 in orioles, usually 3 in figbirds; apple to dull olive-green, with red, reddish-purple, purplish-brown and brown markings. Diet: fruit, insects.

Species include: **African golden oriole** (*Oriolus auratus*), **Black-naped oriole** (*O. chinensis*), **Black oriole** (*O. hosii*), **Black-winged oriole** (*O. nigripennis*), **Eastern black-headed oriole** (*O. larvatus*), **figbird** (*Sphecotheres vieilloti*), **Golden oriole** (*Oriolus*

oriolus), **Green-headed oriole** (*O. chlorocephalus*), **Maroon oriole** (*O. traillii*), **Sao Thomé oriole** (*O. crassirostris*), **Yellow figbird** (*Sphecotheres flaviventris*).

Drongos
Family: Dicruridae
Twenty species in 2 genera.
Africa, S Asia, Philippines to Solomon Islands, Malaysia, N and E Australia. Open country, cultivation, second growth, edges of rain forest, coastal scrub and mangroves. Size: 7–25in (18–64cm) long. Plumage: black with greenish or purplish gloss, gray or some white; hair-like feathers on crest and elaborate tail shape, forked or racket-tipped. Sexes alike. Voice: jumble of harsh metallic notes, musical calls and whistles; some accomplished mimics. Nests: frail structure, placed in fork of branch. Eggs: 2–4, often white, speckled with brown. Diet: predominantly insects, some nectar.

Species include: **Black drongo** (*Dicrurus macrocercus*), **Crested drongo** (*D. forficatus*), **Fork-tailed drongo** (*D. adsimilis*), **Great Comoro drongo** (*D. fuscipennis*), **Greater racket-tailed drongo** (*D. paradiseus*), **Mayotte drongo** (*D. waldenii*), **Mountain drongo** (*Chaetorhynchus papuensis*), **Shining drongo** (*Dicrurus atripennis*), **Spangled drongo** (*D. hottentottus*).

New World orioles or American blackbirds, which are an entirely different family (p118).

All orioles are remarkably similar in shape and size. The figbirds are less bright in plumage than the orioles, and are more heavily built and more sluggish. In the orioles the bill is slightly decurved, while the figbirds have short, stout bills, hooked at the tip. All the species occur in woodland or forest, where they are restricted to feeding in trees, although both the Golden oriole and the Eastern blackheaded oriole will feed on the ground on fallen fruits or insects in the grass layer. Figbirds commonly occur in small parties or flocks, even in mixed flocks with other oriole species, but most of the orioles are solitary, or found in pairs or family parties. The African orioles, African golden, Eastern black-headed and Green-headed orioles occasionally join mixed-species foraging flocks, and, when they do so, move slowly through the forest or woodland with the other birds. When foraging alone, orioles often fly long distances, as much as 0.6–1.2mi (1–2km), from fruiting tree to tree or other food sources. The rather flapping flight in all orioles is heavy, fairly swift and undulating, rather similar to the flight of woodpeckers.

It is on the islands of Indonesia and New Guinea where the greatest diversity of species has developed, and the greatest range of plumage colors may be seen here. In contrast to the African orioles, in which the plumage is yellow and black, or in one species only, clear yellow and olive green, the plumages of orioles in Australasia range from the completely black, with chestnut under tail coverts of the Black oriole, through the crimson and black of the Maroon oriole to the dull yellowish and greenish of the Australian orioles.

Oriole nests are neatly woven, deep baskets of fine material including grass and beard lichens. The lining is of softer, finer material. Nests, particularly those built from beard lichens, often have material trailing down which serves to camouflage the nest to a great extent. In the African orioles, nest sites are more often inside the tree and seldom on the outer edge of the canopy. Figbird nests are shallower and more flimsy than oriole nests, and are placed in the canopy of trees, in forks at the ends of slender branches. Figbirds construct their nests of twigs and grass and do not weave the materials together as the orioles do.

Although orioles are widespread and usually common or frequently seen where they do occur the nests and eggs of several species

remain to be discovered.   WRJD

The **drongos** are generally solitary, tree-dwelling birds, usually encountered resting on some convenient tree-perch from which they sally forth to snap up some suitable passing insect. Many of them make spectacular swoops, curves and twists in pursuit of their prey.

The adoption of this kind of feeding technique in woodland calls for a much greater maneuverability than is necessary when hawking in open country, hence many drongos have acquired long and often lyre-shaped tails. The shape and structure of the tail varies greatly, from cut-off and shallow-forked to very deeply forked. The outer tail

feathers may be extremely long, curled or denuded of barbs and ending in spoon-shaped rackets, as is found in the Greater racket-tailed drongo of India and Southeast Asia, which has a tail length of 12in (31cm) or more. African drongos are conventional in appearance compared with some of the Asiatic species, which have conspicuous crests as well as racket-shaped tails.

Seven species of drongo occur in Africa, Madagascar, the Comoros and on the island of Aldabra, the remainder being found in the Oriental region. The Spangled drongo has the most extensive range of any drongo, extending from the northern Himalayas to China and through the whole of Indo-Malaysia to the Austral-Papuan regions, as far as the eastern Solomons, and in eastern Australia, with some 30 recognized races.

The Black drongo is one of the most abundant and familiar birds of India and is often seen perched on the earth banks surrounding the fields near villages. It often accompanies grazing cattle, snatching insects disturbed by the animals' movements through the grass, or riding upon their backs. Black drongos are considered to be of great usefulness to agriculture, in destroying vast quantities of insect pests. They are bold and pugnacious birds with piratical habits, setting upon foraging birds with great speed and determination, pursuing them relentlessly with agile twists and turns, forcing them to give up their prey. The Black drongo often retrieves the prey in mid-air, then calmly flies back to its perch, where it tears the insect to pieces with its hooked bill, while holding it in its feet. Fired

grassland will attract considerable numbers of Black drongos to hunt and catch the escaping insects. They also have a great liking for winged termites, hunting them till well into dusk, when they are frequently seen flying up vertically to snatch them on the wing.

A nesting pair of Black drongos will fearlessly attack any crow or raptor which crosses its nesting territory, with great ferocity. During the winter, numbers will congregate to roost in company in bamboo clumps. The Black drongo ranges in seven subspecies from southeastern Iran through India to China, and to Java and Bali.

The Fork-tailed drongo of Africa is very similar to the Black drongo, and is sometimes regarded as being the same species. It also shows the same tenacity, often harrying much larger birds than itself. It is widely distributed south of the Sahara in savanna wherever there are trees.

The Shining drongo of West Africa ranges in lowland forest and is difficult to distinguish from the Fork-tailed drongo. However it is more given to joining the mixed bird parties of the forest, preferring the sunlight of the high tree-tops and the edges of the forest clearings.

The drongos of Madagascar, the Comoro islands and Aldabra are closely related to the Fork-tailed drongo. The Crested drongo of Madagascar and Anjouan islands can be distinguished by its small crest, and the Great Comoro drongo is larger with brownish wings and tail. The Mayotte drongo of Mayotte Island is also larger with a more deeply forked tail.   PRC

▲ **Common mynah feeding its young.** The Common mynah (*Acridotheres tristis*) is as common a sight on the roadsides of pastoral New Zealand (where it has been introduced, as in Australia, South Africa and elsewhere) as it is in the dry hills of India. The species is a good mimic, but the Yellow-wattled Hill mynah is even better and therefore more popular as a cage bird.

▶ **Golden oriole nest,** high up in a horizontal fork of a tree. Both parents share incubation of the eggs and care of the young.

◀ **A Crested drongo in Madagascar** awaits its insect prey. The long, forked tail helps the bird to perform the aerobatics required in the pursuit.

NEW ZEALAND WATTLEBIRDS AND AUSTRALIAN MAGPIES

Families: Callaeidae, Corcoracidae, Grallinidae, Artamidae, Cracticidae

Order: Passeriformes (suborder Oscines, part).
Twenty-six species in 8 genera.
Distribution: see maps and table.

New Zealand wattlebirds   Australian mud-nesters   Magpie-larks

Bell magpies   Wood swallows

THERE are relatively few species of birds confined to New Zealand, and many of these have found it difficult to cope with the loss of habitat due to massive clearing for forestry and agriculture, and the efficient introduced predators that accompanied European settlement. The **New Zealand wattlebirds** exemplify this conflict; all have declined in abundance over the past 100 years and one, the huia, has almost certainly become extinct since it was last seen alive in 1907.

The three species that make up this family were all forest-dwellers that spent a proportion of their time foraging at ground level: this and their readily accessible nests are thought to have made them very susceptible to predation by cats and rats. However, it would seem that collecting by both Maoris and the early European settlers significantly hastened the demise of the huia, which, unfortunately, was sought for ornamentation by both cultures.

The family gains its name from the conspicuous hanging face wattles that adorn each species. These are orange colored except for the Northern Island race of the kokako which has blue wattles. The huia is one of the very few birds in which there is a pronounced difference in bill shape between the sexes.

The kokako and saddleback both eat a wide variety of fruits, berries and insects gathered at all levels of the forest. Their legs are well developed and their wings, while not large, are quite adequate for short flights. Breeding is usually in the spring and early summer. The female builds the nest and she alone incubates the eggs. The male feeds the female on the nest and escorts her when she leaves it to forage. Both parents feed the nestlings. Young stay with their parents for several months after leaving the nest but there is no evidence of longer term associations such as might lead to cooperative breeding groups.

Both living wattlebirds have been the subject of much concern to ornithologists in New Zealand, and the Wildlife Service has been active to prevent either following the huia into possible extinction. The establishment of the saddleback on predator-free islands forms one of the few major success stories in the management of endangered species. It is hoped that efforts with the kokako along similar lines will be as successful.   IR

How did the first mud-nest builder recognize that wet mud was a good material to use? Although wet sloppy mud seems to be a most unpromising material no less than 16 different families of birds ranging from flamingos to swallows have recognized that mud dries to a firm shape and use it regularly to build their nests. In Australia and New Guinea two endemic families have been linked in the past solely on the basis of building their nests with mud. But recently, the two magpie-larks have been placed in a family of their own (Grallinidae), leaving the White-winged chough and the apostlebird as the family of Australian mud-nesters (Corcoracidae).

They are neither magpies nor larks, but the **magpie-larks'** pied plumage suggests the former, their feeding the latter. Alternative names include pee-wee, from their call, and mudlark, from their nests. Both the magpie-lark and the Torrent lark are black and white with slight differences between the sexes. The former is starling-like in build and terrestrial gait, but has a slow flapping flight. The Torrent lark is smaller, very active, and an inhabitant of fast-flowing

▲ **Family of apostlebirds at roost.** Young of this east Australian species often stay with their parents and others of the family group for three or four years, rather than dispersing in their first year like most other birds. All family members help to build the nest, incubate the group's single clutch, and care for and feed the young.

▲ **Endangered species,** the kokako ABOVE LEFT or Blue wattlebird of North Island, New Zealand.

◄ **Insect caught on the wing** is brought back by this male Masked wood swallow to the nest. The species inhabits drier parts of Australia, where it rarely breeds in the same place two years running.

streams in upland New Guinea. It persistently wags its tail from side to side. Magpie-larks often feed around the edge of ponds, frequently eating snails.

Magpie-larks have a call-and-response "pee-wee" call, usually initiated by the male. It maintains contact between male and female and proclaims the territory. They are aggressive, attacking other black and white birds, even their own reflections. Breeding starts in late winter and the mud nests are strengthened with wool and grass. Both parents incubate and feed the young, which are dependent for several weeks after fledging. Flocks of young birds gather in late summer.   HAF

Both **Australian mud-nesters** are confined to eastern Australia and since neither has reached Tasmania or shows any signs of different forms throughout its range, this suggests that they are relatively recent arrivals. The plumage of these birds is soft and fluffy (as in many babblers) compared with the smooth, glossy feathering of most passerines (including the magpie-larks). Both spend most of their time foraging on the ground and have well-developed legs in consequence. The White-winged chough has a long slightly curved bill (remarkably similar to that of the unrelated chough of Europe, hence the name) with which it probes into tussocks, digs in soft earth and turns over twigs and pieces of bark to search for insects, its main source of food. Apostlebirds have shorter chunkier "finch-like" bills and although they, too, eat insects they consume a wide variety of seeds as well.

The Australian mud-nesters are very rarely found in simple pairs but in groups of up to 15–20 members, the result of young from earlier years retained within the family group instead of dispersing. Usually, only one female lays in a nest though occasionally two may do so, resulting in a very large clutch.

All members of these groups help to build the nest, to incubate and brood the nestlings and to feed the young in and out of the nest. Sexual maturity is not reached until three or four years from hatching, and during this time the eye color of the birds changes. This feature provides a very useful guide to a bird's age.

Sometimes groups aggregate into large flocks at a localized source of abundant food such as a stubble field recently harvested, or a recently sown cereal crop. This has sometimes caused conflict with farmers in the past but is sufficiently rare that in these days of more enlightened thinking about conservation matters, the species are unlikely to be slaughtered on this account. Most farmers and their families enjoy the presence of these birds which with encouragement may become adapted to man and with their often amusing social interactions add to the variety of country life.

IR

Wood swallows are a distinct group of small birds with strong well-developed wings that enable them to stay aloft for hours scooping up insects in their broad bills. Besides hawking high in the sky, wood swallows have been seen feeding among the blossoms of trees and since they have brush-like tips to their tongues they may gather nectar as well as insects. They have short legs and hop clumsily on the ground. The triangular wing-silhouette closely resembles that of the Common starling and has led to the name in German of Schwalbenstare ("swallow-starling"), which is very apt.

Both members of the pair build the nest, incubate the eggs and feed the young for at least a month. In the Dusky, Little, Black-faced and White-breasted wood swallows groups have been known to attend the nest.

Species in temperate regions breed in spring, those in the tropics during the wet season. Species of the arid inland, such as the Black-faced wood swallow, may breed at any time, responding very rapidly to heavy falls of rain; nests have been built and eggs laid within 12 days of such a downpour. Wood swallows generally nest in loose colonies with their flimsy, stick, cup-nests

▶ **A telegraph pole in Queensland** provides this magpie-lark with a high horizontal "branch," its preferred nest site. "Mudlarks" nest high up, but forage on the ground.

▶ **Pied currawong** BELOW of the Great Dividing Range. Currawongs take insects and other small creatures, and also quantities of fruit. They are named for their gong-like calls.

▼ **Mud nest of a White-winged chough takes shape.** The initial "saddle" of mud (1) is enlarged to a platform (2), raised into a saucer (3), and finally a bowl (4).

In the social White-winged chough and apostlebird, all members of the family group help build the mud nest. Butcherbirds and currawong pairs build their nests without such assistance.

The 5 Families of New Zealand Wattlebirds and Australian Magpies

E Endangered. Ex? Probably Extinct.

New Zealand wattlebirds
Family: Callaeidae
Three species in 3 genera (one probably extinct).

Endemic to New Zealand. Dense forest. Size: 9–20in (22–50cm) long, weight 3–8.5oz (77–240g). Voice: a variety of whistles, clicks, mews and pipes. Plumage: gray, black and white in kokako, black and reddish in saddleback. Eggs: 2–4, whitish with purplish-brown blotches and spots; incubation period 18–25 days; nestling period 27–28 days. Diet: fruit and insects.

Species: **huia** Ex? (*Heteralocha acutirostris*), **kokako** E (*Callaeas cinerea*), **saddleback** (*Philesturnus carunculatus*).

Magpie-larks
Family: Grallinidae
Two species of the genus *Grallina*.
Australia, Timor, Lord Howe Island, New Guinea. Woodland and forest.

Size: 8–20in (20–50cm) long, weight 1.5–12oz (40–350g). Plumage: gray or black and white. Voice: harsh, buzzing and piping calls. Eggs: 3–5, white to pink in color, blotched with red, brown or gray. Incubation period 17–18 days; nestling period 19–23 days. Diet: insects, other invertebrates, including snails, some seeds.

Species: **magpie-lark** (*Grallina cyanoleuca*), **Torrent lark** (*G. bruijni*).

Australian mud-nesters
Family: Corcoracidae
Two species in 2 genera.
Eastern Australia. Woodland and grassland. Size: 13–19in (33–47cm) long, weight 4–15oz (110–425g). Plumage: soft and fluffy; sooty black in White-winged chough, gray and black in apostlebird. Voice: piping whistles. Eggs: 2–5, creamy white with brown, gray or black blotches; incubation period 18–19 days;

nestling period 18–25 days. Diet: seeds and insects.

Species: **White-winged chough** (*Corcorax melanorhamphos*), **apostlebird** (*Struthidea cinerea*).

Wood swallows
Family: Artamidae
Ten species of the genus *Artamus*.
India, SE Asia, Melanesia, New Guinea and Australia. Woodland, shrubland and grassland. Size: 5–9in (12–23cm) long, weight 0.5–2.5oz (14–73g). Plumage: gray and brown, piebald, multi-colored gray, white, reddish and black; juveniles: mottled or speckled. Voice: brisk "preet preet." Eggs: 2–4, creamy white, spotted red brown; incubation period 12–16 days; nestling period 16–20 days. Diet: insects.

Species include: **Ashy wood swallow** (*Artamus fuscus*), **Bismark wood swallow** (*A. insignis*), **Black-faced wood swallow** (*A. cinereus*), **Dusky**

wood swallow (*A. cyanopterus*), **Little wood swallow** (*A. minor*), **Masked wood swallow** (*A. personatus*), **White-backed wood swallow** (*A. monachus*), **White-breasted wood swallow** (*A. leucorhynchus*), **White-browed wood swallow** (*A. superciliosus*).

Bell magpies
Family: Cracticidae
Nine species in 3 genera.
Australia and New Guinea; one introduced to New Zealand. Woodland, shrubland and grassland. Size: 10–20in (25–50cm) long, weight 3–5oz (80–140g). Plumage: gray, white and black. Voice: loud varied carolling. Eggs: 3–5, blue or green, blotched and streaked brown; incubation period 20 days; nestling period 28 days. Diet: omnivorous but mainly insects.

Species include: **Australian magpie** (*Gymnorhina tibicen*), **Louisiade butcherbird** (*Cracticus louisiadensis*), **Pied currawong** (*Strepera graculina*).

rarely within 10ft (3m) of another nest. Family parties remain together long after the breeding season and are very sociable, frequently preening each other and huddling together for roosting even when the night temperature remains above 86°F (30°C); these associations sometimes lead to cooperative breeding. In cold weather, wood swallows may even cluster during the day, and as many as 200 have been seen to gather like a swarm of bees on a tree trunk. A male may courtship-feed his female; copulation is preceded by a characteristic display in which both birds flutter their part-open wings and rotate their half-spread tails.

Some wood swallows remain as residents all the year around while others are regular migrants, returning to the same place to breed each year. The truly nomadic species, the White-browed and the Masked wood swallows, form mixed flocks which annually travel thousands of miles between breeding attempts. They rarely breed in the same place two years running even if there appears to be plenty of food. IR

Australia is widely supposed to be a "land of song-less birds," but the **bell magpies** give the lie to this. They comprise three genera of basically black and white robust birds that are chiefly insectivorous. They differ in the way they catch the bulk of their insect prey: butcherbirds live a shrike-like existence flying from perches well above the ground and even impaling their prey in "larders" as shrikes do. Magpies are heavier birds with longer legs: they spend much more time on the ground foraging, probing into the ground and under branches, cow-pats etc with their bills. Currawongs are larger still and although they too may spend a lot of time on the ground they are adept at foraging in the forest, searching the canopy for phasmids or probing into the bark of living trees.

One butcherbird is endemic to New Guinea: the Louisiade butcherbird; three other species are shared between New Guinea and Australia and the Gray only occurs in Australia. They all have long massive bills, blue-gray with a black, hooked tip which enables them to capture and dismember prey as large as small birds. Usually found in resident pairs or family parties, they all have beautiful piping or carolling calls that are often performed by the pair or group, with calls and responses creating a magnificent performance.

The Australian magpie is the best known of the family. Its social life is complex but basically territorial. Food is varied and ranges from small seeds and ants, through scarabs, ground weevils and grasshoppers to worms, frogs, lizards and mice. This illustrates the versatility of the species, explains the value of a varied territory and the need for the experience of a long-lived resident to exploit it fully.

Currawongs are named from their call, which is loud and ringing. Their bills are large, pointed and very strong; they are skillful predators of other birds' nests and tend to forage over much larger areas than the other two genera. The Pied currawong nests in the forests of the Great Dividing Range and makes annual nomadic movements towards the plains and cities, in large flocks. They may be significant predators of stick insects which at times defoliate large areas of eucalypt forest. IR

BOWERBIRDS AND BIRDS OF PARADISE

Families: Ptilonorhynchidae, Paradisaeidae
Order: Passeriformes (suborder Oscines, part).
Sixty-one species in 26 genera.
Distribution: see map and table.

Birds of paradise   **Bowerbirds**

Bowerbirds are the supreme artists among birds. Not only do the males construct elaborate structures decorated with colorful objects—fruits, berries, fungi, tinfoil and bits of plastic—but some even paint them with natural pigments applied with a tool or "paintbrush" held by the bill.

Nine bowerbirds live only in New Guinea, seven only in Australia and two are common to both. Most inhabit wet forests, up to 13,000ft (4,000m) above sea level in the case of the little-known Archbold's bowerbird, discovered as late as 1940. Many are extremely localized, like the Adelbert bowerbird, confined to the Adelbert Mountains of Papua New Guinea, and the Golden and Tooth-billed bowerbirds, found only in rain forests above 2,950ft (900m) on and around the Atherton Tableland of Queensland, Australia. Other species, notably New Guinea's Flamed bowerbird and Australia's Spotted and Great Gray bowerbirds have extensive continuous ranges, while most others have patchy broken distributions.

Bowerbirds have long been considered close relatives of birds of paradise and recently several ornithologists placed both groups in the family Paradisaeidae. Anatomical and behavioral studies, and the analysis of genetic characters indicate very strongly, however, that the two groups form distinct families. Some genetic studies have

► **Gray-green plumage** of the female Satin bowerbird has its counterpart in the male's glossy black. Those bowerbird species with the greatest color difference between the sexes tend to have the more elaborate bowers.

The Bowerbird and Bird of Paradise Families

Bowerbirds
Family: Ptilonorhynchidae
Eighteen species in 8 genera.
New Guinea, Australia. Tropical, temperate and montane rain forests; riverine and savanna woodland, grassland; dry, arid zones. Size: 8.5–15in (21–38cm) long, weight 2.5–8oz (70–230g); males larger than females except Regent bowerbird, in which the male is smaller. Plumage: nine species predominantly camouflaged brown, gray or green; males of remaining species with yellow or orange crest or cape; or generally gaudy iridescent yellows, reds or blue and their females drab brown, gray or green with barring underneath. Voice: bird mimicry, mechanical noises, cat-like wails. Nests: bulky cup of twigs, leaves, tendrils in fork, vine or crevice. Eggs: 1–2, rarely 3; plain off-white to buff or blotched and scrawled with color about large end. Incubation period

about 19–24 days, nestling period approximately 18–21 days. Diet: fruit, insects, other invertebrates, lizards, other birds' nestlings.

Species: **Adelbert bowerbird** (*Sericulus bakeri*), **Archbold's bowerbird** (*Archboldia papuensis*), **Fawn-breasted bowerbird** (*Chlamydera cerviniventris*), **Flamed bowerbird** (*Sericulus aureus*), **Golden bowerbird** (*Prionodura newtoniana*), **Great gray bowerbird** (*Chlamydera nuchalis*), **Green catbird** (*Ailuroedus crassirostris*), **Lauterbach's bowerbird** (*Chlamydera lauterbachi*), **MacGregor's gardener** (*Amblyornis macgregoriae*), **Regent bowerbird** (*Sericulus chrysocephalus*), **Satin bowerbird** (*Ptilonorhynchus violaceus*), **Spotted bowerbird** (*Chlamydera maculata*), **Spotted catbird** (*Ailuroedus melanotis*), **Striped gardener** (*Amblyornis subalaris*), **Tooth-billed bowerbird** (*Scenopoeetes dentirostris*), **Vogelkop gardener** (*Amblyornis inornatus*), **White-eared catbird** (*Ailuroedus buccoides*), **Yellow-fronted gardener** (*Amblyornis flavifrons*).

Birds of paradise
Family: Paradisaeidae
Forty-three species in 18 genera.
Moluccas, New Guinea, Australia. Tropical and montane forests, savanna woodland, mangroves. Size: 6–44in (15–110cm); males larger than females. Plumage: most males colorful with iridescing ornate feather structures; females camouflaged, often barred underneath. Some monogamous species black or iridescent blue-black all over. Voice: varied, including crow-like notes, gunfire or loud bell-like sounds. Nests: bulky leaf and tendril cup on stick foundation in tree or vines. Several build domed nests, and the King bird of paradise is a hole nester. Eggs: 1–2, rarely 3; pale often pinkish base, colorfully spotted, blotched and, typically, smudged mainly at larger

end. Incubation period: about 17–21 days; nestling period 17–30 days. Diet: most are largely fruit-eaters, some insectivorous; also leaves, buds, flowers, animals.

Species include: **Blue bird of paradise** (*Paradisaea rudolphi*), **Brown sicklebill** (*Epimachus mayeri*), **King bird of paradise** (*Cicinnurus regius*), **Lawes' parotia** (*Parotia lawesii*), **Long-tailed paradigalla** (*Paradigalla carunculata*), **MacGregor's bird of paradise** (*Macgregoria pulchra*), **Magnificent bird of paradise** (*Diphyllodes magnificus*), **Magnificent riflebird** (*Ptiloris magnificus*), **Paradise crow** (*Lycocorax pyrrhopterus*), **Paradise riflebird** (*Ptiloris paradiseus*), **Raggiana bird of paradise** (*Paradisaea raggiana*), **Ribbon-tailed bird of paradise** (*Astrapia mayeri*), **trumpetbird** (*Manucodia keraudrenii*), **Victoria riflebird** (*Ptiloris victoriae*), **Wallace's standardwing** (*Semioptera wallacei*).

▲ **Maypole bower** of the Golden bowerbird. The male adds moss, flowers and fruit to the attractions of the bower, which may attain 6.6ft (2m) in height.

▷ **Avenue and mat bower** OVERLEAF of the Satin bowerbird. A blue plastic lid is part of the show, together with blue feathers and green leaves. The male solicits the female with grating, cackling and squeaking calls, as it dances about with its tail cocked high, jumps over the bower, and points its bill to the decorations. Having entered the bower and mated, the female leaves to build a nest and raise young on her own.

indicated closer relationships between bowerbirds, lyrebirds and Australian scrub-birds than previously acknowledged.

Bowerbirds are stout, strong footed, heavy-billed birds ranging in size from that of a starling to that of a medium crow. As much a part of the physical appearance of adult male bowerbirds is the court or bower. These remarkable external secondary sexual characters—only discovered in 1870—are created to impress females, and possibly also to intimidate rival males, and have nothing to do with nesting, which is entirely

the females' concern. Recent studies of the Satin bowerbird indicate that bower building is not innate but is learned behavior. Young males start with inferior bowers but gradually improve them as they gain experience. Males of bower-tending species are promiscuous, attracting many females to their bower by calls and mating with as many as possible. Most such males are very brightly colored; glimmering gold, or orange, and black as in the Flamed, Adelbert, Regent and Archbold's bowerbirds; iridescent blue-black in the well-known Satin, completely brilliant yellow and golden-olive in the Golden or generally brown with contrasting orange or yellow crest like most of the Gardener bowerbirds. The "avenue" bower building Spotted, Great Gray, Fawn-breasted and Lauterbach's bowerbirds of grasslands and more arid woodlands are generally drab gray or brownish with small pinkish nape crests.

An important generalization is that species with more colorful males build modest bowers while drabber ones build bigger complex structures (see box). Females of promiscuous species wear drab camouflage, being predominantly brown, olive or gray, often with barring or spotting. The sexes of White-eared, Spotted and Green catbirds are similar, being generally green with white spotting on breast, wings, tail and about the head or throat. Sexes of the presumed promiscuous Toothbilled bowerbird are also identical, being olive brown above and heavily streaked brown on dirty white below. Male Toothbills clear a forest floor "court" of litter and lay decorative green leaves on it, and they call almost continuously at it to attract females.

Males of promiscuous species are long lived, taking up to seven years to attain adult plumage from their initial female coloration, whereas females may breed after two years. Some Satin bowerbird bower sites have been used for nearly 50 years.

Most bowerbirds are predominantly fruit eaters, but insects, vegetable matter and some animals are also taken. In winter some of the avenue-building bowerbird species regularly form flocks which may be serious pests to commercial fruit crops, and Satin bowerbird flocks will ground feed on grasses. Most other polygamous species appear to be sedentary and probably solitary. Toothbilled bowerbirds eat considerable amounts of leaves and succulent stems in winter, having a stout "toothed" bill for tearing and chewing leaves. Until recently, promiscuous male bowerbirds were presumed to form breeding colonies or leks,

their bowers being clustered in associated congregations, but no confirmation of this exists. Recent studies show that the Regent, Satin, Fawn-breasted, MacGregor's and Golden bowerbirds certainly do not, their bowers being evenly distributed throughout suitable habitat. In those promiscuous species which have been studied, females defend only their nest site and males only the immediate vicinity of the bower. In the monogamous catbirds an all-purpose territory is maintained year round.

Birds of paradise are so named because of the bizarre appearance of most males, which have fantastic feather and plume structures and wonderful coloration, much of which is iridescent.

Most species are confined to New Guinea where the family doubtless originated, but the Paradise crow and Wallace's standard-wing are confined to the Moluccan Islands and the Paradise and Victoria's riflebirds to eastern Australia. The Magnificent riflebird and the trumpetbird ranges also just reach Australia from New Guinea. Some New Guinea species have extensive lowland distributions but most have restricted and/or patchy ranges in the mountains at definite altitudinal zones. A few are confined to offshore islands. Most species are wet forest birds although a few occur in sub-alpine woodlands, lowland savanna or mangroves.

Birds of paradise are stout crow-like or starling-like, round-winged, very strong-footed birds. Plumage is extremely varied, from black with brilliant areas of metallic iridescence in some to brilliant combinations of rich yellows, reds, blues and browns, with rich pastel areas of specialized display plumes or weird head or tail "wires" of modified feathering in others. Each genus of the polygamous species has a basic male plumage structure peculiar to it which is manipulated in certain ways during ritualized display sequences.

The five generally uniform blue-black manucodes (*Manucodia* species), and the generally black MacGregor's bird of paradise, show no sexual differences in plumage and are monogamous, and the similarly dull-plumaged Paradise crow and the two paradigallas are presumed to be likewise. The other more colorful and sexually dimorphic species are known or presumed to be polygamous, males being promiscuous and females raising the young alone.

Bills of birds of paradise vary enormously, from short stout crow-like generalized bills, and finer starling-like ones, to very long fine sickle shapes specialized for probing under moss and bark for insects and larvae. While most species are predominantly fruit eaters that also take a variety of insects, animals, leaves and buds, the sicklebills and riflebirds

▲ **Bowerbirds without a bower.** The Spotted catbird's plumage is similar in both sexes. Catbirds do not build a bower.

▶ **Raggiana bird of paradise.** Males display to establish their precedence over other males at the breeding ground where females gather. In this species the performance may include the bird hanging upside-down.

The Transferral Effect

In bowerbirds, the gaudy display plumage of the males has been progressively transferred to the bower "displays" that they build. There are various stages of this "transfer"—birds that have retained colorful plumage build dull bowers and the most elaborate bowers are built by dull-looking birds.

There are four basic types of bower: the "court" of the Toothbilled bowerbird, merely a cleared area of forest floor decorated with green leaves; the "mat" of Archbold's bowerbird, being a carpet of mosses and ferns; the "avenue" bowers of the Flamed bowerbird, the Satin bowerbird (1) and the Spotted bowerbird, which have two parallel upright stick walls forming a central avenue; and "maypole" bowers of the Yellow-fronted

gardener and the Golden bowerbird, consisting of stick accumulations about sapling trunks. Three maypole builders build bowers so complex they look just like small towers or thatched buildings, decorated with moss or lichen "lawns," colored flowers, fruits and insect castings.

Maypole, or gardener bowerbirds clearly demonstrate the transferral effect. Within these four species, bowers vary from the

simple stick tower of MacGregor's gardener (2) to the complex hut-like structure of the Vogelkop gardener (3). The males of each species differ in the extent of a colorful crest relative to bower complexity. MacGregor's gardener builds the simplest bower and has a large orange crest. The Striped gardener has a more complex bower (4) but a reduced crest, and the Vogelkop gardener builds the most complicated bower and completely lacks a crest. When the relationship between luxuriance of crest and bower was first noticed, about 30 years ago, the home, bower, and the female of the beautifully crested

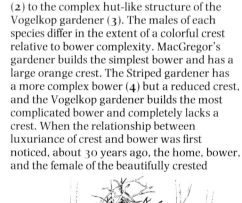

are highly specialized insectivores that eat only some fruit. In the latter, longer billed species, the bill of the female is larger in most species. This is noteworthy as many birds of paradise appear to suffer from limited resources in nonbreeding seasons, when the females move lower down the mountains than the males in order to limit intraspecific competition.

The incredible displays of promiscuous male birds are to impress females or, in birds such as the typical or plumed birds (*Paradisaea* species), which congregate on breeding grounds (leks) to establish a male dominance hierarchy. The six-wired birds (*Parotia* species), like many promiscuous species, display as solitary males at traditional courts or perches which young males eagerly wait to occupy at the first opportunity. Meantime, like young male bowerbirds, they must spend years, perhaps as many as seven, in immature female-like plumage. This situation, with adult males mating promiscuously with many females, means that there are few breeding males in the population relative to females or immature males. Pressure by the latter, in addition to that from rival adult males, ensures that only the

fittest males are able to maintain their place in the breeding community and that only the most vigorous immatures "inherit" display areas or places in leks. Interestingly, captive young male birds of paradise have been noted to breed at a relatively early age in the absence of adult plumage males, suggesting hormonal activity may be restricted by the presence of dominant adult males. No such inhibition however acts on females, which are capable of breeding at two to three years old.

While a breeding system in which few males fertilize many females has brought about evolutionary rapid divergence in the appearance of the males of the various birds of paradise, they remain genetically close. Thus species markedly different in male appearance are nevertheless not genetically isolated and as a result hybrids are a common phenomenon. Not only do species within a genus hybridize, but species of many different genera do so; in which the males of the two parent species are utterly different in appearance. In the case of male offspring from such hybridization the characters of the two contributing species mingle to produce different looking birds, many of which were described as new species to science prior to our understanding of the hybrid situation.

The fact that some birds of paradise, and bowerbirds, are monogamous and territorial, and that some of the polygamous species have displaying areas (leks) where males congregate while others display solitarily, raises the question: how did these different systems arise? It seems that the predominance of tropical forest fruits in the diet is important to the development of polygamy in these bird groups and that the quality of fruit and/or its dispersion in the forest in space and time may dictate the kind of breeding system and/or the way in which males disperse and display.

Several distributionally restricted species may be threatened by habitat destruction but, unfortunately, some species populations, such as several in Irian Jaya (Indonesian New Guinea), are still unknown and urgently require objective assessment. Perhaps the most striking of all species, the Blue bird of paradise, is presently considered to be threatened because the mid-mountain forests vital to it have been reduced by encroaching agriculture. It may be further threatened by potential competition from the Raggiana bird of paradise, which tolerates a wider range of habitats and abuts the lower distributional limits of the Blue bird.   CBF

Yellow-fronted gardener remained undiscovered and it was postulated, therefore, that its bower would prove to be simple in accordance with the inverse relationship exhibited by the other species. Recently, the Yellow-fronted gardener has been discovered in remote mountainous Irian Jaya, and the bower is similar to MacGregor's gardener, as predicted.

Sexual selection, through "female choice," has apparently caused this transfer of visual sexual signals from crest to bower; females select males with superior bowers and thus enhancing bower architecture because only males with superior bowers reproduce. As discerning females selected for improved bowers, males lost their bright plumage: it became disadvantageous, attracting predators.

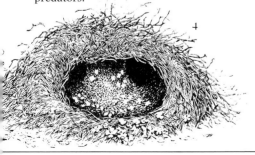

CROWS

Family: Corvidae

Order: Passeriformes (suborder Oscines, part).
One hundred and sixteen species in 23 genera.
Distribution: worldwide, except for the high
Arctic, Antarctic, southern S America, New
Zealand and most oceanic islands.

Habitat: varied, including forests, farmland,
grasslands, desert, steppes and tundra.

Size: 6–26in (15–65cm) long
(including long tails of some
magpie species), weight 2–50oz
(80–1,500g).

Plumage: often all black, or black marked with
white or gray; many jays brightly marked with
blue, chestnut, buff or green. Sexes usually
similar.

Voice: varied range of harsh or more musical
calls; some species capable of mimicry.

Nests: typically bowl-shaped structures of twigs
with lining of fine materials, placed in tree;
some species have domed nests or nest in holes.

Eggs: usually 2–8; ground color whitish, buff,
cream, light blue or light green, often marked
with dark spots or blotches; incubation period
16–22 days; nestling period 20–45 days.

Diet: varied in most species, including fruit,
seeds, insects, small vertebrates, often eggs of
other birds or carrion; many species store food.

Species include: **Alpine chough** (*Pyrrhocorax
graculus*), **American crow** (*Corvus
brachyrhynchos*), **Australian crow** (*C. orru*),
Australian raven (*C. coronoides*), **Biddulph's
ground jay** (*Podoces biddulphi*), **Blue jay**
(*Cyanocitta cristata*), **Carrion crow** (*Corvus
corone*), **chough** (*Pyrrhocorax pyrrhocorax*),
Clark's nutcracker (*Nucifraga columbiana*), **Fish
crow** (*Corvus ossifragus*), **Gray** or **Canada jay**
(*Perisoreus canadensis*), **Green magpie** (*Cissa
chinensis*), **Hawaiian crow** E (*Corvus tropicus*),
House crow (*C. splendens*), **Hume's ground jay**
(*Pseudopodoces humilis*), **jackdaw** (*Corvus
monedula*), **jay** (*Garrulus glandarius*), **Jungle
crow** (*Corvus macrorhynchos*), **Little crow**
(*C. bennetti*), **magpie** or **Black-billed magpie**
(*Pica pica*), **Marianas crow** E (*Corvus kubaryi*),
Mexican crow (*C. imparatus*), **nutcracker**
(*Nucifraga caryocatactes*), **Pied crow** (*Corvus
albus*), **raven** (*C. corax*), **Red-billed blue magpie**
(*Urocissa erythrorhyncha*), **rook** (*Corvus
frugilegus*), **Scrub jay** (*Aphelocoma coerulescens*),
Sinaloa crow (*C. sinaloae*), **Steller's jay**
(*Cyanocitta stelleri*), **White-necked raven** (*Corvus
albicollis*).

E Endangered.

RAVENS, crows and magpies have often
been seen as birds of ill-omen, perhaps
because of their color and size, their
perceived intelligence and their raucous
cries. The raven especially was believed to
have the power of foretelling death. In
Marlowe's words: "The sad presaging raven
tolls the sick man's passport in her beak."

The crow family contains the largest of all
passerines, the ravens, as well as a wide
variety of smaller jays, magpies, and others.
Some of them are regarded as the most intel-
ligent and highly evolved of all birds. Many
of the species are woodland or forest birds,
and most of the jays and magpies of Asia and
South America are almost confined to forests. However, most of the familiar species
of Europe and North America prefer more
open habitats, and there are no forest birds
among the African or Australian representatives.

The most widespread and familiar group
comprises the typical crows and ravens of
the genus *Corvus*. These are large birds with
tails of short or medium length and plumage
that is all-black, black and white, black and
gray or entirely sooty-brown. Because they
diverge further from the typical types of
songbird than most other members of the
family, they are usually regarded as the
most highly evolved of the crows.

In Europe the genus is represented by the
raven, Carrion and Hooded crows, rook and
jackdaw; in southern Asia by the House
crow and Jungle crow among others; and
in Africa by the Pied crow, White-necked
raven and others. In North America and
again in Australia there are a number of all-

▲ **Quick to exploit** any opportunity, crows will seize on an unexpected food source. Here Carrion crows at carrion, the carcass of a calf on a hillside. Crows (genus *Corvus*) are the largest of the passerines and are considered the most evolutionarily advanced of all birds.

◄ **The Azure-winged magpie** (*Cyanopica cyana*) has actions like a magpie's. The species is unusual for its patchy distribution, for it is found in Spain and Portugal and the Far East (chiefly China, Korea, Japan) but not in-between. The tree-fork nest site is typical for the species.

black crows that resemble each other rather closely in structure and appearance but differ in their voices. Thus the American crow, Fish crow, Sinaloan crow and Mexican crow are more readily separable by voice than appearance, and in Australia the Australian crow, Little crow, Australian raven and others are difficult to identify except by their calls. The genus *Corvus* has been more successful than others of the family in colonizing remote islands, resulting in development of species with local distributions in the West Indies, Indonesia, the southwest Pacific and Hawaii.

The chough and Alpine chough resemble *Corvus* in their glossy all-black plumage, but differ in having more slender downcurved bills colored red or yellow. They are mainly mountain birds, extending to elevations of nearly 27,000ft (9,000m) in the Himalayas, but also occuring near rocky sea-cliffs in some regions.

Two species of nutcracker inhabit Eurasia and North America, respectively. The European nutcracker is mainly chestnut with white streaks, whereas the American Clark's nutcracker is mainly gray. Both feed largely on seeds of nuts and rely on hidden supplies during the winter.

The magpies include not only the familiar piebald magpie of Europe, Asia and North America, but also a number of more brightly colored species from southern Asia such as the Green magpie and Red-billed blue magpie. They all have short strong bills and very long graduated tails. The dividing line between the Asian magpies and jays relies mainly on the length of the tail, but the American jays include both short-tailed and rather long-tailed forms. Among the American jays there is a large proportion of species of rather small size, some of them no bigger than large thrushes, and also a large proportion with much blue in the plumage.

Among several atypical groups placed in the crow family, the ground-jays of central Asia are unusual in being predominantly ground-dwelling. They inhabit dry semi-desert and steppe regions and usually run from danger rather than taking to the air. Hume's ground jay is particularly small and lark-like and there is uncertainty about whether this species rightfully belongs in the crow family.

However, allowing for this and a very few other exceptions, the crow family is fairly well defined. The combination of large to very large size, robust build, a strong bill with the external nostrils covered by bristle-like feathers, and strong legs, serves to distinguish most crows from other songbirds, although certain starlings, drongos and birds-of-paradise share some features.

The adaptability and versatility of crows shows most clearly in their diets and feeding behavior. Most species take both animal and plant foods, and many are quick to exploit new and artificial food sources. The manipulation of food is made easier by the robust, generalized bill widespread in the family, and in most species also by use of the feet to hold food while it is dismembered. Many species have been recorded "dunking" or washing food, and this may be an adaptation to counter stickiness. Food-hiding is also prevalent in the family (see pp150–51). It has often been suggested that crows can survive on almost any food, but the poor physical condition of many captive birds strongly implies that their nutritional requirements are similar to those of most other birds.

The longevity of crows has probably been overestimated by casual observers because of the tendency for them to persist from generation to generation in suitable territories. Thus we have the old folk saying that "a crow lives three times as long as a man, and a raven lives three times as long as a crow." However, the maximum age recorded in captivity for a raven was 29 years, and that bird died of senile decay, suggesting that wild birds do not often live as long. Recoveries of ringed birds of several crow species show that one-third to one-half of young birds may die in the first year, and that few adults live to be older than 10 years. Nevertheless, some of the larger crows would thus appear by passerine standards to be long-lived.

Several studies of marked birds have shown that individuals do not start to breed until they are two years old, although in the Carrion crow and magpie they may be paired and holding territories during the second year of life. This deferment of sexual maturity may allow the young birds to gain additional experience before attempting to breed.

Crafty Corvines

The quick-wittedness and great adaptability of many of the typical black crows (genus *Corvus*) may partly account for their wide distribution over four continents. At any event, intelligence accounts for the versatility in feeding behavior that has allowed them to survive in such harsh environments as deserts, tundra and cities.

Experimental studies with ravens have suggested that under some controlled conditions they can "count" up to five or six. This species and the jackdaw performed better than parrots, pigeons and chickens in simple experiments designed to test intelligence.

Wild crows appear to use their intelligence to good effect in obtaining food. For example, Carrion crows learned to drop freshwater mussels from the air onto land surfaces so as to break them open and obtain the soft body of the animal within. Accompanying Herring gulls would repeatedly drop the mussel onto soft mud, but the crows were much quicker in learning to select hard surfaces.

Another example was reported by a gamekeeper who had been checking on the location of pheasant nests with clutches of eggs. On returning to several of the pheasant nests he found they had all been robbed by crows along several hundred feet of hedgebank. Later observations showed that a Carrion crow had learnt to watch the gamekeeper in order to obtain information on the location of the nests.

Other instances have been reported of ravens, Carrion crows and jackdaws being quick to rob nests of gulls or birds of prey during brief periods when they were left unattended owing to presence of birdwatchers in the vicinity. Indeed, nests of some of the scarcer birds of prey such as eagles are less likely to be deserted as a result of human disturbance than they are to be robbed by crows while the parent birds have been frightened away from the nest.

A majority of members of the crow family defend exclusive breeding territories in which they nest. As examples, the raven, jay and Blue jay all defend territories from which both birds of the pair threaten intruders. A few species nest colonially, notably the jackdaw, which has rather loosely spaced colonies nesting in holes, and the rook which nests in denser colonies in the tops of trees. The colonial nesters are gregarious throughout the year, and many of the species that hold breeding territories flock outside the breeding season, some of them occupying large communal roosts. Studies of marked birds of several species have shown that the same territories are occupied year after year and that the pair-bond often lasts for life.

Several different species of crows are known to have breeding seasons that are timed to take advantage of peak food supplies for the nestlings. Thus, in England the rook lays in March to take advantage of the peak in earthworm abundance in April, whereas the jay lays in late April or May to take advantage of the late May and early June peak in abundance of defoliating caterpillars on trees.

Incubation is carried out by the female alone in most species (by both sexes in nutcrackers), and the female is usually fed on the nest by the male. Because incubation often starts when the first egg of the clutch is laid, the nestlings differ in size as they hatch over a period of several days. When food is short the smallest of the brood often dies. Both parents feed the young on food that is mostly carried to the nest concealed in the throat of the adult bird. The fledglings of most if not all species are fed by their parents for some weeks after they leave the nest, and in at least some species they may remain in the parents' territory for many months after they become independent. Florida Scrub jay young may stay for a year or more. This species is known to breed cooperatively.

Several species of crows are significant pests of agriculture. The rook makes severe inroads as a pest because of its depredations on cereal sowings in winter and early spring. During World War II it was estimated that rooks in Britain caused damage costing £3 million per annum, but no recent estimates of this damage are available.

DTH

◄ **The Pied crow** FAR LEFT is common throughout most of tropical and southern Africa and is the only corvid found in Madagascar.

◄ **Displays of the rook** BELOW. In late winter and early spring, the cawing that accompanies the territorial bowing and tail-fanning display (1) is the characteristic sound of a rookery. In males, the display may develop into the pre-copulatory display (2), especially early during the breeding season. In fighting over food, rooks and other corvids adopt an aggressive "take-off" posture (3).

▲ ▼ **Representative species of crows.**
(1) White-necked raven (*Corvus albicollis*). (2, 2a ABOVE, in flight) Jackdaw (*Corvus monedula*). (3, 3a) Chough (*Pyrrhocorax pyrrhocorax*). (4, 4a) Magpie (*Pica pica*). (5, 5a) Raven (*Corvus corax*). (6) Nutcracker (*Nucifraga caryocatactes*). (7) Jay (*Garrulus glandarius*). (8) Steller's jay (*Cyanocitta stelleri*). (9) Green magpie (*Cissa chinensis*). (10) Red-billed blue magpie (*Urocissa erythrorhyncha*).

Squirreling crows

How crows cache food

Most members of the crow family that have been studied in detail in the wild have been seen to hide food. In captivity, many ravens, magpies and jays appear to have a compulsion to hide food. Often the food is carried inside the throat of the bird, so that it is only when the bird is seen to regurgitate or when the food caches are discovered that the extent of food-hiding becomes clear.

Food-hiding behavior is usually not seen when the food consists of such small, well-hidden, living items as insects or earthworms. However, when a surplus of bread is supplied to wild jays or crows they quickly begin to hide away supplies. They typically use small holes in the ground, under debris or vegetation, but sites above ground on trees or buildings may also be used. A deliberate effort is usually made to cover the hidden food by raking loose material on top of it, or by walking a short distance to find a stone or other object to place on top.

Several instances have been reported of very hungry ravens and crows, when suddenly faced with an abundance of food, taking the trouble to hide a large quantity before beginning to eat. However, the extent to which food is deliberately stored for later use varies widely between species. Where there are no seasons of major shortage the hiding and later recovery of food is on a small scale, as for example with magpies and jackdaws in England. Other species use stored reserves of food to allow survival through harsh winter conditions when only scanty food supplies remain available.

The Gray jay inhabits forests of spruce and other conifers over large areas of northern Canada. During the winter, food supplies are very scarce in these forests and the thick and extensive snow cover would prevent the jays from recovering food hidden in the ground. Instead, spruce seeds and other food are stored in the foliage of the conifers stuck to the leaves with saliva. For this purpose, the Gray jay has evolved especially large salivary glands.

Food-hiding may serve two functions in addition to, or instead of, the provision of a food supply during periods of shortage. One suggestion was that the extensive transport and surface-burial of acorns by jays and of hazel-nuts by nutcrackers was aimed at the spreading and perpetuation of these trees.

The second suggestion was that the Blue jay may carry and hide food in order to remove surplus food from its territory. This was argued to have the effect of discouraging other Blue jays from trespassing in search of food, and hence perhaps of competing for food later when it may be scarce. Despite these possible explanations, several studies have suggested that at least some members of the crow family derive a significant part of their diet from stored reserves

▲ **Hard times** for the gregarious rook of Eurasia. It is less common for such social species to cache food for the winter—mates and other flock members are watching! But for some corvids squirrel-like provisioning appears to be an important aid to surviving the winter.

◄ **Acorns are a major food** of the European jay, which makes large stores in the fall for use in the following winter and spring.

► **The Gray or Canada jay** favors coniferous and spruce forests in its North American home. The species caches food in conifer foliage, not on the ground as most other corvids do, because this becomes too deeply covered with snow in winter.

during a season of food shortage. Hence it seems likely that this is the main function of food-hiding.

The crows' memory for the whereabouts of hidden food is good. European nutcrackers spend much of the fall hiding hazel nuts or pine seeds in holes in the ground, often carrying them over half a mile. During the winter, the diet of the nutcrackers includes a high proportion of this stored food, and they can excavate food from beneath 8in (20cm) or more of snow cover. There are records of nutcrackers feeding hazel nuts to their nestlings in the late spring and these nuts were presumably hidden the previous fall. Nonetheless, some of the hidden nuts and pine seeds are not recovered and these may germinate, having been both dispersed and "planted" by the nutcrackers.

By comparison with the European nutcracker, a study of jays in Holland suggested they were less efficient at recovering acorns, relying in part on the development of a growing shoot to reveal the hiding place. However, jays also recover many acorns before they germinate, and there is one instance recorded of them digging through snow to find them.

Social crows such as the rook may have difficulty in hiding food where it will not be discovered by other members of the flock. There are several observations of the mate or other birds of the flock watching food being hidden and then quickly trying to find it. In these instances the bird often appears to have difficulty in locating the exact spot, whereas the bird that hid the food may be immediately successful in recovering it.

DTH

BIBLIOGRAPHY

The following list of titles indicates key reference works used in the preparation of this volume and those recommended for further reading.

Ali, S. (1977) *Field Guide to the Birds of the Eastern Himalayas*, Oxford University Press, Delhi.

Ali, S. and Ripley, S. D. (1983) *A Pictorial Guide to the Birds of the Indian Subcontinent*, Bombay Natural History Society/Oxford University Press, Delhi.

Ali, S. and Ripley, S. D. (1984) *Handbook of the Birds of India and Pakistan*, Oxford University Press, Delhi.

Baker, R. R. (1984) *Bird Navigation—the Solution of a Mystery?* Hodder and Stoughton, Sevenoaks, Kent.

Baker, R. R. (1978) *The Evolutionary Ecology of Animal Migration*, Hodder and Stoughton, Sevenoaks, Kent.

Blakers, M., Davies, S. J. J. F. and Reilly, P. N. (1984) *The Atlas of Australian Birds*, Melbourne University Press, Melbourne.

Bock, W. J. and Farrand, J. (1980) *The Number of Species and Genera of Recent Birds: a Contribution to Comparative Systematics*, American Museum of Natural History, New York.

Bond, J. (1979) *Birds of the West Indies: a Guide to the Species of Birds that Inhabit the Greater Antilles, Lesser Antilles and Bahama Islands*, Collins, London.

Brown, L. H., Urban, E. K. and Newman, K. (1982) *The Birds of Africa*, vol I, Academic Press, London.

Brudenell-Bruce, P. G. C. (1975) *The Birds of New Providence and the Bahama Islands*, Collins, London.

Campbell, B. and Lack, E. (1985) *A New Dictionary of Birds*, T. and A. D. Poyser, Stoke-on-Trent.

Clements, J. (1981) *Birds of the World: a Checklist*, Croom Helm, London.

Cramp, S. (1978–85) *Handbook of the Birds of Europe, the Middle East and North Africa: the Birds of the Western Palaearctic*, vols I–IV, Oxford University Press, Oxford.

Dementiev, G. P. *et al* (1966) *Birds of the Soviet Union*, vols I–IV, Jerusalem.

Dorst, J. (1962) *The Migration of Birds*, Heinemann, London.

Falla, R. A., Sibson R. B. and Turbott, E. G. (1979) *The New Guide to the Birds of New Zealand*, Collins, Auckland and London.

Farner, D. S., King, J. R. and Parkes, K. C. (1971–83) *Avian Biology*, vols I–VII, Academic Press, New York and London.

Farrand, J. J. (1983) *The Audubon Society Master Guide to Birding*, 3 vols. Knopf, New York.

Ferguson-Lees, J., Willis, I. and Sharrock, J. T. R. (1983) *The Shell Guide to the Birds of Britain and Ireland*, Michael Joseph, London.

Finlay, J. C. (1984) *A Bird Finding Guide to Canada*, Hurtig, Edmon.

Flint, V. E., Boehme, R. L., Kostin, Y. V. and Kuznetzov, A. A. (1984) *A Field Guide to Birds of the USSR*, Princeton University Press, Princeton, N.J.

Forshaw, J. M. and Cooper, W. T. (1977) *The Birds of Paradise and Bower Birds*, Collins, Sydney and London.

Gallagher, M. and Woodcock, M. W. (1980) *The Birds of Oman*, Quartet, London.

Glenister, A. G. (1971) *The Birds of the Malay Peninsula, Singapore and Penang*, Oxford University Press, Kuala Lumpur.

Godfrey, W. E. (1966) *The Birds of Canada*, National Museum of Canada, Ottawa.

Goodwin, D. (1976) *Crows of the World*, British Museum (Natural History), London.

Goodwin, D. (1982) *Estrildid Finches of the World*, British Museum (Natural History), London.

Gruson, E. S. (1976) *A Checklist of the Birds of the World*, Collins, London.

Halliday, T. (1987) *Vanishing Birds: their Natural History and Conservation*, Sidgwick and Jackson, London.

Harris, M. (1982) *A Field Guide to the Birds of Galapagos*, revised edn, Collins, London.

Harrison, C. J. O. (1975) *A Field Guide to the Nests, Eggs and Nestlings of British and European Birds, with North Africa and the Middle East*, Collins, London.

Harrison, C. J. O. (1978) *A Field Guide to the Nests, Eggs and Nestlings of North American Birds*, Collins, London.

Harrison, C. J. O. (1982) *An Atlas of the Birds of the Western Palaearctic*, Collins, London.

Harrison, C. J. O. (ed) (1978) *Bird Families of the World*, Elsevier-Phaidon, Oxford.

Howard, R. and Moore, A. (1980) *A Complete Checklist of the Birds of the World*, Oxford University Press, Oxford.

Irby Davis, L. (1972) *A Field Guide to the Birds of Mexico and Central America*, Texas University Press, Austin.

King, A. S. and McLelland, J. (1975) *Outlines of Avian Anatomy*, Baillière Tindall, London.

King, B., Woodcock, M. and Dickinson, E.C. (1975) *A Field Guide to the Birds of South-East Asia*, Collins, London.

Krebs, J. R. and Davies, N. B. (1981) *An Introduction to Behavioral Ecology*, Blackwell Scientific Publications, Oxford

Lack, D. (1968) *Ecological Adaptations for Breeding in Birds*, Methuen, London.

Leahy, C. (1982) *The Bird Watcher's Companion: an Encyclopedic Handbook of North American Birdlife*, Hale, London.

McFarland, D. (ed) (1981) *The Oxford Companion to Animal Behavior*, Oxford University Press, Oxford.

McLachlan, G. R. *et al* (1978) *Roberts' Birds of South Africa* (4th edn), Struik, Cape Town.

Moreau, R. E. (1972) *The Palaearctic-African Bird Migration Systems*, Academic Press, London.

National Geographic Society (1983) *Field Guide to the Birds of North America*, NGS, Washington.

Newton, I. (1972) *Finches*, Collins, London.

Newman, K. (1983) *The Birds of Southern Africa*, Macmillan, Johannesburg.

Nørgaard-Oleson, E. (1973) *The Tanagers*, Skibby Books, Denmark.

O'Connor, R. J. (1984) *The Growth and Development of Birds*, Wiley, New York.

Penny, M. (1974) *The Birds of the Seychelles and the Outlying Islands*, Collins, London.

Perrins, C. M. (1976) *Bird Life: an Introduction to the World of Birds*, Elsevier-Phaidon, Oxford.

Perrins, C. M. and Birkhead, T. R. (1983) *Avian Ecology*, Blackie, London.

Peters, J. L. *et al* (1931–) *Checklist of Birds of the World*, Museum of Comparative Zoology, Cambridge, Massachusetts.

Peterson, R. T. (1980) *A Field Guide to the Birds East of the Rockies* (4th ed), Houghton Mifflin, Boston, Mass.

Peterson, P. T., Mountford, G. and Hollom, P. A. D. (1983) *A Field Guide to the Birds of Britain and Europe* (4th edn), Collins, London.

Pizzey, G. (1980) *A Field Guide to the Birds of Australia*, Collins, Sydney.

Schauensee, R. M. de (1982) *A Guide to the Birds of South America*, Academy of Natural Sciences of Philadelphia.

Schauensee, R. M. de and Phelps, W. H. (1978) *A Guide to the Birds of Venezuela*, Princeton University Press, Princeton, N.J.

Schauensee, R. M. de (1984) *The Birds of China Including the Island of Taiwan*, Oxford University Press, Oxford, Smithsonian Institution Press, Washington, D.C.

Serle, W., Morel, G. J. and Hartwig, W. (1977) *A Field Guide to the Birds of West Africa*, Collins, London.

Simms, E. (1979) *Wildlife Sounds and their Recording*, Elek, London.

Skutch, A. F. (1975) *Parent Birds and their Young*, University of Texas Press, Austin, Texas.

Slater, P. (1971, 1975) *A Field Guide to Australian Birds*, vol I, Oliver and Boyd, Edinburgh; vol II, Scottish Academic Press, Edinburgh.

Snow, D. W. (1982) *The Cotingas*, British Museum (Natural History), London.

Tyne, J. van and Berger, A. J. (1976) *Fundamentals of Ornithology* (2nd edn), Wiley, New York.

Watson, G. E. (1975) *Birds of the Antarctic and Sub-Antarctic*, American Geophysical Union, Washington, D.C.

Wild Bird Society of Japan (1982) *A Field Guide of the Birds of Japan*, Wild Bird Society of Japan, Tokyo.

Williams, J. G. and Arlott, N. (1980) *A Field Guide to the Birds of East Africa*, Collins, London.

GLOSSARY

Adaptation features of an animal that adjust it to its environment. NATURAL SELECTION favors the survival of individuals whose adaptations adjust them better to their surroundings than other individuals with less successful adaptations.

Adaptive radiation Where a group of closely related animals (eg members of a family) have evolved differences from each other so that they occupy different NICHES and have reduced competition between each other.

Adult a fully developed and mature individual, capable of breeding but not necessarily doing so until social and/or ecological conditions allow.

Air sac thin-walled structure connected to the lungs of birds and involved in respiration; extensions of these can occur in hollow bones.

Albino a form in which all dark pigments are missing, leaving the animal white, usually with red eyes.

Alpine living in mountainous areas, usually above 5,000ft (1,500m).

Altricial refers to young that stay in the nest until they are more or less full grown (as opposed to PRECOCIAL). See also NIDICOLOUS.

Aquatic associated with water.

Arboreal associated with or living in trees.

Avian pertaining to birds.

Beak see BILL.

Bill the two MANDIBLES with which birds gather their food. Synonymous with beak.

Bolus a ball (of food).

Boreal zone the area of land lying just below the north polar region and mainly covered in coniferous forest.

Broadleaved woodland woodland mainly comprising angiosperm trees (both deciduous and evergreen), such as oaks, beeches and hazels, which is characteristic of many temperate areas of Europe and North America.

Brood group of young raised simultaneously by a pair (or several) birds.

Blood-parasite a bird that has its eggs hatched and reared by another species.

Call short sounds made by birds to indicate danger, threaten intruders or keep a group of birds together. See also SONG.

Canopy a fairly continuous layer in forests produced by the intermingling of branches of trees; may be fully continuous (closed) or broken by gaps (open). The crowns of some trees project above the canopy layer and are known as emergents.

Carpal the outer joint of the wing, equivalent to the human wrist.

Casque bony extension of the upper MANDIBLE.

Cecum diverticulation or sac of the hind-gut.

Class a taxonomic level. All birds belong to the class Aves. The main levels of a taxonomic hierarchy (in descending order) are Phylum, Class, Order, Family, Genus, Species.

Cloaca terminal part of the gut into which the reproductive and urinary ducts open. There is one opening to the outside of the body, the cloacal aperture, instead of separate anus and urinogenital openings.

Clutch the eggs laid in one breeding attempt.

Colonial living together in a COLONY.

Colony a group of animals gathered together for breeding.

Comb a fleshy protuberance on the top of a bird's head.

Communal breeder species in which more than the two birds of a pair help in raising the young. See COOPERATIVE BREEDING.

Congener a member of the same genus.

Coniferous forest forest comprising largely evergreen conifers (firs, pines, spruces etc), typically in climates either too dry or too cold to support DECIDUOUS FORESTS. Most frequent in northern latitudes or in mountain ranges.

Conspecific a member of the same species.

Contact call CALLS given by males in competition.

Contour feathers visible external covering of feathers, including flight feathers of tail and wings.

Convergent evolution the independent acquisition of similar characters in evolution, as opposed to the possession of similarities by virtue of descent from a common ancestor.

Cooperative breeding a breeding system in which parents of young are assisted in the care of young by other adult or subadult birds.

Coverts the smaller feathers that cover the wings and overlie the base of the large FLIGHT FEATHERS (both wings and tail).

Covey a collective name for groups of birds, usually gamebirds.

Creche a gathering of young birds, especially in penguins and flamingos; sometimes used as a verb.

Crest long feathers on the top of the heads of birds.

Crop a thin-walled extension of the foregut used to store food; often used to carry food to the nest.

Crustaceans invertebrate group which includes shrimps, crabs and many other small marine animals.

Cryptic camouflaged and difficult to see.

Deciduous forest temperate and tropical forest with moderate rainfall and marked seasons. Typically trees shed leaves during either cold or dry periods.

Desert areas of low rainfall, typically with sparse scrub or grassland vegetation or lacking vegetation altogether.

Dimorphic literally "two forms." Usually used as "sexually dimorphic" (ie the two sexes differ in color or size).

Disjunct distribution geographical distribution of a species that is marked by gaps. Commonly brought about by fragmentation of suitable habitat, especially as a result of human intervention.

Dispersal the movements of animals, often as they reach maturity, away from their previous HOME RANGE. Distinct from **dispersion**, that is the pattern in which things (perhaps animals, food supplies, nest-sites) are distributed or scattered.

Display any relatively conspicuous pattern of behavior that conveys specific information to others, usually to members of the same species; often associated with courtship but also in other activities, eg "threat display."

Display ground the place where a male (or males) tries to attract females.

DNA deoxyribonucleic acid; the key substance of chromosomes—important for inheritance.

Dominance hierarchy a "peck-order"; in most groups of birds, in any pair of birds each knows which is superior and a ranking of superiors therefore follows.

Double-brooded (also triple- or multiple-brooded) birds which breed twice or more each year, subsequent nests following earlier successful ones, excluding those when the first or all earlier nests fail, in which case the term **replacement nests** applies.

Echolocation the ability to find one's way by emitting sounds and gauging the position of objects by timing the returning echo.

Erectile of an object, eg a crest, that can be raised.

Faculative optional. See also OBLIGATE.

Family either a group of closely related species, eg penguins, or a pair of birds and their offspring. See CLASS.

Feces excrement from the digestive system passed out through the CLOACA.

Fledge strictly to grow feathers. Now usually used to refer to the moment of flying at the end of the nesting period when young birds are more or less completely feathered. Hence **fledging period**, the time from hatching to fledging, and **fledgling**, a recently fledged young bird.

Flight feathers the large feathers of the wing, which can be divided into PRIMARY FEATHERS and SECONDARY FEATHERS.

Fossorial burrowing.

Frontal shield a fleshy area covering the forehead.

Frugivore eating mainly fruits.

Gallery forest a thin belt of woodland along a riverbank in otherwise more open country.

Generalist an animal whose life-style does not involve highly specialized strategems (cf SPECIALIST), for example, feeding on a variety of foods which may require different foraging techniques.

Genus the taxonomic grouping of species. See CLASS.

Gizzard the muscular forepart of the stomach. Often an important area for the grinding up of food, in many species with the help of grit.

Gregarious showing a tendency to congregate into groups.

Guano bird excreta. In certain dry areas the guano of colonial sea birds may accumulate to such an extent that it is economic to gather it for fertilizer.

Gular pouch an extension of the fleshy area of the lower jaw and throat.

Habitat the type of country in which an animal lives.

Hallux the first toe. Usually this is small and points backwards, opposing the three forward-facing toes.

Harem a group of females living in the territory of, or consorting with, a single male.

Hatchling a young bird recently emerged from the egg.

Helper an individual, generally without young of its own, which contributes to the survival of the offspring of others by behaving parentally towards them. See COOPERATIVE BREEDING.

Herbivore an animal which eats vegetable material.

Holarctic realm a region of the world including North America, Greenland, Europe and Asia apart from the Southwest, Southeast and India.

Homeothermic warm-blooded, having the ability to keep body temperature constant.

Home range an area in which an animal normally lives (generally excluding rare excursions or migrations), irrespective of whether or not the area is defended from other animals.

Hybrid the offspring of a mating between birds of different species.

Hypothermy a condition in which internal body temperature falls below normal.

Incubation the act of incubating the egg or eggs, ie keeping them warm so that development is possible. Hence **incubation period**, the time taken for eggs to develop from the start of incubation to hatching.

Insectivore an animal that feeds on insects.

Introduced of a species that has been brought from lands where it occurs naturally to lands where it has not previously occurred. Some introductions are natural but some are made on purpose for biological control, farming or other economic reasons.

Irruption sudden or irregular spread of birds from their normal range. Usually a consequence of a food shortage.

Keratin the substance from which feathers are formed (and also reptile scales, human hair, fingernails etc.)

Krill small shrimp-like marine CRUSTACEANS which are an important food for certain species of seabirds.

Lamellae comb-like structures which can be used for filtering organisms out of water.

Lanceolate of (feathers) referring to the lance-like (pointed) shape.

Lek a display ground where two or more male birds gather to attract females. See DISPLAY.

Littoral referring to the shore-line.

Mallee scrub small scrubby eucalyptus which covers large areas of dryish country in Australia.

Mandible one of the jaws of a bird which make up the BILL (upper or lower).

Melanin a dark or black PIGMENT.

Metabolic rate the rate at which the chemical processes of the body occur.

Migration usually the behavior in which birds fly (migrate) from one part of the world to another at different times of year. There is also local migration and altitudinal migration where birds move, eg on a mountain side, from one height to another.

Molt the replacement of old feathers by new ones.

Monoculture a habitat dominated by a single species of plant, often referring to forestry plantations.

Monogamous taking only a single mate (at a time).

Monotypic the sole member of its genus, family, order etc.

Montane pertaining to mountainous country.

Montane forest forest occurring at middle altitudes on the slopes of mountains, below the alpine zone but above the lowland forest.

Morph a form, usually used to describe a color form when more than one exist.

Morphology the study of the shape and form of animals.

Natural selection the process whereby individuals with the most appropriate ADAPTATIONS are more successful than other individuals and hence survive to produce more offspring and so increase the population.

Neotropical originating in the tropics of the New World.

Nestling   a young bird in the nest, hence **nestling period**, the time from hatching to flying (see FLEDGE).

Niche   specific parts of a habitat occupied by a species, defined in terms of all aspects of its life-style (eg food, competitors, predators and other resource requirements).

Nidicolous   young birds which remain in the nest until they can fly. See ALTRICIAL.

Nidifugous   of young birds that leave the nest soon after hatching. See PRECOCIAL.

Nomadic   wandering (as opposed to having fixed residential areas).

Obligate   required, binding. See also FACULATATIVE.

Oligotrophic   of a freshwater lake with low nutrient levels; such lakes are usually deep and have poor vegetation.

Omnivore   an animal that eats a wide variety of food.

Opportunistic   an animal that varies its diet in relation to what is most freely available. See GENERALIST, SPECIALIST.

Order   a level of taxonomic ranking. See CLASS.

Organochlorine pesticides   a group of chemicals used mainly as insecticides, some of which have proved highly toxic to birds; includes DDT, aldrin, dieldrin.

Pair bond   the faithfulness of a mated pair to each other.

Palaearctic   a zoogeographical area roughly comprising Europe and Asia (except the Indian subcontinent and Southeast Asia).

Pampas   grassy plains (of South America).

Parasitize   in the ornithological sense, usually to lay eggs in the nests of another species and leave the foster parents to raise the young. See BROOD-PARASITE.

Passerine   strictly "sparrow-like" but normally used as a shortened form of Passeriformes, the largest ORDER of birds.

Pecten   a structure lying on the retina of the eye.

Pigment   a substance that gives color to eggs and feathers.

Polyandry   where a female mates with several males.

Polgamy   where a male mates with several females.

Polymorphic   where a species occurs in two (or more) different forms (usually relating to color). See MORPH, DIMORPHIC.

Polygyny   where a bird of one sex takes several mates.

Population   a more or less separate (discrete) group of animals of the same species.

Prairie   North American steppe grassland between 30°N and 55°N.

Precocial   young birds that leave the nest after hatching. See ALTRICIAL.

Predation   where animals are taken by a predator.

Predator   birds that hunt and eat other vertebrates hence "anti-predator behavior" describes the evasive actions of the prey.

Preen gland   a gland situated above the base of the tail. The bird wipes its bill across this while preening the feathers, so distributing the waxy product of the preen gland over the feathers. The exact function of this is not known; some groups of birds do not possess preen glands.

Primary feather   one of the large feathers of the outer wing.

Primary forest   forest that has remained undisturbed for a long time and has reached a mature (climax) condition; primary rain forest may take centuries to become established. See also SECONDARY GROWTH.

Promiscuous   referring to species where the sexes come together for mating only and do not form lasting pair bonds.

Pyriform   pear-shaped.

Quartering   the act of flying back and forth over an area, searching it thoroughly.

Race   a subsection of a species which is distinguishable from the rest of that species. Usually equivalent to SUBSPECIES.

Radiation   see ADAPTIVE RADIATION.

Rain forest   tropical and subtropical forest with abundant and year-round rainfall. Typically species rich and diverse.

Range   geographical area over which an organism is distributed.

Raptor   a bird of prey, usually one belonging to the order Falconiformes.

Relict population   a local group of a species which has been isolated from the rest for a long time.

Resident   an animal that stays in one area all the year round.

Roosting   sleeping.

Sahara-Sahelian zone   the area of North Africa comprising the Sahara Desert and the arid Sahel zone to its south.

Savanna   a term loosely used to describe open grasslands with scattered trees and bushes, usually in warm areas.

Scrape   a nest without any nesting material where a shallow depression has been formed to hold the eggs.

Scrub   a vegetation dominated by shrubs—woody plants usually with more than one stem. Naturally occurs most often on the arid side of forest or grassland types, but often artificially created by man as a result of forest destruction.

Secondary feather   one of the large flight feathers on the inner wing.

Secondary forest   an area of rain forest that has regenerated after being felled. Usually of poorer quality and lower diversity than PRIMARY FOREST and containing trees of a more uniform size.

Sedentary   nonmigrating. See RESIDENT.

Sequential molt   where feathers (usually the wing feathers) are molted in order, as opposed to all at once.

Sexual selection   an evolutionary mechanism whereby females select for mating only males with certain characteristics, or vice versa.

Sibling group   a group containing brothers and sisters.

Sibling species   closely related species, thought to have separated only recently.

Single-brooded   birds which only make one nesting attempt each year, although they may have a replacement clutch if the first is lost. See DOUBLE-BROODED.

Solitary   by itself.

Song   a series of sounds (vocalization), often composed of several or many phrases constructed of repeated elements, normally used by a male to claim a territory and attract a mate.

Specialist   an animal whose life-style involves highly specialized strategems, eg feeding with one technique on a particular food.

Species   a population, or series of populations, which interbreed freely, but not with those of other species. See CLASS.

Speculum   a distinctively colored group of flight feathers (eg on the wing of a duck).

Spur   the sharp projection on the leg of some game birds; often more developed in males and used in fighting. Also found on the carpal joint of some other birds.

Staging ground/place   an area where birds may pause to feed during migration.

Steppe   open grassy plains, with few trees or bushes, of the central temperate zone of Eurasia or North America (prairies), characterized by low and sporadic rainfall and a wide annual temperature variation. In cold steppe, temperatures drop well below freezing point in winter, with rainfall concentrated in the summer or evenly distributed throughout the year, while in hot steppe, winter temperatures are higher and rainfall is concentrated in winter months.

Stooping   dropping rapidly (usually of a bird of prey in pursuit of prey).

Strutting ground   an area where male birds may display.

Subadult   no longer juvenile but not yet fully adult.

Sublittoral   the sea shore below the low-tide mark.

Suborder   a subdivision of an order. See CLASS.

Subspecies   a subdivision of a species. Usually not distinguishable unless the specimen is in the hand; often called races. See CLASS.

Subtropics   the area just outside the tropics (ie at higher latitudes).

Taiga   the belt of forests (coniferous) lying below (at lower latitudes to) the TUNDRA.

Tarsus   that part of the leg of a bird which is just above the foot. Strictly the tarso-metatarsus bones formed from the lower leg and upper foot.

Temperate zone   an area of climatic zones in mid latitudes, warmer than the northerly areas but cooler than the subtropical areas.

Terrestrial   living on land.

Territorial   defending an area, in birds usually referring to a bird or birds which exlude others of the same species from their living area and in which they will usually nest.

Territory   area that an animal or animals consider their own and defend against intruders.

Thermal   an area of (warm) air which rises by convection.

Thermoregulation   the regulation and maintenance of a constant internal body temperature.

Torpor   a temporary physiological state, akin to short-term hibernation, in which the body temperature drops and the rate of METABOLISM is reduced. Torpor is an ADAPTATION for reducing energy expenditure in periods of extreme cold or food shortage.

Totipalmate feet   feet in which three webs connect all four toes. (Most birds have only two webs between the three forward pointing toes, with the hind claws free).

Tribe   a term sometimes used to group certain species and/or genera within a family. See CLASS.

Tropics   strictly, an area lying between 22.5°N and 22.5°S. Often, because of local geography, birds' habitats do not match this area precisely.

Tundra   the area of high latitude roughly demarcated by its being too cold for trees to grow.

Upwelling   an area in the sea where, because of local topography, water from deep down in the sea is pushed to the surface. Usually upwellings are associated with rich feeding conditions for birds.

Vermiculation   (on feathers) fine markings.

Wattle   a fleshy protuberance, usually near the base of the BILL.

Wetlands   fresh- or salt-water marshes.

Wing   front limb of a bird transformed into an organ for flight.

Wing formula   statement of relative lengths of wing feathers, especially of primary feathers. Used as a defining characteristic for many species.

Wing spur   a sharp projection at or near the bend of the wing. See SPUR.

Wintering ground   the area where a migrant spends the nonbreeding season.

Zygodactyl   having two toes directed forwards and two backwards.

INDEX

Picture Acknowledgments

Key *t* top. *b* bottom. *c* center. *l* left. *r* right

Abbreviations A Ardea. AN Agence Nature. ANT Australasian Nature Transparencies. BCL Bruce Coleman Ltd. J Jacana. FL Frank Lane Agency. NHPA Natural History Photographic Agency. OSF Oxford Scientific Films. SAL Survival Anglia Ltd.

Cover BCL. 1 BCL. 2–3 BCL. 4–5 BCL. 6–7 BCL. 8–9 BCL. 10 A. 11 Eric and David Hosking. 12*b*, 12–13, 14–15 ANT. 15*b* A. G. Wells. 18*b* A. 18–19 NHPA. 21*t*, 21*b*, 22*b*, 22–23, 23*b* A. 26, 27 BCL. 29*l* AN. 29*r* A. 30–31 AN. 34, 36–37 FL. 37*b* NHPA. 38 BCL. 39 A. 42 FL. 43*r* Nature

Photographers. 43*b* M. King & M. Read. 44–45 NHPA. 46–47 BCL. 48 NHPA. 49 A. 50 M. King & M. Read. 52*b*, 52–53 ANT. 54*b*, 54–55, 58*t*, 58–59 BCL. 59*r* A. 61*t* AN. 61*b* SAL. 63 AN. 64 A. 65 NHPA. 66 Nature Photographers. 67 BCL. 68 Nature Photographers. 69 A. 74 BCL. 75*t* A. 75*b* NHPA. 76*b* A. 76–77 Nature Photographers. 78 ANT. 80–81 A. G. Wells. 84–85 A. 84*b*, 85*b* BCL. 88–89, 88*b* A. 89 Eric and David Hosking. 90*t* M. King & M. Read. 90*b* FL. 91, 92–93 BCL. 95 A. 96 NHPA. 97 ANT. 98–99 OSF. 99*b* ANT. 101 J. 102 A. G. Wells. 103 ANT. 104–105 J. 106, 107*b* A. 107*t* BCL. 108–109 A. 112–113 BCL. 113*t* NHPA. 115, 117 A. 118 BCL.

119, 120*b* A. 120–121, 124–125, 124*b* BCL. 126*b* Nature Photographers. 126–127 BCL. 127*b* A. 130–131 J. 133 M. King & M. Read. 134–135 FL. 135*b* BCL. 136*t*, 136*b*, 137 ANT. 139*t* SAL. 139*b* FL. 140 Frithfoto. 141 ANT. 142–143 FL. 144 ANT. 145 Frithfoto. 146*b*, 146–147 A. 148 Michael Fogden. 150*b* J. 150–151 A. 151*b* BCL.

Artwork

Abbreviations IW Ian Willis. SD Simon Driver. SM Sean Milne. NA Norman Arlott. LT Laurel Tucker. TB Trevor Boyer. AC Ad Cameron. DO Denys Ovenden. ML Mick Loates.

17 DO. 20 IW. 24 DO. 28 IW. 33 DO. 35 IW. 39, 40 SD. 41 NA. 43 IW. 57 SM. 62 ML. 73 NA. 79*t* DS. 79*b* IW. 83, 87 NA. 90 IW. 92 SD. 94 IW. 101 SD. 110 LT. 116, 119 IW. 122, 129 TB. 138, 144, 148 IW. 149 AC.

Maps and scale drawings SD.